THE LOCKHART PLOT

JONATHAN SCHNEER

THE
LOCKHART
PLOT

Love, Betrayal, Assassination and
Counter-Revolution in Lenin's Russia

OXFORD
UNIVERSITY PRESS

OXFORD

UNIVERSITY PRESS

Great Clarendon Street, Oxford, OX2 6DP,
United Kingdom

Oxford University Press is a department of the University of Oxford.
It furthers the University's objective of excellence in research, scholarship,
and education by publishing worldwide. Oxford is a registered trade mark of
Oxford University Press in the UK and in certain other countries

Published in the United States of America by Oxford University Press
198 Madison Avenue, New York, NY 10016, United States of America

British Library Cataloguing in Publication Data
Data available

Library of Congress Control Number: 2020933781

ISBN 978-0-19-885298-8

Printed and bound in Great Britain by
Clays Ltd, Elcograf S.p.A.

CONTENTS

CONTENTS

LIST OF PHOTOGRAPHS

LIST OF PHOTOGRAPHS

LIST OF MAPS

GLOSSARY OF NAMES

(These brief notes are meant to provide only the most basic relevant information for readers of this book.)

Alexeyev, Mikhail 1857–1918

Chief of the Russian General Staff during World War I, Alexeyev played a primary role in organizing the White Volunteer Army. The British hoped to use the Volunteer Army against Germany, and against the Bolsheviks.

Balfour, Arthur James (first Earl of Balfour) 1848–1930

He had been Conservative prime minister from 1902 to 1905. Lloyd George made him Foreign Secretary at the end of 1916. Lockhart reported to him.

Benckendorff, Djon von 1882–1919

One of Russia's junior diplomats stationed in prewar Berlin, there he met and in 1911 married Moura Zakrevskaia, the sister of a colleague. The couple returned to Russia when war broke out in 1914 and Djon became an aide-de-camp to the Tsar. After the October Revolution in 1917, he left his wife in Petrograd and with his two children moved to Yendel, his country estate in Estonia, where he was murdered in 1919.

Benckendorff, Moura von 1892–1974

Daughter of a wealthy Ukrainian lawyer and landowner, she married the junior Russian diplomat Djon Benckendorff in 1911, separated from him in 1918, and fell in love with Bruce Lockhart. Devastated when he jilted her, nevertheless she went on to survive and flourish.

Berzin, Eduard 1894–1938

Born in Latvia, he served as a captain in the Latvian Rifle Brigade during World War I, continuing in that position after the Bolshevik Revolution.

He and Jan Sprogis (disguised as Shmidkhen) approached Lockhart and fooled him, and Berzin went on to play a leading role in defeating Lockhart's plot. Afterward, he oversaw prison work camps in the gulag system. The Stalinists accused him of having always been a Latvian nationalist and executed him in 1938.

Briedis, Friedrich Andreevich 1888–1918

He was a heroic commander of one of the Latvian Rifle Battalions during World War I, where he came to know Eduard Berzin. Unlike his friend, he resigned his commission after the Bolshevik Revolution. He took part in the counter-revolutionary uprising organized by Boris Savinkov and paid the price. First, however, Dzerzhinsky and Peters persuaded him to write for them a letter of introduction to Captain Cromie.

Buikis, Jan ("Bredis")

Working for Felix Dzerzhinsky and Jacov Peters of the Cheka, he took the pseudonym "Bredis," in the operation to penetrate Cromie's counter-revolutionary organization in Petrograd. Someone recognized him, and he withdrew from the operation. In 1963, a KGB officer, V. F. Kravchenko, "discovered" him living in retirement in Moscow. There followed a series of articles, by both Kravchenko and Buikis, about the Lockhart Plot. Buikis claimed for himself the role actually played by Jan Sprogis, whose pseudonym had been "Shmidken."

Cecil, Robert (first Viscount Cecil of Chelmwood) 1864–1958

The cousin of Arthur Balfour (and son of Conservative prime minister Lord Salisbury), himself a Conservative MP, Cecil served from 1915 to 1918 as Britain's parliamentary undersecretary of state for foreign affairs. He believed the Bolsheviks to be German puppets. He believed the only way to win World War I was to reconstitute an Eastern Front. He favored supporting anti-Bolsheviks in Russia, and therefore he opposed Lockhart's initial mission to establish relations with them. When Lockhart turned and decided to oppose the Bolsheviks too, Cecil formed a more positive opinion of him. After World War I, Cecil went on to become a prominent advocate of the League of Nations.

Chicherin, Georgy 1872–1936

He replaced Trotsky as the Bolshevik Commissar for Foreign Affairs. As such, he often had dealings with Bruce Lockhart.

Cromie, Captain Francis Allen Newton 1882–1918

A daring, handsome, submarine commander, he became Britain's naval attaché in Lenin's Russia. He sank his flotilla of submarines in the Baltic to keep them from German hands and planned to sink Russia's entire Baltic fleet. He also became deeply involved in the Petrograd counter-revolutionary world. On August 30, 1918, the Bolsheviks went to arrest him at the British embassy building, a gun battle ensued, and Cromie died.

Denikin, General Anton 1872–1947

A former general in Russia's imperial army, he opposed the Bolsheviks and joined General Alexeyev to help form the counter-revolutionary Volunteer Army over which eventually he took military command. This was the army Britain hoped would help reconstitute an Eastern Front against Germany, and possibly even overthrow Bolshevism.

Dzerzhinsky, Felix 1877–1926

He became a revolutionary socialist while still a student in Livno, rose to the top of the Lithuanian revolutionary socialist movement, suffered numerous imprisonments, made numerous escapes, helped to organize the October Revolution in Russia and then became leader of the All-Russia Extraordinary Commission to Combat Counterrevolution and Sabotage, or (from its initials) VCheka, shortened, when speaking, to Cheka. No one worked harder, longer, or more effectively. He planned the operation that defeated Lockhart's plot.

Engel'gardt, Alexander ("Shtegel'man")

Almost all we know of this individual is that he was descended from a prominent Latvian family, and that Dzerzhinsky chose him to lead the three-man team of Chekists sent to penetrate Cromie's organization in Petrograd. He took the alias "Shtegel'man." He and a fellow Cheka agent, Lieutenant Sabir, were present at the British embassy building in Petrograd when Cromie met his death there.

Fride, Lieutenant Colonel Alexander ?–1918

He worked for the Bolsheviks as chief of military communications, but through his sister, Maria, passed information to the British spy, Sidney Reilly, and to the American agent Xenophon Kalamatiano. When the Bolsheviks broke up Lockhart's plot they arrested Fride and tried and executed him.

Garstin, Denis 1890–1918

A graduate of Sydney Sussex College, Cambridge, where he had edited the literary magazine, *Granta*, Garstin volunteered for service when World War I broke out, received his commission as captain, and took part in the early battles to defend France. Because he knew Russia from before the war, the army sent him to work in the British embassy in Petrograd in 1916. Later he would work with Lockhart. He hoped a liberal democratic regime would replace the Bolsheviks. When General Poole occupied Archangel, Garstin joined him and then took part in the advance south. He perished shortly thereafter in battle.

Grenard, Fernand 1886–1959

He was the French Consul General in Moscow who worked closely with Lockhart and helped subsidize Russian counter-revolutionaries.

Hall, Harold Trevenen 1884–1947

A British SIS agent working with Cromie in Petrograd, Hall made the mistake of trusting Engel'gart/Shtegel'man and Lieutenant Sabir. He was at the British embassy when Cromie died.

Hicks, William ?–1930

An expert in gas warfare, he met Moura while serving in Moscow sometime before the Revolution. He met Lockhart in London in December 1917 and joined his small team when it returned to Russia. He and Lockhart shared rooms, first in Petrograd where he brought Moura to lunch, thus facilitating the Lockhart–Moura romance, and later in Moscow. When the Cheka came for Lockhart, it arrested Hicks too (but did not re-arrest him several days later, as it did Lockhart). He and Lockhart remained friends for life, but there is no evidence that he participated in the Lockhart Plot.

Hill, George Alexander 1892–1968

A commissioned officer in the Royal Flying Corps, like Sidney Reilly, he worked in Russia for the Secret Intelligence Service. Hill established a network of agents, safe houses, and couriers to relay information from Russia. Reilly kept him apprised of the Lockhart Plot and, when it failed, he helped Reilly to escape. The Bolsheviks permitted Hill to leave Russia with Lockhart's party on October 3, 1918.

Kalamatiano, Xenophon Dmitrievich 1892–1923

He directed an information bureau in Russia gathering sensitive materials for American Consul General De Witt Clinton Poole. One of his agents was Alexander Fride. Kalamatiano coordinated loosely with British and French agents in the Lockhart Plot. When the Cheka broke the plot, it arrested Kalamatiano and, although it sentenced him to death, freed him in 1921.

Kannegisser, Leonid 1896–1918

A young poet, with anti-Bolshevik but socialist political inclinations, Kannegisser assassinated Moisei Uritisky, head of the Petrograd Cheka on August 30, 1918. He may have had some connection to Boris Savinkov. Probably he had no connection to Lockhart.

Kaplan, Fanny 1890–1918

She is the woman whom the Cheka accused of shooting Lenin on the night of August 30, 1918. Probably she belonged to the Socialist Revolutionary Party, which may have plotted the attempted assassination. The Cheka executed her several days later.

Knox, General Alfred William Fortescue 1870–1964

Britain's military attaché in Moscow at the time of the February Revolution, Knox hated the Bolsheviks and opposed Lockhart's initial conciliatory attitude towards them. He engaged with Lockhart in a struggle to influence the Foreign Office. He won.

Lenin, Vladimir Ilyitch 1870–1924

Leader of the Bolshevik Party, with Leon Trotsky a prime organizer of the October Revolution, as Chairman of the Council of Peoples' Commissars of the Soviet Union he led the new Russian government that Lockhart attempted to subvert.

Litvinov, Maxim 1876–1951

The Bolsheviks chose him to be their representative in London. The British government accorded him informal recognition when the Bolsheviks did the same for its emissary, Bruce Lockhart. When the Bolsheviks arrested Lockhart, the British arrested Litvinov. Then the two governments worked out an exchange of prisoners.

Lloyd George, David (first Earl of Dwyford) 1863–1945

British prime minister from December 1916 until 1922, he sent Lockhart back to Russia at the beginning of 1918 to establish informal contact with the Bolshevik government and persuade it to stay in the war against Germany, or if it insisted on quitting, to make a peace not detrimental to Allied interests. But he did not defend Lockhart from his British critics or oppose his agent when he turned.

Lockhart, Robert Hamilton Bruce 1887–1970

Britain's vice consul in Moscow 1912–17, and then Britain's emissary to the Bolsheviks, first he advocated working with them, then advocated working in Russia in spite of them, and finally advocated overthrowing them—which he attempted to do.

Lombard, Reverend Bousfield Swan 1866–1951

He was chaplain of the British embassy and English church in Petrograd, and of the Royal Navy submariners during World War I. He provided safe haven for Captain Cromie in a secret room in his attic during the dangerous weeks before Cromie's death on August 30, 1918. In fact, he took tea with Cromie at the embassy building on that day and suffered a month's-long imprisonment afterward.

Malkov, Pavel 1887–1965

An early Bolshevik, he took part storming the Winter Palace, became commandant of the Smolny Institute in Petrograd, where the Bolsheviks initially made their headquarters, and then he became commandant of the Kremlin when the Bolsheviks moved their government to Moscow. He led the party that arrested Bruce Lockhart.

Marchand, René 1888–?

Ambassador Noulens mistakenly believed him to be a French secret service agent and invited him to the August 25 meeting at which genuine agents detailed their plans for sabotage in Russia. Marchand, who was a journalist and Bolshevik sympathizer, promptly reported the meeting to the Cheka.

Milner, Alfred (first Viscount Milner) 1854–1925

A high-powered member of Lloyd George's War Cabinet, he first met Lockhart in Russia in 1917, was impressed by him, and played a key role in assigning him to return to Russia in January 1918.

Noulens, Josef 1864–1944

He was the anti-Bolshevik French ambassador to Russia who helped finance the counter-revolutionaries, including the Socialist Revolutionaries and Boris Savinkov. He led them to believe that Anglo-French forces would arrive in north Russia by early July 1918, knowing that they would not.

Peters, Jacov 1886–1938

A Latvian revolutionary who fled to London after the 1905 revolutions, he probably had something to do with the infamous robbery and murders that led to the Sydney Street Siege, but the jury did not convict him. He was Felix Dzerzhinsky's second-in-command of the Cheka and took over briefly when Dzerzhinsky stepped back in the summer of 1918. He took a primary role in designing the counter-plot to defeat Lockhart. He was kind to Moura Benckendorff while she was imprisoned, possibly in order to recruit her to work for the Cheka. In 1938, the Stalinists tried him for having been a Latvian nationalist all along and executed him.

Poole, DeWitt Clinton 1885–1952

Served as the American vice consul general in Moscow during 1917–18, employed Xenophon Kalamatiano and cooperated with the French Consul General Grenard, and with Lockhart, including when the latter launched his plot. He hosted the meeting on August 25, when René Marchand learned about the plot, was horrified by it, and reported it to the Bolsheviks.

Poole, General Frederick Cuthbert 1869–1936

He served as Britain's General Officer Commanding North Russia Expeditionary Force during 1918–19. The original intent of his mission was first to secure the material in the ports Murmansk and Archangel so that the Germans could not take it, and then to march south to rally Russians loyal to the war in order to reconstitute an Eastern Front—and if that led to the downfall of Bolshevism, so much the better.

Ransome, Arthur 1884–1967

Journalist, author, secret service agent, Ransome loved Russia. *In situ* before the war began, and having returned to it after, he came to know many leading Bolsheviks. Once they took power he had unique access to them. He reported sympathetically on them in newspaper articles, and to the Foreign Office; probably he talked frankly about Britain to the Bolsheviks. He supported Lockhart's initial conciliatory approach. They remained friends, even though Lockhart reversed his position.

Reilly, Sidney George (formerly Shlomo ben Hersh Rozenbluim) 1874–1925

His origins, and much that he did, remain obscure. During our period he worked with Lockhart on the plot to overthrow the Bolsheviks. He may have been Ian Fleming's model for the fictional James Bond. He has been termed the "Ace of Spies."

Robins, Raymond 1873–1954

He made a fortune in the gold rush in Alaska, converted to Christianity, and became a social reformer, although an anti-socialist. He ran unsuccessfully on the Progressive Party ticket to become US Senator from Illinois. In Russia he headed the American Salvation Army project to provide and distribute food. Also, he had received from US President Wilson instructions similar to Lockhart's: make contact with the Bolsheviks, try to keep them in the war. Robins advocated non-intervention and recognition of the new regime. He returned to the US to lobby for these goals.

Lieutenant Sabir

Posing as a counter-revolutionary, he attempted to make contact with Captain Cromie and was turned away. Then Engel'gardt/Shtegel'man vouched for him. The two of them led Cromie and Harold Trevenen Hall down the garden path and were present when Cromie died.

Savinkov, Boris 1879–1925

A terrorist associated with the Socialist Revolutionary Party during pre-war years, he served as Kerensky's Assistant Minister for War and turned to counter-revolution after the Bolsheviks seized power. Despite French and British subsidies, neither country could offer military support, and his anti-Bolshevik uprising in July 1918 failed. Yet he remained one of Bolshevism's most ardent and effective foes until lured back to Russia in 1925. Then he was captured and either killed by the Bolsheviks or died by his own hand.

Spiridonova, Maria 1884–1941

Sent by the Tsar's courts to Siberia for life for terrorist activities, freed after eleven years by the February Revolution, she became a leader of the left SRs. She plotted the assassination of German ambassador Wilhelm von Mirbach, whose death she vainly hoped would force Russia back into war with Germany. The Bolsheviks arrested her, then let her go, made her life a misery until finally re-arresting her in 1937, and shooting her in 1941.

Sprogis, Jan ("Shmidkhen")

In the Cheka operation directed by Dzerzhinsky and Peters, he, posing as "Shmidken," along with Buikis ("Bredis") and Engel'gardt ("Shtegel'man") penetrated Captain Cromie's counter-revolutionary organization in Petrograd. He and Captain Eduard Berzin then approached Lockhart in Moscow and encouraged him to believe they could deliver the Latvians to his plot. Sprogis' end is obscure.

Trotsky Leon 1879–1940

As Lenin's Commissar of Foreign Affairs, he conducted at Brest-Litovsk the brilliant but doomed Bolshevik negotiations to end the war with Germany. At first, he allowed Lockhart to think that Britain and Bolshevik Russia could cooperate, but as the German threat to Bolshevism faded so did Trotsky's interest in cultivating Britain. Replaced as Commissar by Georgy Chicherin, Trotsky built and led the Red Army, which ultimately saw off the foreign and Russian counter-revolutionary threat. Later, of course, Stalin had him murdered, as he did many other old Bolsheviks.

Uritsky, Moisei 1873–1918

He was the head of the Petrograd Cheka. The poet Leonid Kannegisser murdered him on the morning of August 30, 1918, thereby precipitating the Bolshevik decision to immediately close down the Lockhart Plot.

A NOTE TO READERS

The Lockhart Plot was a conspiracy developed by British, French, and American agents during the spring and summer of 1918, when the outcome of World War I still hung in the balance. Its aim was to murder the Bolshevik leaders Vladimir Lenin and Leon Trotsky, to overthrow their recently and precariously established communist regime, and to install another that would continue the war against Germany on the Eastern Front. The men and women who planned it, and those who thwarted them, worked in the shadows, for obvious reasons. They exchanged no letters or only innocuous ones, they wrote no incriminating diary entries, and at least on the British, French, and American sides, they received no government instructions directly explaining what was to be done. Of course, there is a documentary record, but it contains no "smoking gun" directive proving that any Allied government ordered its agents to overthrow the Bolsheviks. Perhaps the record has been vetted, that is to say, sanitized. But also, in 1918, Allied governments feared that the Bolsheviks had broken their cyphers, and therefore they wrote to their agents with great circumspection. Sometimes, the agents wrote back with equal guardedness. When they wrote frankly, they often did not understand their own position or motivations, so murky and freighted was the situation.

There may be much pertinent and significant material in the archives of the Russian secret police, today known as the FSB, but it is not available to Western researchers, nor have Russian scholars quoted it much, and what they have quoted is hardly revelatory. Of course, there are contemporary newspaper reports, but the historian must use them cautiously. Compounding difficulties, once the plot had been broken and became public knowledge, the protagonists who wrote about it did so for self-interested reasons. Their accounts are all unreliable. Lockhart, in his memoirs, entirely denied responsibility for the plot, which is what the British government wanted of him; conversely, the self-aggrandizing Sydney Reilly, history's "Ace of Spies," claimed primary responsibility for it, quite falsely. On the Russian side, the only major figure to write about the plot at any length purposely mixed up his own role with the more important part played by one of his colleagues—but this was many years later, and the colleague long dead, and therefore unable to contradict him.

Despite all this, the plot has not lacked for American, British, French, and Russian historians. But the many authors who have tried to tell the story, in journal articles, chapters of books, and sections of chapters, all had to pick their way through a maze of opaque papers, reports, and cables, and then through a minefield of intentionally misleading accounts and statements, false trails, and outright lies. They have been more or less credulous, more or less creative, more or less successful. To a greater or lesser extent, every historian faces similar difficulties no matter the project; all written histories are imperfect and incomplete—but the Lockhart Plot is a more difficult subject than most.

This is the first book-length account of it. I have had to deal with the same obstacles and pitfalls faced by my predecessors, but I have done so in a different way. Where the evidence is contradictory, as it often is, I say so in the text. Where it is incomplete, I tell the reader. When I have to guess at the motivations of one or another of the conspirators or their opponents because there simply is not enough evidence to be certain, I explain that is what I am doing. Also, where the documents themselves contain judgements that may or may not be accurate, I note it. For example, agents of the French and British secret services, whose reports many historians accept as gospel, were as likely to make unsubstantiated judgements and statements as anyone else, especially when discussing the main female figure in this book, the alluring, charismatic, Moura von Benckendorff. She was the object of incessant gossip, rumor, and innuendo, much of it cruel and sexist. That is what the agents were repeating—and some historians too.

This is the most complete account of the Lockhart Plot yet written, but it cannot be definitive, for all the reasons just explained. Let the reader beware, then—but also let him or her enjoy an attempt to accurately recount in full an extraordinary, even thrilling, episode in Russian history, replete with derring-do, intrigue, betrayal, romance, violence, even tragedy. It really happened, and it might have shaken the world. Today, in the time of Putin and Trump, we may, from a long distance, and over the passage of many decades, still perceive its enduring relevance.

PART I

LOCKHART BEFORE
THE FALL

CHAPTER 1

THE MAKING OF
BRUCE LOCKHART

January 11, 1918: a gray and somber day in London during the
fourth year of a war that had devastated half the world and
whose outcome no one could yet predict. Two Russians representing the Bolshevik regime that had taken power in Russia the
previous October, and two Britons representing the government
of their own country, sat across from one another at a table in the
Lyons Corner House in the Strand near Trafalgar Square. In such
modest and incongruous settings the world may be shaped, or
undone. The quartet had just finished lunch. Now, in a room
barely lit by a few weak bulbs, and by the feeble, slanting rays of an
overcast northern winter sky, one of the Russians was writing a
letter in Cyrillic characters. He used the table at which they had
just dined as his desk. When he finished, his companion quickly
provided an English translation. The letter was addressed to
"Citizen Trotsky, People's Commissariat for Foreign Affairs," and
the first paragraph read:

> *Dear Comrade, – The bearer of this, Mr. Lockhart, is going to Russia with an*
> *official mission with the exact character of which I am not acquainted. I know*
> *him personally as a thoroughly honest man who understands our position*
> *and sympathizes with us. I should consider his sojourn in Russia useful from*
> *the point of view of our interests.*

While the two Britons nodded their satisfaction, the author of the letter ordered a French dessert—"pouding diplomate" (diplomat pudding)—but the waiter returned a few moments later to say there was none left. This was a poor augury for the "official mission" referred to in the letter, yet, when the meal concluded and the four men departed the restaurant, at least one of them disappeared down Whitehall into the darkening afternoon with a spring in his step. Maxim Litvinov had been denied his "pouding diplomate," but as usual, young Bruce Lockhart, whom the British government was about to send to Moscow to parlay with Lenin and Trotsky, had gotten just what he wanted. This time, it was a reference letter from the only person in England who could smooth his way with the Bolshevik government in Russia. Of course, he had no inkling that also he had set into motion a train of events that would culminate in the audacious plot that bears his name.

* * *

In 1918, Bruce Lockhart was 31 years of age. He stood, according to his passport, five-foot seven inches tall (the average height of a British soldier at that date was about five-foot five). He had blue eyes, brown hair above a high forehead, ordinary nose, medium mouth, and square face. He had jug ears and a stocky frame. He stares coolly from the century-old passport photo with an assessing, slightly skeptical, self-assured and intelligent gaze.[1] It is a true and revealing photograph, the impression it makes only reinforced by a description of Lockhart's speaking voice provided later by one of his friends: "assertive and modest, arrogant and humorously depreciative at the same time."[2]

He was born in 1887 in Anstruther, Fife, Scotland, and proudly claimed to have no drop of English blood in his veins. He had

4

Figure 1. Robert Hamilton Bruce Lockhart in 1915, on his way to Russia

spent his childhood in the bosom of a large, happy, close-knit and prosperous family. His mother's side owned an old established distillery, Balmenach, at Cromdale near Grantown-on-Spey; his father's side held extensive interests in the rubber plantations of Malaysia. His parents sent young Lockhart to the exclusive Fettes College in Edinburgh, where he distinguished himself not as a scholar but as an athlete. In fact, he inherited outstanding athletic ability. It gave him self-confidence—perhaps too much.

Upon leaving Fettes he did not go to Cambridge as his father had done, and where sports might again have distracted him, but rather to the "Institute Tilley" in Berlin, where he learned German and, finally, "how to work," and then to Paris where private tutors took him in hand. The results were gratifying: the teenager who loved sports now found that he could pick up languages easily (he would claim to "speak some six or seven" only a few years later),[3] displayed a wonderful memory, and discovered a passion for literature, poetry, theater, and art that never left him. Soon he could recite by heart passages from Heine in the original German, and the works of the aesthete and travel writer Pierre Loti in the original French.

In 1908 he returned to England to prepare for the Indian Civil Service exam. He buckled down to study for a serious test; he knew now that he could compete with the best students; a real career beckoned. Then one of the rubber plantation uncles visited the family and excited the young man's imagination with tales of the romantic, mysterious Orient. Lockhart impulsively dropped his books and sailed east with his relative.

He was 21 years old, impetuous but formidable. He learned the Malay language as he had learned French and German, with ease. "He has exceptional abilities," wrote his first employer in Malaya.[4] Recognizing them, his uncle sent him to open up a new rubber estate near Pantei, in Nigeri Sembilan. The young man made a success of this too. But along with high intelligence, natural authority, and acute perception, he would soon display a dangerous streak of recklessness.

Early in 1910, he gave a party. His gaze fell upon the most beautiful girl he had ever seen, "a radiant vision of brown loveliness." Her name was Amai, and he knew that he must have her. That she was about to marry into the highest reaches of local society did not deter him; perhaps the challenge excited him. His campaign of seduction nearly amounted to stalking, but he won her. Characteristically, he did not consider what might come after; and if he thought about the sacrifices Amai would have to make— and then did make—to be with him, they did not weigh heavily on his mind.

Everyone opposed the match, including some who might take deadly measures to end it. After a period of months characterized

by bliss with her and strife with practically everyone else, Lockhart
fell desperately ill, probably with malaria, but possibly from poison.
His suffering was intense, but he was too proud to seek professional help. Eventually Amai summoned a doctor who prescribed
immediate flight, not directly to Lockhart, but on the young man's
behalf to his uncle. The next day this gentleman and a cousin
bundled the weakened young Scot into an automobile and conveyed him to the ship that would provide the first leg of his journey home. Lockhart later claimed that he had protested—but
could his relatives have overborne him if he truly had been determined to stay?

The elegiac tone of a 1936 memoir suggests that on one level he
always regretted the end to this affair.[5] But also it had been a narrow
escape, for the life of a colonial planter never could have satisfied
him, which he surely knew. At any rate, here was a pattern that
would recur: more than once in the years to come, Lockhart would
ignore convention and his own better instincts while pursuing an
attractive young woman; would experience initial success and
delight; but then would face the disapproval of powerful figures
whom he dared not oppose, and to whom, after some heartburning, he would yield. The affair with Amai was a harbinger.

Back in Scotland, momentarily chastened, this time he agreed
to take the Consular Service exam. He listed as referees the man-
agers of the Malayan plantations on which he had worked, confident they would overlook his amorous misadventure. They did.
"At all times honest, sober and well conducted," wrote one of
them. "I have the highest opinion of his character and capacity,"
wrote the other.[6] From his former headmaster he obtained the
following testimonial: "R. H. B. Lockhart was educated at Fettes
College. He had considerable intellectual capacity and was very

prominent in games. I recommended his Father to endeavour to find him a career in the Consular Office, in which I think his abilities should make him very serviceable."[7] With this endorsement in his pocket, Lockhart headed for London to cram for the exam. This time he really did buckle down, which meant that no one could beat him. When the grades were made public his name appeared at the top of the list. He had come first in every category.

And reaped the reward. His first posting was a plum: vice consul in Moscow. A week before his departure his parents threw a farewell party in his honor. There he spied another vision of loveliness, this time of the Australian variety. Her name was Jean Adelaide Haslewood Turner. As with Amai, he knew immediately what he wanted, and did not think beyond. He had only seven days to gain his objective, but again he mounted an irresistible whirlwind campaign. In this instance no powerful forces intervened, and the pair would marry the first time he came home on leave a year later. But it would not be a happy marriage.

* * *

In January 1912, Bruce Lockhart, betrothed, charming, formidably intelligent, adventurous beyond common sense, determined and competitive (not merely on the playing fields), strong-willed but only to the penultimate point, arrived in Russia. He drank his first glass of vodka; ate caviar for the first time. During Moscow's long winter nights, he rode in horse-drawn sleighs, their bells jingling, over snow-covered streets, under star-filled skies. During summer, he wandered through the city's elaborate Hermitage Summer Gardens, marveling at their splendor. He attended grand dinners in homes like palaces, where champagne flowed freely. He played football for a factory team owned by two English brothers whom he met through his consular duties. It must have been very high-level play since it attracted crowds of ten to fifteen thousand. He helped the team to win a series of Moscow league championships.

During those two and a half years before the outbreak of World War I, he came to know many Tsarist officials. But also, his Russian language teacher, a liberal dissident, introduced him to critics of the regime, including leading members of the once radical but increasingly moderate Constitutional Democratic, or Kadet, Party, and the Socialist Revolutionary Party, an incarnation of the old terrorist Populist Party dedicated to peasant revolution, now containing not only populists but also various inharmonious and therefore fissiparous liberals, urban intellectuals, and socialists of varying stripes. These often-colorful figures appealed to him more than the Tsar's apologists did, and he appealed to them. He befriended his neighbor, Mikhail Chelnokov, the Kadet Party's Mayor of Moscow. Convivial and confident, knowledgeable and well connected, young Lockhart circulated among the city's elite. Culturally, at least, he was no snob. Gypsy music fascinated him. Cabaret drew him. He quickly learned to speak perfect Russian.[8] When his wife joined him early in 1913, he was complete.

To cap this magical period, Jean became pregnant. Her due-date was June 20, 1914. What followed, however, beggared every expectation. On the 21st, Jean lost her baby during a botched delivery which nearly cost her life too, and from which she recovered slowly in hospital in miserable conditions, a devastating experience for both parents. Then exactly a week after the death of their infant, a Serbian nationalist in Sarajevo, Gravilo Princip, assassinated Franz Ferdinand, heir to the Austrian throne. That was the trigger for worldwide tragedy. When Austria decided to punish Serbia, Russia came to the defense of her Slavic "little brother." But then Germany backed her Austrian ally. That brought France and Britain into the conflict; they supported Russia, their partner in the Triple Entente. Thus, Princip's pistol shots proved to be the first salvo in a war that would wreak unimaginable destruction. The Lockharts' personal misfortune had been subsumed in a global catastrophe.

*   *   *

He coped by losing himself in work. Contacts and knowledge gained over three years paid off. As the war ground on, he began sending regular reports on the situation in Moscow to Sir George Buchanan, Britain's ambassador to Russia, who was stationed in the Russian capital, Petrograd—as Russian patriots had renamed St. Petersburg because it sounded less German. Buchanan judged the reports good and began forwarding them to London. In fact, they were better than good. They contained astute observations and literary flourishes that bear comparison with those of T. E. Lawrence (of Arabia), another British agent working at this time, albeit in a different corner of the world. For example, in June 1917, after witnessing Russia's new leader, Alexander Kerensky, address an enormous, adoring crowd at Moscow's Big Theatre, on the theme that "nothing worth having can be achieved without suffering," Lockhart wrote:

> [Kerensky] himself looked the embodiment of suffering. The deathly pallor of his face, the restless movements of his body as he swayed backwards and forwards, the raw almost whispering tones of his voice, which was yet heard as clearly as a bell in the farthest gallery of the vast building, all helped to make his appeal more terrible and more realistic....And when the end came the huge crowd rose to greet him like one man. Men and women embraced

each other in a hysteria of enthusiasm. Old generals and young *praporshicks* [ensigns] wept together over the man...Women gave presents of jewellery. Officers sacrificed their orders.

And then the needle to puncture the balloon and his own novelistic prose, thereby demonstrating his own perspicacity: "Common sense, however, makes one hesitate..." For both before and after the cheering of the bourgeoisie and Socialist Revolutionaries at the Big Theatre, other voices, socialist voices, more influential voices, at other meetings addressed by Kerensky even on the same day, had been "demand[ing] explanations of his policy of the necessity of attacking," that is to say, of continuing the war by launching a great offensive.[9] The doubters would prevail in the end, as Lockhart already suspected they would.

He kept in touch with Moscow's most prominent men and women during these first three years of the war, in and out of politics, supporters and opponents of the regime. Curious, fearless, determined, he attended private political meetings at which probably he was the only foreigner, providing translations of speeches and resolutions; he joined outdoor demonstrations, strikes, and processions at which probably he was the only non-socialist, describing them in pungent, penetrating prose, including translations even of the slogans daubed on placards and banners. He delivered employment statistics and production statistics. He assessed the morale of troops stationed in the city. He recorded the views of reactionaries, liberals, socialists, professors, authors, musicians, economists.

For the most part he kept his political views to himself in his reports. Still, the dispatches reveal him to have been not only remarkably industrious, knowledgeable and literate, but also open-minded and rather idealistic. In a country infamous for anti-Semitism, at a time when many in the British diplomatic and consular services did not hesitate to express anti-Semitic views, and moreover at a time when it was common to assert that "the Jews" dominated not only Russia's revolutionary movement but the world revolutionary movement—and world finance as well— he wrote with admirable sympathy and understanding: "A Jewish pogrom [in Russia] is far more probable than a revolutionary movement financed and fomented by Jews."[10] His cables sided openly with Russia's "Progressives" in their struggle against "the Blacks" for reform. Only a year into the war, he warned about that struggle: "the triumph of the reactionary party…must be regarded with considerable anxiety."[11] He often referred admiringly to his liberal friends, Prince Georgy Lvov, a former Kadet, who would try in 1916 to persuade the Tsar to abdicate, and when that failed to organize a bloodless palace coup, and most frequently to Mayor Chelnokov (a man "of unimpeachable honour and integrity"), who championed "the Moscow of the refugees, of the hospitals, and of the factories."[12]

With regret, however, he came to recognize that his Kadet friends lacked political effectiveness. He did not favor revolution in Russia during wartime, but he began warning early on that one was possible, even likely. Who would lead it? Unfortunately, the Kadet Party, and the "intelligenzia" who dominated it, did "not seem to be of the stuff of which revolutions are made."[13] When the Tsar fell, not through their efforts alone by any means, and the Kadets nevertheless helped to form a provisional government, he soon realized that the future belonged to parties further left: "One is bound to admit that the Socialists are far more energetic." His own sympathies moved leftwards as a result. In July 1917, he wrote admiringly of M. Urnof, the Socialist Revolutionary president of the Moscow Soldiers' Council and vice president of the Moscow Duma: "He is a man of great force of character and of very high ideals and is altogether one of the most interesting personalities in Moscow."[14] But he never favored the Bolsheviks, "who have for their motto 'the worse things are, the better for us.'"[15] The Bolsheviks, he charged, were carrying on "a harmful and dangerous agitation" not only against the "bourgeois and imperialistic" governments of France and Britain,[16] but "louder than ever" against the new provisional government, and even against other socialists.[17]

The Foreign Office read his cables eagerly. "Mr. Lockhart's report is … well written, convincing," noted a Whitehall official in September 1915.[18] "I only wish we got as clear and interesting reports from more quarters than Moscow," wrote another mandarin.[19] By early 1917, Lockhart's views were circulating at the highest levels. The Foreign Secretary, Arthur Balfour, regularly passed his cables to Prime Minister David Lloyd George. The young Scot did not know how high his reputation had climbed, but soon had an inkling. When Britain's Consul General in Moscow transferred to New York City, Lockhart received instructions to stay where he was and to take his place. Not yet 30, he had the attention of Britain's top men. He had become their eyes and ears at what would soon be the storm center of world affairs.

* * *

Three years of war had passed and the catastrophes for Russia had mounted—at the front where shortages, especially in heavy guns, led to casualties of astonishing proportions (five million); and at home, where transportation broke down utterly, corruption reigned, food grew scarce, and bellies empty. Russia always had been a country of awful contrasts between rich and poor, but the war exacerbated the disparities to a terrible degree. So long as he held power, the Tsar dismissed anyone who called for reform and appointed arch reactionaries in their place. Then he assumed control of the army, which was beyond his ability to manage. This act had the unintended result of saddling him with personal responsibility for all the ensuing military failures. By 1917, sensible men and women even among the aristocracy, normally his most loyal and natural supporters had begun to fall away. He had long since forfeited the support of middle-class liberals and urban workers.[20]

In his reports, Lockhart traced the developing tragedy with clear eyes. In mid-February 1917, when Alfred Milner, a member of Lloyd George's War Cabinet arrived in Moscow, Lockhart arranged a meeting for him with his friend Prince Lvov. The Prince warned there could be revolution in Russia within three weeks. Milner was impressed—as much by the young man who made the introduction and served as interpreter—as by the man who made the prediction.

Almost exactly three weeks later, food riots in Petrograd escalated into the very revolution Lvov had predicted. The Tsar abdicated and Lvov himself emerged initially as head of a new provisional government. Liberals in France and Britain rejoiced. Lockhart, however, knew that Russian liberalism had gained only a precarious victory. The revolution had unleashed vast forces with which his friends would be unable to cope. He wrote another report entitled "On the Moscow Revolution of March 12th to March 17th," expressing his reservations. "It is improbable," he warned presciently, "that a country in the state in which Russia is at present can pass through so disintegrating an upheaval of her forces without further revolutions and counter-revolutions."[21] In his diary, he was more certain: "It seems impossible that the struggle between the bourgeoisie and the socialist elements or proletariat can pass off without further bloodshed."[22]

Bruce Lockhart, 30 years old, had found his voice and audience. His future looked well set. But the youth who had dropped his books and sailed to Malaya, and who had run a plantation with great success until he spied Amai, still lived. This time, "Madame Vermelle" (almost certainly a misspelling, it should have been "Vermel"), "a Russian Jewess," as he called her in his memoir, caught his eye. Historians have written that she may have been French not Russian, and may not have been Jewish. Certainly, she was not the first woman with whom he dallied in Russia.[23] In fact probably the woman in question was Vera Lutse, a Polish soprano famous for her interpretation of Madam Butterfly in the Puccini opera, who went on to marry a prominent Russian physician called Vermel.[24] Whoever she was, the ambassador ordered Lockhart to drop her. Eventually he did.

This episode deserves further attention. First of all, it is unlikely that the diplomatic set prized monogamy in 1917 or thought its non-observance a great crime. Moreover, if Lockhart had been unfaithful to his wife previously, why did the ambassador intervene this time only? Perhaps because Vera Lutse was too prominent a personage and the affair too visible? Or could she perhaps have had unsuitable (Bolshevik?) political associations?[25] At any rate, Lockhart did as his superior advised—for "exactly three weeks." Then: "One day the telephone rang and I went back."[26] Now the ambassador told him that he and his spouse must return to England. The obvious inference is that Buchanan was determined to protect the future of a man who had earned the appreciation of Lloyd George and Arthur Balfour. And Lockhart acquiesced—just as he had done in Malaya.

The episode practically recapitulates the earlier one. Amorous and impetuous, Lockhart had pursued an unsuitable woman, knowing he should not. He had jeopardized relationships (most importantly this time, with his wife) and risked his position. Ultimately, he bowed to more senior figures who disapproved and sent him home, leaving the woman on her own. What Jean thought of all this goes unrecorded, but she knew her husband had strayed.[27] Somehow, he made it up to her; after all, he was a charmer and a rogue as well as a brilliant observer and reporter, and within weeks she was pregnant again.

* * *

Back in London, September 1917 now, he went to work at the recently created Ministry of Overseas Trade as a Russia expert. He had little to do, actually, because war and revolution had so disrupted Anglo-Russian trade that there was not much of it, but his reports from Moscow had made his reputation. No one in Whitehall knew the reason for his reappearance—or if they did know they did not care—and important people still listened to him. Lockhart warned that the country he had just left faced further troubles.

Events justified him right away, which can only have heightened his reputation. Led by Lenin and Trotsky, the Bolsheviks seized power from the provisional government in October (according to the Russian calendar—November according to the Western calendar to which Russia would convert a few months later), calling for international proletarian insurrection and an end to the world war. The more insistently they called, the more suspicious the Allies became. They knew Germany had helped Lenin return to Russia via the famous "sealed train" that brought him and select colleagues from Switzerland through Germany to the Finland rail station in Petrograd.[28] They believed, and historians have confirmed, that Lenin continued to accept German favors, or rather "German gold," as it was called at the time.[29] Allied leaders deemed the Bolsheviks to be nothing more than German puppets who now were stabbing their country's erstwhile partners in the back. The British, French, and American governments prepared to recall their ambassadors from Petrograd.

Lockhart opposed this move. He knew enough about the "bolsheviki" to argue that Lenin and Trotsky had no allegiance to the Kaiser even if they had accepted his help—they had used Germany as much as Germany had used them. Moreover, they would hold power for the foreseeable future, because their opponents, whom he knew well, were weak and divided. Better, then, to recognize the new Bolshevik government, and try to turn it against the Central Powers. He made these arguments to anyone who would listen.

Near the midpoint of December, he dined again with Lord Milner. The persuasive, knowledgeable, imposing young expert presented his views to the War Cabinet minister, who must have recalled his initial positive impression. There can be no better testimony to Lockhart's persuasiveness than this: "When he went away," Lockhart remembered, "he told me that I should hear from him very soon."[30]

On December 21, he received a summons to 10 Downing Street, to meet the prime minister. "I was ushered into a long narrow room which seemed to me all table…Lord Milner took me up to Lloyd George. 'Mr. Lockhart?' he said…'The Mr. Lockhart?…From the wisdom of your reports I expected to see an elderly man with a grey beard.'"³¹ Then, as Lockhart recounted in his memoir, the prime minister gave him his marching orders: return to Russia as Britain's unofficial envoy to the Bolsheviks (if they would deal with him, then Britain would deal on a like, unofficial, basis with their representative, Maxim Litvinov, in London); persuade the Bolsheviks to stay in the war against Germany; failing that, persuade them to make a peace with Germany that did not threaten British interests.

The young Scot accepted the commission immediately, joyfully. Miraculously, he was the coming man after all. His career resurrected, he would be the prime minister's emissary to revolutionary Russia. The meeting with Litvinov at the Lyons Corner Shop at which there was no "pouding diplomate" soon followed.

But he had accepted an unofficial mission, shrouded in secrecy that is still difficult to penetrate. Lockhart "should leave England as quietly as possible," advised the Foreign Office. After his departure Trotsky would be informed that "men in sympathy with the Russian Democracy," and "worthy of [his] confidence" were approaching.³² This must be an oblique reference to the lines of communication Lockhart had developed during his vice-consular stint, not merely with the liberal opponents of the Tsar but with more radical elements. Members of the British government, unacquainted with the fine gradations that separated one group of Russian socialists from another (the First Lord of the Admiralty, Lord Edward Carson, asked Lockhart to explain to him the difference between Maximalists and Bolsheviks),³³ may have thought that Lockhart, who knew "socialists," therefore would know how to talk to the ones currently in power, and they to him.

Nevertheless, his appointment gave rise to confusion, firstly among Bolsheviks who did not know where in the diplomatic hierarchy Lockhart stood, and secondly among British officials still in Russia who would soon be finding him too cocksure by half. Moreover, no one quite knew to whom he ultimately reported—for an emissary of the Foreign Office he would develop closer than usual links with certain agents belonging to the Secret Intelligence Service (SIS).[34] And was he an envoy of the Foreign Office or of the fraction of the War Cabinet which had conceived his mission? Some Britons in Russia, and in London too, may not have appreciated the ambiguity, and may have protested to their superiors—to no avail at first, his authority ran so deep.[35]

Or seemed to. Perhaps he should not have been cocksure—for acute though he was, he misunderstood his position; and charmer though he was, he did not realize that he himself had been charmed, dazzled really, by Milner and Lloyd George. He was not their indispensable man but a tool, to be dispensed with the moment he put a foot wrong in Russia. The prime minister "would leave anyone in the lurch if it suited his purpose," one of his colleagues was writing at just about this time.[36] Young Bruce Lockhart's confidence was misplaced.

He spent Christmas 1917, his last two weeks in London, preparing for his mission. He conferred often with Milner. He met with most cabinet ministers and with the most important members of the Foreign Office, including the languid, aristocratic Balfour, and the parliamentary undersecretary for foreign affairs, Robert Cecil, Balfour's unusually tall, cadaverously thin, younger cousin and chief aide. These two would loom large in his future. Lockhart wrote in his diary, "Milner is the only one who strikes me as really efficient…Neither he nor Ll.G. think much of the F[oreign] O[ffice], in particular of Balfour."[37]

A little more than a week later, he and the small team he had assembled to help him in Russia boarded a train at King's Cross station in London. It would bring them to Rosyth, Scotland, where a cruiser lay waiting to bear them to Stockholm, from which they would travel by rail, in stages, to Petrograd.[38] At Edinburgh, his wife joined him to see him off, but his thoughts were not with her. "Adventure tugs at the heart-strings of youth…I had had a colossal stroke of luck."[39] In truth he had no idea how exciting his mission would be—or how perilous. He was headed for great danger, but also for a great romance, one that would mark him more deeply than the risky liaison with Amai, the clandestine affair with "Madame Vermelle," or even the whirlwind courtship he had mounted to win his wife. He could not know it but he was on his way to the greatest adventure—and love—of his life.

CHAPTER 2

THE EDUCATION OF
BRUCE LOCKHART

The Bolsheviks believed in nothing less than reordering the world, beginning with their own country. As one of their earliest decrees put it: "All the classes of society existing up to now in Russia, and all divisions of citizens into classes, all class distinctions and privileges, class organizations and institutions and all civil grades, are abolished."[1] Such breath-taking pronouncements evoked exhilaration and surging hope among some, but also skepticism, hostility, disgust, even terror among others, and not just in Russia: every government in the world grimaced with distaste at what the Bolsheviks proposed to do. Few believed the revolutionaries would hold power long enough to realize their egalitarian dreams; indeed, the revolutionaries themselves did not. But they were determined to try, if only to establish an historical marker for future generations of communists to measure themselves against, and to attempt to surpass. If they must go down, they would go down fighting. Meanwhile, Russia slid toward complete breakdown.

In revolutionary Petrograd, Russia's capital, chaos reigned at the beginning of 1918. Trams seldom ran and rarely followed their posted routes when they did. If one appeared, it was necessary to ask the conductor where it really was going, whatever the signs might promise.[2] That was only one indication of breakdown. At the railway stations "intellectuals, aristocrats and others, most of them women," offered for sale whatever they thought they could spare from their homes in order to purchase food at fantastic prices.[3] Potatoes cost seventy times what they had before the war; cheese cost thirty times.[4] "We sit in cold rooms, without electric light…with 1b [sic] of black sour bread handed out for 2 days' ration…no meat, chickens at £1 apiece [about £56 today]," reported an English journalist.[5] In the streets, armed bandits and gangs ran wild: "Heaps of my friends have been held up, robbed, even of their clothes," recounted a British officer. "Which wouldn't be so bad in summer, but now is hardly recommended. So, we all go armed." He described "Unemployment…starvation…murder… trade absolutely stopped."[6] It is "anarchy," he concluded.[7]

Application of communist principles to daily life seemed both arbitrary and sporadic. The Bolsheviks had yet to establish their grip. For example, it snowed in mid-February, after a brief thaw. Before the revolution, the municipality had employed teams of men with shovels to clear the streets and sidewalks; after the Bolsheviks seized power, municipal authority vanished at first. During the early winter months of 1917–18, snow piled high in the thoroughfares of Petrograd, "banked like mountains." But, wrote the officer again, "Now everyone is put on to clear [it away]. Everyone: officers, bourgeois, aristos, financiers, everyone. And my turn will probably come."[8]

Bolshevik Red Guards did not shovel snow, however. Rather they stalked the city looking for former army officers to harass. "You know that new Russia is a democracy where all men are equal," one Guard scolded a former colonel who stood trembling with barely suppressed rage and humiliation before a crowd of onlookers, not all of whom sympathized with him. "How can you wear shoulder straps when it is against the express orders of the revolutionary military control? Be careful comrade....Another patrol might not be so gentle as we have been." Then he sliced off the unfortunate man's decorations with a long, wicked-looking, razor-sharp knife.[9]

Bolshevism had turned Russia upside down, and Lockhart entered the great charivari on the evening of January 30. At seven o'clock that night, his train chugged into the very Finland Station in Petrograd where Lenin had alighted the previous April to launch his party upon its earth-shaking course. What Lockhart saw when he left the station and headed for his temporary quarters at the British Embassy, unnerved him. The horse that pulled his sleigh "looked like it had not had a square meal for weeks." Another horse lay dead in the road near the Troitski Bridge, frozen solid.[10] The rock-hard snow and ice on Petrograd's streets made driving on them seem "something like a scenic railway—without the security."[11] Pedestrians reminded him of "ghosts...shuffl[ing] along in a dismal sort of way...No one smiles." Soon he learned about the gangs of bandits plaguing the city. "It is dangerous and unpleasant going about alone at night," he confessed to his wife in his first letter home since returning to Russia. "It is a very subdued and quiet little Bertie sitting here now. He was very upset and missed his little Jeany-peany very much indeed. England seems miles away."[12]

Such a resilient character could not remain subdued and quiet for long, however, and quickly he plunged into work. He found allies right away. Indeed, he would come to occupy the center of a remarkably gifted, idealistic, and purposeful circle of friends and political confederates, now largely forgotten. For the most part, it consisted of men who had gone to Petrograd, as he had, to facilitate Allied–Russian relations.

On the evening of his third day in Petrograd, Sunday, February 3, he dined with, among others, an American colonel, Raymond Robins. The latter's mission in Russia was to do for the United States what Lockhart was supposed to do for Britain. As he was a colonel in the American Red Cross, not the US Army, he lacked Lockhart's status, but he was an imposing and charismatic figure anyway: tall and burly, black-haired and swarthy, with piercing dark eyes, and a penetrating gaze, a powerful voice, eloquence to go with it, and a theatrical, commanding presence.

Having made a fortune prospecting for gold in Alaska and then having invested wisely, Raymond Robins thought capitalism was superior to socialism. Belief in the value of competition, however, did not interfere with his visceral sympathy for underdogs which was rooted in his Christian faith. In America, that meant working with Jane Addams at her famous settlement house in Chicago, and with various trade unions, and with Senator Robert La Follette and other Progressives, including Teddy Roosevelt, who had suggested that President Wilson send Robins to Russia in the first place. In Russia, it meant working with the Bolsheviks, whom he viewed as belonging to the only party in the country with sufficient power and determination to give underdogs their day in the sun. He would have believed in working with the Bolsheviks even if President Wilson had not sent him to Russia to do so.

Robins wanted to go further than his government did, however. He advocated formal recognition of the communist regime. That night, dining with Lockhart, he "made out a splendid case for recognizing" it. Afterwards the young Scot wrote admiringly that the American "would have convinced anyone."[13] Probably Robins

Figure 2. Raymond Robins

deployed at the dinner table the same arguments he had made some weeks earlier to a reporter for the *Chicago Daily News*: "This [Bolshevik] Government is a solid thing, deriving its power with primitive directness from the largest body of persons in Russia, the workmen, the soldiers, and sailors and the peasants. It has both the armed and the moral force which in combination make governments…Failure to recognize it will not induce it to go away but [rather]…will add more and more to the economic resources of the Central Powers and will tend increasingly to drive it to a separate peace with them."[14]

The next day Lockhart re-met Arthur Ransome whom he had known earlier in the war while serving as vice consul in Moscow. A ginger-haired, mustachioed, bohemian journalist who once had kept a pet snake in a cigar box in his Petrograd hotel room, Ransome had journeyed to Russia before 1914, partly to escape an unhappy marriage in England, partly to learn and write about

Russian folk and fairytales. (He would go on to pen the famous *Swallows and Amazons* series of children's books set in England's Lake District.) Then he fell in love with the country and its people, with whom he sympathized deeply. By 1917, he understood Russia well enough to know that her soldiers would not go on fighting, even when the Allied and Russian Provisional Governments demanded that they should. He predicted further revolution, for which conventional society mocked him, and prophesied that he would come to a bad end. "I hope to live to see you hanged," the British ambassador informed him. "Your head first," the impertinent Ransome replied.[15] Then came the October Revolution, and ambassador Buchanan, his head nearly in a metaphorical noose, returned to England. The journalist felt vindicated.

Even before the October Revolution, Ransome had befriended Bolsheviks. Their idealism appealed to him and, like Raymond Robins, he did not much consider the ruthless aspects of Leninism. Now that the Bolsheviks had taken power, he saw them as human beings trying to build a new and just society, faced with nearly insurmountable difficulties, struggling to overcome them, willing to sacrifice their lives if necessary. He sympathized—to such a degree that he fell in love with Leon Trotsky's secretary, Evgenia Petrovna Shelypina, a young woman whom other foreign correspondents called "the Big Girl" because she stood six foot two inches tall.[16] Eventually Ransome divorced his first wife and married her. A genuine British liberal, tolerant, humane, essentially apolitical (although not so in his present extraordinary circumstances), he earned the trust of leading members of the Bolshevik government, who gave him unprecedented access to their meetings and musings.

Figure 3. Arthur Ransome

As a result, Ransome wrote the best-informed newspaper articles to emerge from revolutionary Russia. His government did
not approve his outlook but read him closely. It could not afford
not to. Eventually it hired him as an intelligence agent (which is
not the same as a spy; Ransome never spied, but rather reported
honestly to his masters in London what he had seen in Russia.
What he probably did not tell them, however, was that also he
reported honestly to his Bolshevik friends what he knew about
the country of his birth). The remaining skeleton staff at the British
embassy thought this man, who seemed to have one foot in either
camp, to be a rather slippery character, which perhaps he was—
but they debriefed him regularly too. They recognized that he was
an invaluable source of information. Now, on February 4, 1918,
Bruce Lockhart was shaking him by the hand and complimenting
him on his journalism: "It's your fault that we're here."[17]

Captain Denis Garstin, son of the Newlyn School painter, Norman Garstin, brother of the writer Crosbie Garstin, himself a graduate of Sydney Sussex College, Cambridge where he had edited the literary magazine *Granta*, joined Lockhart's small staff in Russia and became a member of his inner circle too. Garstin had gone to the Crimea as a tutor in 1912 and was still in Russia when war broke out. He made his way home immediately and volunteered for the army, which commissioned him captain in the 18th Hussars. He served with a machine gun squadron in the terrible early campaigns in France: Ypres, Thiepval, Albert, and Loos, and earned a Distinguished Service Order and Military Cross. Because he spoke Russian, and had literary talent, the army sent him back to Russia, in September 1916, to work in the embassy's propaganda office, which is where Lockhart found and poached him. In Russia, Garstin already had won two medals more: the Russian Order of St. Vladimir and the Order of St. Anne.

This young man wrote three books during 1915–17, two about his experiences on the battlefields of France, the other about life in Russia before and during the war.[18] They have not achieved the renown of war memoirs written by, say, Robert Graves or Siegfried Sassoon, but they bear comparison. Closely observed, sympathetic, sensitive, they are also hard edged, as befitted the work of a survivor. He was an enthusiast and an idealist who thought the February Revolution "the greatest thing in the history of our times—the finest thing." Then came the Bolsheviks. He wrote: "the Kingdom of God was come upon Earth...The Bolsheviks have taught the people to think";[19] and: "I really believe that Lenin means well."[20] Sadly, however, Garstin leaves the slimmest record

Figure 4. Denis Garstin as a schoolboy

of them all (only his books and a few letters). There is a painting of him aged 16 at Blundell's boarding school, but I could find no suitable photograph.

The outlier in the group was Captain Francis Allen Newton Cromie, but because in the end he worked more closely with Lockhart on the great Plot than any other, he deserves a closer look.[21]

Cromie did not yet live in Petrograd, but rather at the British naval base at Reval (Tallinn today) in Estonia. What made him an outlier in the circle was not his location, however, but that he appeared, on first impression, to be a conventional imperial Briton and typical military martinet. The others loved Russia and its people. They truly believed in Anglo-Russian cooperation. Cromie wrote: "A Russian only understands a big stick and a big threat, anything else is taken for weakness. One must not forget that one is not dealing with a European, but with a cunning and cruel savage."[22] He loved order and hierarchy; he despised the social leveling carried out by revolutionaries: "The local Governor General cannot read or write," he reported disgustedly to the

Admiralty from Bolshevik-controlled Helsingfors (Helsinki). "The practical C-in-C [used to be] a stoker; the Second Marine Minister was a ship's cook."[23]

At this stage, Cromie had just become his country's naval attaché in Russia. Previously he had commanded submarines. In 1915, he had guided his own craft past hostile vessels and through minefields from Britain to Reval, a perilous and difficult passage in itself. He had demonstrated his martial capacity soon after, capturing and sinking five German commercial vessels in a single day. For this, and other extraordinary exploits, he was promoted first to commander, then to acting captain. He earned one medal after another, more even than Garstin did. They included the British DSO, the French Legion of Honor, and the Russian Orders of St. George, St. Vladimir, and St. Anne.[24] Soon he had assumed command of all seven British submarines in Baltic waters.

Cromie possessed unexpected qualities. He was an accomplished raconteur, a fine singer, a talented painter of marine scenes in watercolor; he played tennis; he learned the Russian language. He was something of a peacock, and always in cold weather wore a dashing overcoat with an astrakhan collar. He was incorruptible. All this, when combined with his tall figure, improbably chiseled features, and row of medals across his broad chest, opened many doors for him, including those of the most socially exclusive in Russia, despite his comparatively modest origins. Although married, he probably had an affair with a young war-widow, the Baroness Shilling, who made her bed with black silk sheets. He fell in love with another Petrograd socialite, the Princess Sophie Gagarin, with whom he dallied regularly. As the Revolution took hold, he began helping his new wealthy friends to hide their assets or transfer them to Britain.

Cromie also possessed diplomatic skills. He used them to settle disputes during increasingly difficult times: between his men and Russian naval ratings, between Russian naval officers and their subordinates, between Russian Bolsheviks and non-Bolsheviks. When most of the British embassy staff returned home, his government made him a diplomat in fact. He did not enjoy being the British naval attaché, but he earned plaudits. Ransome, who admired the Bolsheviks for example, knew Cromie despised them. Nevertheless, he thought Cromie "one of the best Englishmen who ever worked in Russia, a man who had the sympathy and imagination to understand and work with Soviet authorities."[25]

Above all, Cromie was a British patriot who knew his duty. With Russia's navy in disarray, German warships could menace any vessel including submarines that ventured from the safe harbor of Reval, where Cromie's flotilla of seven subs had stationed. They could menace the port itself, or any other Baltic port, even the port of Petrograd. They might eventually dominate the entire Gulf of Finland. Cromie drew the logical conclusion and began planning the destruction of his little navy to keep it from German hands. He blew it up, all seven submarines, just before the Germans arrived; they saw it happen. Then he arranged repatriation for his men, but stayed on in Russia himself, and with his Russian navy contacts began plotting the destruction of the Russian Baltic Fleet too. At first, Trotsky and his aides encouraged him because they did not want their ships controlled by Germany either, but as the German threat subsided, their attitude changed.

Cromie's did not. He went on plotting. By early May he was cabling to London that it would cost "Six hundred thousand

Figure 5. Captain Francis Allen Newton Cromie

rubles and seven thousand five hundred pounds" to sink a Russian Dreadnought, and "two hundred and fifty thousand rubles and one thousand five hundred pounds" to sink a Destroyer—without Bolshevik permission. He needed additional money for "Agitation Propaganda" and for transport out of Russia for his Russian co-conspirators. He would block the entrance to Kronstadt by sinking three British steamers, "cost estimated about one million rubles and one thousand five hundred pounds Sterling payable in England."[26] Russia and Germany were no longer at war, but Cromie and Germany were, and Cromie was now proceeding without regard to Bolshevik susceptibilities.

Thus, Lockhart's circle at the outset: brave, sanguine, ambitious, capable, indeed, formidable. Within eight months, two would be

Map 1. Captain Cromie's World (I)

dead, one would be in jail, one had returned home in disgrace, and another had taken refuge in Stockholm.

* * *

At this early stage, everyone belonging to the circle rejected conventional anti-Bolshevik wisdom, even Cromie. Idealists they may have been—with the exception of Cromie—and in the springtime of enthusiasm and excitement for their mission, but all of them claimed to be realists. As such, they all doubted those who said the Bolsheviks were doomed. They ridiculed the charge that Lenin and Trotsky were German puppets. They believed that the Allies

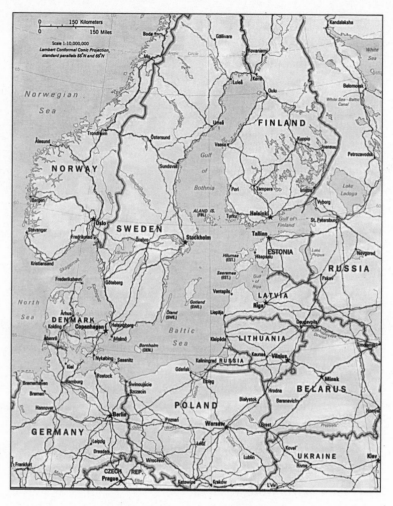

Map 2. Captain Cromie's World (II)

and Bolsheviks could work together. That would lead to formal recognition of the new regime, which even Cromie favored, albeit for a short time only in his case. Then the Bolsheviks would turn against Germany—and the Allies would win World War I.

Quickly, however, Lockhart realized that his group, however talented and determined, was politically isolated. Conventional wisdom held that the Bolshevik grasp of power was tenuous, that one good push would dislodge it. After all, the economy remained in crisis; inflation had rendered paper money practically meaningless; cholera, typhus, and typhoid waxed and waned but did not disappear; many people had not enough to eat; and the Bolsheviks were resorting increasingly to strong-arm tactics to keep hold of power. Only among urban workers was the new regime still popular. Most of the aristocracy and middle class despised it. The officer class in the armed forces did too. Indeed, counter-revolutionary forces already were grouping in the Don region and the northern Caucasus, led by an imposing array of former Tsarist generals: Kaledin, Kornilov, Alexeyev, Denikin.

Most of the peasantry, which constituted the vast majority of the population, likewise despised the new regime. It just had voted overwhelming for Socialist Revolutionaries (SRs) in elections to a Constituent Assembly that would replace the Duma, and that would rival the government of soviets favored by Bolsheviks.[27] The Bolsheviks, who garnered 24 percent of the vote, as opposed to the SR's 46 percent, hastily dispersed this body early in January—with the support of the left SRs, who had hived off from the old SR Party at the start of World War I. The call to reconvene the Constituent Assembly would reverberate—and worry the Bolsheviks—for years.

In these circumstances, non-Bolshevik and anti-Bolshevik Russians, some of them Lockhart's Kadet friends, opposed any effort that might legitimate or strengthen the new regime (e.g., his own mission). Many would welcome a German invasion to overthrow it. Most of the diplomats and officials he interviewed, said they wanted the Bolsheviks gone too, although they did not want the Germans to make them go. They too thought his undertaking a fool's errand, as did half the remaining British embassy staff. Lockhart discovered to his dismay that the British navy, army, and intelligence departments had sent agents into Russia and almost all had been offering to "support counterrevolutionary movements."[28]

Soon he discovered that the very British government he represented held mixed views of his assignment as well. In London, Lloyd George and Milner backed him, but the elusive Balfour remained lukewarm, while most cabinet ministers and Foreign Office and War Office mandarins, including Robert Cecil, opposed him outright. To win the war they aimed not to propitiate Bolsheviks, but to occupy three Russian ports, Vladivostok, Archangel, and Murmansk, by invitation if possible, but by force if necessary. This might cause difficulties for the Bolsheviks, but at this point the primary goal was to keep caches of Allied weapons and supplies in those towns from German hands.[29] Moreover, two of the ports held strategic importance: Vladivostok was the terminus of Russia's railway in the Far East; Archangel was the terminus of her railway from Moscow in the northwest. Here were additional reasons to keep the Germans out of them.

But there was more to it even that that. On February 9, merely a week after Lockhart set to work in Petrograd, the Russia Committee of the British government met at the Foreign Office to discuss the three ports and their significance. Captain Alex Proctor, recently returned from Archangel, told assembled committee members that although the Bolsheviks would object to Allied occupation of them, the mass of Russian people would not because they despised Bolsheviks as Jews and German instruments. Proctor, whom the

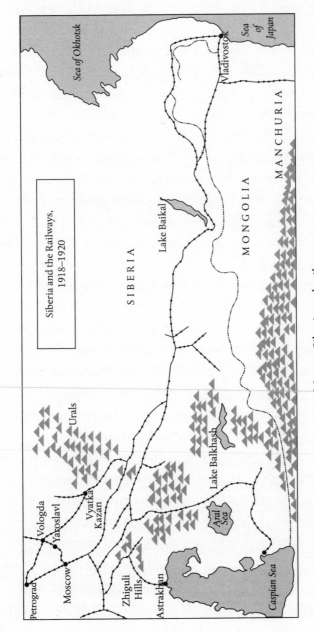

Map 3. Siberia and railways

Map 4. Western Russia

British government would intern as a Nazi sympathizer during World War II, had bigger ideas than mere occupation of ports, however. From Vladivostok, he explained, Japanese troops could "advance along the Siberian Railway, leaving guards as required at stations, bridges, etc., and finally reach Vologda [northern point of a triangle linking Petrograd and Moscow] without anyone knowing of their coming prior to their actual arrival." From Murmansk and Archangel, French and British troops could travel south—also to Vologda. Then, joined with the Japanese and tens of thousands of re-enthused Russian soldiers, ex-deserters who would flock to their banners, they could head west to confront the Germans.[30]

Fantastic though it may appear (and, when they learned of it, to Lockhart and his friends, it did indeed appear fanciful—or worse) this soon became the main thrust of Allied Russia policy. At a time when no other front in the war offered hope of decisive victory, the regeneration of Britain's erstwhile ally as a fighting partner in the East beguiled the minds of otherwise sober and realistic men. Robert Cecil, who chaired the committee that day in the absence of his cousin, the Foreign Secretary, came to believe it was "the only real solution to the question."[31] In his mind, and not only in his, occupation of the three ports, however attained, as the preliminary to reconstituting the Eastern Front was key to winning World War I. This would remain his outlook, and that of leading members of the government, even after Russia signed the infamous peace treaty of Brest-Litovsk with Germany on March 3.[32]

No one at the meeting addressed by Proctor said that after the Allies converged on Vologda they should attack Petrograd and Moscow, destroying the revolutionary regime once and for all before turning on the Germans, but that possibility hung over the meeting. Disdain for Bolshevism permeated the atmosphere. Everyone realized the possibilities. They had only to grasp the counter-revolutionary nettle. Once they did, however, a series of questions would arise concerning Bruce Lockhart. For example, why permit him to continue pursuing the chimera of Allied-Bolshevik understanding; why not alter his instructions; better still, why not call him home?[33]

* * *

As storm clouds gathered in London, Lloyd George's emissary was developing his very different line of attack in Petrograd. It hinged upon Russian resentment, now growing into hatred, of

Germany. Bolshevik doctrine taught that one band of "imperialist pirates" as Lenin called them, was as bad as another, but Germany seemed to be disproving this theory: she was worse.

On December 22, 1917, just as Lockhart was meeting the prime minister and cabinet in London, and learning his mission, the Russians and Germans were opening peace negotiations in a desolate military outpost, Brest-Litovsk, on the bleak Belorussian plain. There, despite Leon Trotsky's brilliant defense of his country's interests, Germany persisted in demanding that Russia give her the Baltic states and cede additional territory in the south to Turkey. German negotiators also required Russia to withdraw her troops from Finland; disarm her warships in the Black, Baltic, and Arctic seas; accept a German puppet government in Ukraine, and a host of disadvantageous commercial obligations; and pay an indemnity of six billion German gold marks.

These demands caused a crisis in the Bolshevik Party. At the crucial meeting of the party's central committee, Trotsky, who had returned to Petrograd in order to attend, argued that Russia should stop fighting, but refuse to accept the German demands: "No War, No Peace." A left communist faction led by Nikolai Bukharin, member of the party central committee and editor of *Pravda*, favored revolutionary war, in this case against the German invaders, who represented capitalism and imperialism, even if it meant moving the government to safety somewhere beyond the Ural Mountains. Lenin argued, against Trotsky, that the German demands be accepted, lest they make demands even more draconian; and against Bukharin that Russia simply did not have the power to wage any kind of war. After anguished debate that brought the party as near to a formal split as it ever came, he prevailed by the narrowest of margins: four votes for his position; three for Bukharin's; four abstentions, including Trotsky's.[34]

"Now was the chance of the Allied governments," Georgy Vasilyevich Chicherin, Deputy Commissar for Foreign Affairs, exhorted Lockhart on February 12, while Trotsky remained fighting his forlorn battle at Brest-Litovsk, and before Russia finally accepted the awful terms.[35] He meant that his country now needed Britain as a counterweight against Germany and might come to some sort of arrangement with her. Britain's agent immediately repeated Chicherin's prediction to Balfour, adding coyly: "Colonel Robbins [sic] who has been wonderfully correct in his summing up of situation is convinced real opportunity for Allies has now arrived."[36] Balfour wired back with greater coyness: "We are of course most anxious to come to any practical arrangements which will prevent Germany from obtaining supplies."[37] That did not preclude occupying the three ports, but Lockhart did not yet have sufficient knowledge to understand.

He had to wait nearly two weeks for Trotsky to return from Brest-Litovsk, but finally met him the day after the Bolsheviks adopted the Gregorian calendar, a Friday, February 15 (by the conventional system of reckoning), at the Smolny Institute, a former school for the daughters of St. Petersburg aristocrats. Now Smolny had become the Bolshevik headquarters, bustling with workers, soldiers, sailors, and commissars. They rushed from room to room, carrying papers, folders, dossiers; they were smoking, spitting, and calling to one another: they were making history despite the Germans, despite the Allies, despite their home-grown enemies. Consciously, excitedly, they were fashioning the world's first communist state.

Lockhart, craftily pretending to be casually carrying a red-bound copy of Marx's *Das Kapital*, entered this hubbub that morning, climbed a staircase, weaving and dodging and jostling amidst the noisy, hurrying crowd. Then he found and followed to the end a long corridor where stood a workingman in ordinary clothes, with rifle and bandolier slung over his greatcoat. This imposing figure guarded a modest doorway to which had been affixed a scrap of paper bearing the handwritten words: "People's Commissary for Foreign Affairs." Lockhart may have had a moment to register that this was not much like heading into an audience with Britain's Foreign Secretary, Lord Balfour, at the intimidatingly grand Foreign Office in Whitehall. Then the Red Guard passed him through the doorway into a plain anteroom occupied by a single secretary, who passed him through again, into an unexceptional office containing only a birch wood writing table, two chairs, telephone, red rug, and wastebasket.[38]

Unpretentious though the room might be, Lockhart speedily took in Trotsky's arresting presence behind the desk, his eagle

Figure 6. Leon Trotsky

eyes, broad forehead and "wonderfully quick mind."[39] The Briton wanted to impress in turn, by appearing to be obliging, not hostile like the Germans. He immediately announced his intention "to find a modus vivendi" with Russia. Trotsky may not have been aware of the Russia Committee in Whitehall, but he knew enough to hear Lockhart out—and laugh. Did not Britain "openly sympathize with and secretly support every anti-Bolshevik movement in Russia?"[40] Lockhart did not know yet about the Russia Committee either, but he did now know about British agents supporting counter-revolutionaries. He did not contradict Russia's Commissar for Foreign Affairs.

Nevertheless, Trotsky took up Chicherin's point—and Lockhart's. Actually, cooperation between Britain and Russia was both possible and desirable. "While he hated British capitalism almost as much as German militarism, he could not unfortunately fight the whole world at once." Meanwhile, Russia required economic assistance. "He was therefore willing to cooperate with us, although he stated quite frankly that on both sides this must by its very nature be an agreement of calculation and not of love."

Trotsky's need for British aid "offers basis for a successful policy," Lockhart enthusiastically cabled to Balfour. "If handled tactfully he can become very valuable asset against Germany." This would be the crux of his position for the next few months. Britain should end aid to anti-Bolshevik parties and organizations. She should abandon plans for intervening anywhere in Russia unless explicitly invited to do so. The Bolsheviks would deliver "all sorts of things" in return.[41] He meant they would offer an invitation to occupy the three ports. He meant they would eventually re-form the Triple Entente that would win the war. They would never do it if the Allies invaded uninvited.

The next week, a great storm broke. This was when the Bolshevik government was hesitating to accept the awful Brest-Litovsk Treaty, and Germany, which already occupied southern, western and northwestern portions of the former Russian Empire, suddenly sent in additional troops. There was no Russian army to oppose them. German soldiers arrived within striking distance of Petrograd. The upper and middle classes of the city, giddy with delight, prepared to welcome their deliverers from Bolshevism. The laborers in the factories grimly prepared to fight for their lives and revolution. The Bolshevik government prepared to flee to Moscow. Bukharin and his supporters secretly approached the leaders of the left Socialist Revolutionary Party, with which the Bolsheviks were currently allied, broaching the possibility of replacing Lenin, and then defying the Germans with a holy war. These talks proved abortive. But surely Raymond Robins was right when he wrote in his diary, "Sense of impending doom,"[42] and of Lenin: "The tiger is at bay."[43]

It was an extraordinary time to be in Petrograd, those last weeks of February and first weeks of March 1918: exciting, perilous, exhilarating. The lives of the Bolshevik principals and of the Allied representatives, hung in the balance, for given the opportunity the Germans would have made short shrift of them all. Foreign embassies feverishly prepared to evacuate staff via Finland. Lockhart arranged the departure of most remaining British embassy personnel and other British officials, but bravely declined to join them, cabling London: "I shall remain in the country as long as there is the slightest hope."[44] Ransome, Robins, Garstin, and Cromie likewise stayed. Other diplomatic personnel found their exits blocked, however. They took refuge in Vologda. That was the sleepy but strategically important town linking

Archangel, Moscow, and Petrograd by rail. Suspicious Bolsheviks took note.

The emergency only reinforced Lockhart's sense that his was the correct strategy. "The Bolsheviks must fight German militarism or perish miserably," he predicted. They could not fight it alone, but needed Allied help, and therefore "will go a long way towards meeting us."[45] He thought they soon would issue "direct invitation to…cooperate in organization of Archangel, Vladivostok, etc." That was only the beginning. "My policy promises you in a short time recommencement of war on this front."[46]

It was the opposite of what the mandarins, who believed in occupying the three ports immediately, whether invited or no, wanted to hear. They preferred the advice of Captain Proctor who continued to advocate immediate occupation. More importantly, they preferred the advice of General Alfred Knox, the former military attaché in Petrograd and chief liaison with the Russian army under the Tsar.[47] This flinty Ulsterman could wield a pen dipped in vitriol, and he hated everything Bruce Lockhart was presently promoting.

Knox prepared for the War Cabinet a scorching rebuttal of Lockhart's recommendations, entitled "The Delay in the East."[48] He wrote, "The policy of flirtation with the Bolsheviks is both wrong as a policy and immoral." Britain should declare for the anti-communists: "If we wish to win the war…we must support openly the non-Bolshevik elements who form the majority in Russia." Like Proctor, Knox wanted to "bring the Japanese as far West as possible," first to help reconstitute the Eastern Front—but equally "to form a rallying point for such Russian elements…as have still a sense of nationality and some respect for the national Church." He too deemed the Bolsheviks to be nothing more than

German pawns. He did not, in the memorandum, use the word "counter-revolution," but that was what he favored.

Lockhart may have been accustomed to the vicissitudes of romance, but he had no experience of serious professional opposition. Now confronted with Foreign Office skepticism and refusal to follow his counsel, his telegrams to Whitehall grew waspish: "I think there is still a game to be played here...but you are not making it easier";[49] and two days later: "If His Majesty's Government consider suppression of Bolsheviks is more important than complete domination of Russia by Germany I should be grateful to be informed."[50] In another telegram he practically accused the Foreign Secretary of having led him down the garden path, even of lying to him.[51]

This was not the way to work the Foreign Office. Some of its members began to think their young emissary was a Bolshevik himself, or at least a Bolshevik sympathizer. Or perhaps they had thought that from the outset. Now they scribbled notes on his cables, as they passed them from desk to desk: "Mr. Lockhart's advice may be bad, but we cannot be accused of having followed it."[52] "He is hysterical and has achieved nothing."[53] "His telegrams are impertinent in tone and substance."[54] Robert Cecil wrote a letter to Arthur Balfour: "Don't you think the time has come when we should hint to Lockhart that it is his business to persuade Trotski that we are right, not to persuade us that Trotski is right?"[55]

Arthur Balfour, famed for his flexibility and philosophical cast of mind, liked to have advisors offering contradictory opinions. Lockhart and Knox certainly did that. Now the pair engaged in a full-fledged contest for his support. As might have been expected, Lockhart, to whom Balfour had forwarded Knox's paper, fought hard. "This is most delicate situation...it is not a task for...a man of the type of mind of General Knox."[56] He wrote a week later: "I should be more than sorry if at this critical hour a man of General Knox's hasty and changeable judgment should be considered as a more reliable authority than myself."[57] But, as a friend in Whitehall now warned him, when it came to contending for the allegiance of Arthur Balfour: "It all depends who has the last word with him."[58] By virtue of his location, Lockhart never could have the last word. Knox, by virtue of his location, always could. So, although Balfour would not completely disown the man in Moscow, and occasionally indicated support, in the end he plumped for Knox.

What of the man who had sent Lockhart to Russia in the first place? David Lloyd George never pursued a single political line. He always pursued several and did not mind if they conflicted.[59] In this instance, although he had sent Lockhart to establish relations with the Bolsheviks, he was perfectly prepared to listen to General Knox advise against establishing them. He said of the general: "There is no man in the British army who knows Russia as Knox does."[60] The words were shrewdly chosen, as Lockhart was not in the army. But when the preponderance of evidence gathered by the Foreign Office seemed to weigh in Knox's favor, and when the Foreign Office made clear its own preference, the prime minister had no difficulty cutting Lockhart loose.

That left only Lord Milner in Lockhart's corner, but with the Foreign Secretary and the prime minister out of it, he would have seen little point staying there alone.

What would have happened if the Foreign Office had taken Lockhart's advice to meet the Bolsheviks halfway? The Bolsheviks already had accepted limited British and French aid reconstructing their military. Trotsky and Captain Cromie had begun discussions on scuttling the Russian fleet in the Baltic to keep it from

German hands. Lenin and Trotsky had said they would trade stores the Allies wished to remove from the three ports for British manufactured goods. These were signs that Anglo-Bolshevik cooperation was possible, that an invitation to occupy might be forthcoming, that Lockhart was on the right track. He insisted the moment was pregnant with possibility.

On the other hand, a Bolshevik invitation to the Allies to come into the three ports might have provoked German occupation of Petrograd in return. No Russian government could risk that when it had no military to resist if the Germans tried it. This was Lockhart's political blind spot and the limiting factor to any Allied–Russian rapprochement. In this regard, if not in others, General Knox saw more clearly than he.

But really, no one on the British side was seeing clearly now. Lockhart thought Britain needed Russia to win World War I and would antagonize her if she occupied the three ports without invitation. Knox and most of Whitehall thought Britain needed to reopen the Eastern Front to win World War I and must occupy the ports to do so, although an invitation from Russia would not be forthcoming. They also thought that former Russian soldiers hated the Bolsheviks and would flock to the invaders' banners. In fact, events would demonstrate that Britain did not need Russian soldiers, or a reopened Eastern Front. She and her Allies, including fresh American troops, would defeat Germany by prevailing in the West. Given all this, surely Lockhart had the better argument over all, despite his blind spot, because good Anglo-Bolshevik relations might have alleviated Russia's sense of isolation and jeopardy, and softened Bolshevik domestic and foreign policies, in which case Russian and world history might have been very different and less bloody.

Meanwhile, another factor soon became apparent. Although Russia had no army with which to resist a German invasion, soon Germany would have no army with which to invade Russia. General Ludendorff was planning a last great offensive on the Western Front, for which he would need every man Germany could provide. When the Bolsheviks began to realize that the German threat was easing, their need for an Anglo-French counterweight eased as well. Then they began to prevaricate: they postponed selling port supplies to the Allies; they ceased to talk with Cromie about scuttling their Baltic fleet; they would issue no invitation to the Allies to occupy any part of their country.

Lockhart remained certain that Anglo-Russian rapprochement was the best option for both countries. But: "I lacked the moral courage to resign and to take a stand which would have exposed me to the odium of the vast majority of my countrymen."[61] His personal history also hinted at what was coming: in his love-life at least, the man had a history of first opposing common expectations and then finally of bowing to them. Recall that when his uncle opposed the relationship with Amai, Lockhart ended it—although he did not want to; when ambassador Buchanan told him to leave Madame "Vermelle" he did so, despite his personal inclinations. Given this pattern, what happened next is not surprising. Faced with strong opposition in Whitehall, the young man from Scotland commenced to waffle. No doubt there was more to it than a desire to please: he sensed the Bolshevik's changing attitude towards Allied occupation of the ports, he was increasingly offended by their mounting reliance upon strong-arm tactics, he found it hard to ignore the wishes and arguments of old friends, like Chelnokov. Thus, he persuaded himself: if he could not convince the policymakers in London to meet the

Bolsheviks halfway, which is what he still really thought they should do, then he would cease advocating it. Britain's emissary to the Bolsheviks, while still believing in conciliating and cooperating with them, began contemplating how to perform a political volte-face.

CHAPTER 3

THE TEMPTATIONS OF BRUCE LOCKHART

Moura Benckendorff and Bruce Lockhart first set eyes upon one another on February 2, 1918, at the very outset of his second stint in Russia, only three days after his arrival in Petrograd, the day before he met Raymond Robins. "Went round to the Soldatenkoff's," Lockhart recorded in his diary that evening. (These may have been descendants of a well-known publisher and art collector; probably he had come to know them during his previous spell in Russia.) "Met there the Benckendorffs." That night he wrote nothing more about the meeting, but later he recorded that she had been playing bridge when he came into the room, and that he had shaken her hand.[1] In his memoir, he recalled, "I was too busy, too pre-occupied with my own importance, to give her more than a passing thought."[2]

That was uncommon. Usually Moura Benckendorff (neé Zakrevskaia) made a striking impression. Brought up in an enormous manor house in the Ukrainian countryside, tended by "masses of servants," she had been beautiful, poised, and something of a show off from the start. Also, precocious: as a little girl, she used to entertain her father's guests, standing on a table, reciting poetry to them. In fact, she often sat at the dinner table with her cosmopolitan, illustrious, liberal lawyer father, and with the cultural and political luminaries he brought home. They might speak English, French, or German in addition to, or instead of, Russian; it did not matter to Moura, who learned these languages early. Her son, Paul, thought such experiences sparked Moura's lifelong love of literature and the arts and politics, and her lasting desire to be among people with expert knowledge of them.[3] It may also have sparked or reinforced the romance to come with Lockhart, who had similar inclinations.

In 1909, while Lockhart was in Malaya, one of Moura's sisters married a diplomat serving in Berlin. Her brother, who had entered the diplomatic service, received a posting there too. They invited 17-year-old Moura to join them: "Bring your smartest clothes as there will be plenty of parties."[4] The teenager, whose father had died recently, and who had been chafing increasingly at her isolation in rural Ukraine, did not hesitate. Then, soon after her arrival, her brother introduced her to an up-and-coming Russian diplomat also working at the Berlin embassy, Djon Alexandrovich von Benckendorff, a nobleman of Baltic German descent, ten years her senior. Handsome, smart, very tall, very rich, and descended from an ancient, prestigious family (one of his uncles was Russia's ambassador to Britain), he seemed at first to be everything she wanted. And vice-versa: no one writes that Benckendorff swept Moura off her feet; she swept him off his. They married on October 24, 1911.

Nearly three years of life at the apex followed, hardly interrupted by the birth of her son, Paul, in 1913. She cut a wide swath in Berlin society; and in St. Petersburg, where they spent her husband's leaves, and where they kept an extravagant rococo house; and at "Yendel," Djon's country estate in Estonia, an hour's journey by train from the capital Reval, and a convenient overnight

Figure 7. Imperious
Moura von Benckendorff

trip by rail from St. Petersburg. They spent holidays there, entertaining lavishly. Yet quickly the marriage showed signs of strain.
Moura loved the world of high culture, and high politics, and
being at the center of things; Djon loved Yendel. A glittering diplomatic career beckoned to him, but he preferred family to friends,
country life to city life, perhaps even livestock to people. His son
wrote: "As long as he could remain on his estate and go on looking
after it in the same manner as his father and his ancestors had, he
would probably have been happy under any regime."[5]

With the outbreak of war, the couple immediately returned to
Russia. Djon joined the army as a staff officer; he would become
an aide-de-camp to the Tsar. Moura, pregnant again, gave birth to
a daughter, Tania, in January 1915. When Djon had leave, the family would visit Yendel. Inevitably, the couple met and befriended
British officers, Russia's wartime allies, at the nearby naval base
in Reval. That is how Moura came to know Francis Cromie.

Figure 8. "Yendel," Djon von Benckendorff's manor house, Yendel, Estonia

In Petrograd, she took a crash course in nursing, volunteered as a Red Cross "sister of charity" at a war hospital called St. George's, and there met Meriel Buchanan, daughter of the British ambassador.[6] Through Meriel perhaps, she gained access to the British embassy, and soon had a job in the propaganda office. That is probably how she met Captain Denis Garstin.

Interestingly, she launched a regular salon in their grand rococo Petrograd house at about this time.[7] Here was a time-honored way for ambitious upper-class women to transcend at least some of the barriers placed before them because of their sex. If successful, a salon might offer its hostess access to men with influence and power, and perhaps the chance to wield power herself, if indirectly, through her guests. Moura von Benckendorff, highly intelligent, deeply cultured, increasingly cosmopolitan, must have made an excellent hostess. Undoubtedly, she now began collecting the literati, glitterati, and influential personages who would flock to her later in her life.

Given her recent associations in Berlin, the salon predictably attracted members of the city's expatriate German community.[8] A rumor began to circulate that Moura Benckendorff was a German spy. Wounded soldiers who sang her praises at the hospital repeated this tale.[9] So, in 1921, did the French intelligence service, and so in 1924 did the Russian.[10] So, finally, did Anthony West, son of H. G. Wells, who said that sometime in the 1930s Moura told it to his father, who told it to him.[11] Maybe it was true, but a British officer who recalled "Madame B.'s" pro-German salon claimed she really worked for Russian counter-intelligence.[12] Another rumor had her reporting directly to Prime Minister Alexander Kerensky, with whom she was said to be having an affair.[13] There is no corroborating evidence. Kerensky, however, did once tell a friend that Moura had spied for the British.[14] A century on, who can tell? The conflicting reports testify to the impact that a well-connected, ambitious, highly intelligent, beautiful woman who liked to be at the center of events might have—and to the regard for her that others had: she was not only mysterious and alluring, but smart enough to be a spy, brave enough, tough enough, well-enough connected, well-enough trusted.

*   *   *

She happened to be at Yendel with Meriel Buchanan when the February Revolution to overthrow the Tsar broke out. By the time they had returned to Petrograd, the most eventful and dangerous days had passed, and for people such as themselves it seemed at first as though daily life was little affected. Moura lived in the city as always, in great luxury, attending opera and ballet, lunching and dining with friends in Petrograd's still elegant, if increasingly expensive, restaurants. Her husband remained with the Russian Army, for even though the Tsar had gone, the war continued, carried on by the new, moderate regime. Then came October, and the great Bolshevik upheaval. That was different. First the Bolsheviks signed a ceasefire with Germany. Then they turned their class-conscious and leveling attention to the domestic scene.

Djon von Benckendorff left his army post and returned to the capital to join his family. It is easy to imagine what this aristocratic landowner and army officer thought of recent events. It is less easy to know what Moura thought. During her stint as a nurse, she had learned from wounded soldiers of chaos and mismanagement and general governmental ineptitude. It opened her eyes. Who knows what she learned at the salon? Certainly, she did not sympathize with the Bolsheviks, but nor, probably, did she lament the fall of the Tsar. She had begun as a spoilt child of great privilege, she still lived a life of great privilege, but she was no longer sequestered in the Ukrainian countryside. Moreover, she always thought for herself. There is evidence that she and her husband quarreled about politics.[15] In early December, just before the British government recalled ambassador Buchanan and his family, the pair attended a Christmas party at the British embassy. This would be the last party ever held there, and it was an unhappy one. Toward the end, someone began to play the former Russian national anthem, now a hymn of defiance.

> God save the Tsar!
> Strong and majestic,
> Reign for glory,
> For our glory!
> Reign to foes' fear,
> Orthodox Tsar.
> God, save the Tsar!

Meriel Buchanan noticed the look of misery on Djon von Benckendorff's face as he listened to these words. She did not mention what Moura's face revealed; perhaps it revealed nothing.

Djon left for Yendel a few weeks later "to look after his estate."[16] His son and daughter soon joined him, but Moura did not. She stayed in Petrograd, to look after her increasingly frail widowed mother, she said. The fact is, however, that Yendel appealed to her for holidays, not for life. No matter the situation, Russia's capital appealed far more, especially during this epochal time. Perhaps she wanted to witness the making of history, the Bolshevik broom sweeping everything clear. Perhaps she simply was glad of an excuse to separate from her husband, even if it meant separating from her babies too. At any rate, there she was, playing bridge at the Soldatenkoff's on Saturday night, February 2, 1918, her husband and children far away, and Bruce Lockhart, newly returned to Russia, just arrived in Petrograd, standing before her.

* * *

That was how they met. They would flirt for two months, February and March 1918, and launch their affair in April. Their increasing intimacy provided the backdrop to his dawning realization of his political isolation in London, and to the political somersault he would perform.

In Petrograd in February, Lockhart shared rooms with an Englishman he had coopted onto his small staff, Captain William Hicks, the expert in gas warfare, who had met Moura earlier in the war.[17] Two weeks after the Soldatenkoff party Hicks brought her home to dinner. Lockhart must have noticed Moura this time because she reappeared to dine again on February 23 and again on March 8 and yet again on March 15. On March 6, she joined him, Garstin, Hicks, and others for what Raymond Robins termed "a great lunch. Five liquors."[18] On March 12, she gave a luncheon party in turn, for Cromie, Garstin, Hicks—and her new friend, Bruce Lockhart.[19] By this time, clearly, they had established easy relations. "I wrote a doggerel verse for each guest," Lockhart would recall. "Cromie made one of his witty speeches. We toasted our hostess and laughed immoderately."[20]

Lockhart was a married man who had strayed at least once already, and who was supposed to be patching things with his pregnant wife. His mission to Russia complicated the process, but he kept patching by post. "Dear Little Girl," he wrote to Jean, "I am very grateful for all you have done for me and for the way you have stood by me."[21] He wrote to her on February 28: "I want to tell you how sorry I am for all the pain I have brought you. I never realized till I came out here, this time without you, how much I loved you. My thoughts are with you always."[22] He had dined only twice with Moura at this point and had done nothing yet to bring his sincerity in these letters into question.

As for Moura: she had two children, but maternal instincts were not her strong suit. She had a husband, from whom she felt increasingly estranged, and who anyway had gone to Estonia. Social conventions meant little to her, and in fact letters she wrote later suggest that, like Lockhart, she too already had extramarital experience. Meanwhile, everything about Lockhart appealed to her: his high spirits and wit; his understanding and knowledge of history, literature, and the arts; his liberal political outlook and sympathy for Russia; his central role in current events; his good looks. It is fair to say that she attracted him for almost the same reasons. What followed seems inevitable.

On March 16, Lockhart moved to Moscow in order to be near the government, which had just fled Petrograd fearing German invasion and occupation. He traveled in the same railway carriage as Trotsky, the only foreigner to do so. This would have been the time to end things with Moura, and perhaps it is what he told himself he would do. He had enough on his plate already. Remember, however, that he had tried to break with "Madame Vermelle" the year before, and that when she had telephoned him he returned to her immediately. It had taken the intervention of the ambassador himself to end the liaison. This time he received a telegram, not a phone call, and there was no ambassador to remind him of his responsibilities. "Dear Lockhart," Moura wired to Moscow, "I am in bed with a bad attack of 'flu and feel very miserable and lonely. Why don't you write or telegraph? I am so disappointed not to have any news. Goodbye and take care of yourself, Moura Benckendorff."[23]

Lockhart and Moura picked up where they had left off. They exchanged letters every day and telephoned most evenings. Soon she was planning to visit. The crucial moment came on Saturday, April 21, when she arrived at the Hotel Elite, at 17 Neglinnaya Street, an exclusive part of Moscow, where Lockhart and Hicks now shared a suite. He came downstairs to greet her. "She was standing by a table, and the spring sun was shining on her hair. As I walked forward to meet her, I scarcely dared to trust my voice. Into my life something had entered which was stronger than any other tie, stronger than life itself."[24]

He succumbed despite the fact that his wife Jean had recently demonstrated her loyalty to him and concern for his career by warning him by letter of his waning reputation in Whitehall, and, more importantly, despite the fact that only two weeks earlier she had written to tell him she had just suffered a miscarriage. Upon receiving that letter, he had written back immediately, April 9: "All our hopes…bitterly disappointed…It is horrible…not to be with you."[25] Five days before Moura appeared at the Hotel Elite with the sun shining on her hair, he had written again to Jean: "My Dearest Girl…so sad I cannot be with you…everything will come well again…there are happier days ahead for us both."[26]

*   *   *

Raymond Robins once wrote in his diary: "Lockhart, able and free of guile."[27] This says more about the man who made the judgement than it does about the man being judged. Lockhart was capable of enormous guile, as we have just seen. It was Robins who, perhaps to his cost, never learned to dissemble and who remained a credulous ally of the younger man almost until the end. All through April and into May he and Lockhart continued to meet daily, Ransome making a habitual third. Sometimes Garstin, sometimes Cromie, sometimes other Allied officials and military officers joined them, but this trio constituted the nucleus. They talked policy, compared notes, tried to concert their efforts and each in their own way to influence policy, or rather, Robins and Ransome thought that was what they were doing.

But Lockhart was a quick study. With one part of his mind occupied by Moura, nevertheless, by mid-April, he secretly began putting out feelers to Bolshevism's legal and illegal opponents. How would they respond to Allied intervention? He learned that most monarchists looked for salvation to Germany.[28] But the Menshevik Party, the left and right Socialist Revolutionary Parties, the now illegal Kadet Party, and various counter-revolutionaries belonging to smaller political bodies, all said they wanted the Allies to help Russia re-launch the war with Germany. All but the left Socialist Revolutionaries really wanted Allied intervention to lead to the downfall of Bolshevism. The right Socialist Revolutionaries said they would help the Allies when they arrived.[29]

Lockhart undoubtedly understood the counter-revolutionary aims of the anti-Bolsheviks, but he himself would move towards counter-revolution in three distinct stages. At this stage, he favored occupation of the ports only as an anti-German measure to help the Allies win the war, and he continued to hope that he could induce the Bolsheviks to request it. Almost every day he pushed someone at the Russian Foreign Office to invite Allied troops into Vladivostok, Murmansk, and Archangel.

But also, he was seeking to ingratiate himself with the Foreign Office at home, which brought him to stage two. To the Whitehall mandarins, he began advocating occupation of Vladivostok, Murmansk, and Archangel whether Russia gave permission or not. And when he grasped how much the anti-Bolshevik parties in Russia longed for foreign intervention, he began pressing for it to happen right away: "Further delay is both dangerous and foolish."[30] Soon he had ceased to mention Bolshevik permission at all. "We should hold on by hook or by crook in this country, concealing as far as possible our intentions until we are ready to strike."[31]

Guile? Lockhart had plenty of it. Now when he met Bolsheviks, he promised that Britain would never come ashore without permission. Meanwhile, he was advising Whitehall to come ashore right away: "The most we can hope for is that when they are faced with accomplished fact, Bolsheviks will not afford us serious opposition."[32]

Recognizing the improbability of *invited* intervention, he began planning how to carry out an *uninvited* one. First, the British government should muzzle the press at home, so no word of a scheme reached German or Russian ears.[33] It should "continue to play with the Bolsheviks," but at the right moment should issue a "well-worded declaration...demanding...consent [to occupation of the ports]." He submitted a draft of the declaration, whose publication should coincide with "simultaneous landing[s] at Murmansk, Archangel and Far East."[34] He calculated that intervention in Archangel alone would require "no less than 2 Divisions," ten to twenty thousand men.[35]

He also began to consider ramifications of landing uninvited, and this led him to stage three. Suppose the revolutionary government resisted? "If we are to intervene without Bolsheviks, as now seems probable, it will be absolutely necessary for us to destroy Baltic fleet...I have had several conversations with Captain Cromie on this subject."[36] But with the German threat in the Baltic ebbing, surely the Bolsheviks would oppose destruction of their own navy. Therefore: "It would be advantageous to support an anti-Bolshevik movement."[37] Thus the former champion of cooperation with Bolshevism and opponent of any Allied landings in Russia at all, came first to advocate landing with Bolshevik permission, then to landing without it, and finally to landing in concert with anti-Bolsheviks who aimed at counter-revolution. He would still have said the whole point was to win World War I, but he knew that counter-revolution could be a by-product.

What had happened to his earlier idealism? A draft of the proposed declaration suggests he was trying to square intervention with his conscience. The "Allied Governments... have no desire to interfere with any Government which has [the] support and confidence of [the] people of Russia," he wrote, "nor... of retaining for themselves any portion of Russian territory which they may be forced to occupy as a military measure."[38] But idealism warred with deceit, for every day he was smilingly and charmingly meeting with, and seeming to agree with, not only Bolsheviks who, of course opposed any landings, but also with his friends Ransome and Robins, unreconstructed champions of Allied–Bolshevik understanding. Finally, Robins at least began to sense something had gone amiss. "Lockhart... is too gay," he confided to his diary in April.[39] In mid-May, he wrote: "We are all alone."[40] He meant he was alone now, not that he and Lockhart were alone together. Many years later, he would accuse his former colleague of having been a "rat."[41] He was right. "Colonel Robins... was useful to Allies while there was hope of gaining Russian Government's consent to intervention," Lockhart now was advising Balfour, "But he is fanatic on Bolshevism, and situation has completely changed..."[42] As for his friend Ransome: "He can put the case for working in with the Bolsheviks better than anyone. I would however beg you not to consider his views as altogether representing my own."[43]

On May 9, he met someone who would tempt him further down the counter-revolutionary road, a British intelligence officer recently arrived from Britain, darkly handsome and magnetic, a man who never thought small. Sidney Reilly arrived in Russia musing: "A Corsican lieutenant of artillery trod out the embers of the French Revolution. Surely a British espionage agent…could make himself master of Moscow?"[44] Lockhart wrote that day in his diary: "He is either mad, or he is a crook," and this extraordinary character may have been one or the other or both. Nevertheless, the new Bruce Lockhart would meet this latest member of his circle more than halfway. He had already gone far to salvage his career, but with the help of Sidney Reilly he would go much farther.

PART II

DEFENDERS OF THE FAITH

CHAPTER 4

IRON FELIX DZERZHINSKY

The Bolshevik organization charged with defeating counter-revolutionaries was called "The All-Russian Extraordinary Commission for Combating Counter-Revolution and Sabotage," the VCHEKA, from its initials, pronounced Cheka (emphasis on the last syllable). By coincidence, the date of its foundation, December 23, 1917, was also the date Lockhart formally accepted his new mission to Russia. The British agent would come to know a good deal about the Cheka and the two men who led it, Felix Dzerzhinsky and his second-in-command, Jacov Peters. In the end these two would have the power of life or death over him.

Dzerzhinsky was a scion of Polish-Lithuanian gentry. Little in his early life suggested its eventual outcome: that he would rise to head Russia's secret police, and that from the Bolshevik Revolution in 1917 until his death in 1926 even the mention of his name would inspire terror. Born on September 11, 1877, he experienced his early childhood as a rural idyll in imperial Russia's province of Vilnius, today part of Lithuania. He lived on the modest estate his family had owned since the seventeenth century. It was perfect for a self-sufficient boy who liked to explore woods and fields, to pick mushrooms and wild flowers, and to swim and fish, as Felix did and always would.

Like the young Stalin, young Dzerzhinsky aspired to become a Catholic priest, perhaps to please his mother, whom he adored. Signs of his unbending will surfaced early: he insisted that his siblings pray with him; he once confided to a brother that if he lost his faith he would kill himself. As a boy he was, "thin and demure…with the face of an icon," but also "noisily mischievous [and] impertinent." At the Vilno gymnasium, which he began to attend in 1887, the year of Lockhart's birth, the impertinence soon manifested. He and like-minded students read and discussed forbidden socialist texts. They gathered on Gedinimas Hill, above the center of Vilno, and swore "to fight against evil to the last breath." Dzerzhinsky really meant it.

Fifteen years later at Fettes, Lockhart ignored his studies to play sports. In Vilno, young Dzerzhinsky ignored his classes to read Marx and Engels. He turned from Catholicism to a new religion, which he studied with great intensity. "I simply cannot give only half of my spirit. I either give all or nothing."[1] It was true then, it would be true all his life. He became a socialist student leader, and attended an illegal socialist student congress in Warsaw. He joined the illegal Lithuanian Social Democratic Party. When his mother passed away in 1896 (his father had died while Felix was still a child), he quit school altogether to become a full-time revolutionary.

The masses did not take kindly to a teenage schoolboy lecturing them. When he tried to harangue factory workers, they beat him. But they could never deter him, and eventually he learned not to harangue, but to befriend and to coax. He had great organizational skills and he labored tirelessly. His reputation among Vilno socialists grew. They sent him to Kovno to establish a branch of the party. Here too he worked indefatigably and successfully, and so drew the attention of police. On July 17, 1897, they arrested him, and sent him to prison. He told them nothing, despite threats, punishments, and more beatings. The head of the Kovno police wrote to the prosecutor in Vilno, "Felicks Dzierzynski, considering his views, convictions and personal character, will be very dangerous in the future, capable of any crime."[2] The prosecutor drew the logical conclusion and argued successfully that he be sentenced to three years' exile in Nolinsk, Viatka province in western Siberia.

It was an awful trip. One section he traveled by riverboat, with hundreds of other convicts, naked, packed into the steamer's hold, which was nearly airless and without light. But neither ten months in jail nor the dreadful passage, nor even the daunting prospect of three years' banishment to this far-off outpost, dampened Felix Dzerzhinsky's ardor. No sooner did he arrive in Nolinsk than he commenced an anti-tsarist agitation. For this, the governor of the province exiled him yet further north, to a tiny hamlet called Kaigorodsk. Here too he soon annoyed the local authorities, this time by helping peasants write petitions and protests to various government agencies.

There were no jobs in Kaigorodsk. He had funds from relatives back home, but even so had to hunt for food in harsh conditions, no matter the season or weather. Unsurprisingly he developed bronchitis, emphysema, anemia, and trachoma in both eyes, (this last due to the trip in the hold of the riverboat). A doctor told him he had tuberculosis and not much longer to live. His response was not to rest and try to recover his health, let alone to seek out pleasure during the brief time on earth predicted for him, as Bruce Lockhart undoubtedly would have done if given a similar diagnosis, but rather to re-dedicate himself to the socialist movement. In another age, he would have become a religious martyr. In Russia at the end of the nineteenth century, he made a conscious decision to sacrifice his life to the cause of socialism. "To be a bright torch for others, to be able to shed light—that is the supreme happiness which man can achieve."[3] He plotted an escape from Kaigorodsk, and carried it out, pretending to have gone on a five-day fishing expedition, in fact setting out immediately, and first of all in a row-boat, later by speedier means of transportation, for Vilno, which he reached on a chilly night in the autumn of 1899. Upon which he plunged immediately into revolutionary activity again.

* * *

The Party sent him to Warsaw. Still quite ill, he nevertheless threw himself into the attempt to establish a united Polish and Lithuanian

Figure 9. Young Felix Dzerzhinsky

Social Democratic Party. In less than half a year, always working with an eye peeled for the police, always sharpening his skills as an agitator outside the law, he and his comrades achieved this goal. Next, he began urging the newly united party to merge with the Russian Social Democrats. He wanted all workers in the Russian Empire to work together. His pace was feverish, perhaps because he thought he was living on borrowed time, perhaps because he knew it was only a matter of time before the authorities came for him again. They did: on February 4, 1900, while he was addressing a meeting.

This time they sentenced him to five years' exile in eastern Siberia. It meant another awful journey and his health so bad now that along the way at the town of Verkolensk on the Lena River, his captors left him in hospital. He was coughing blood. Yet, with another Social Democrat, he immediately escaped. They stole a boat and headed back downriver, taking turns at the oars. Although it was June it was cold, and mist lay thick upon the waterway. Caught in a stretch of rapids they capsized. He went under. His companion rescued him. Both were drenched and freezing. Dzerzhinsky built a fire before which they stripped and dried their clothes. Some peasants appeared. Dzerzhinsky told them he and his friend were merchants. He offered five rubles for transport to the nearest railway station. The peasants brought them there. A jarring note surfaced in his account: "What fools you are, muzhiks! Have you ever seen such an unlikely pair of merchants? What fools!"[4] It was a disturbing adumbration of a later attitude: one that finally would justify requisitioning grain from contemptible peasants who might starve, so that urban workers could live.

He returned to Warsaw, so obviously ill that his party comrades insisted he enter a sanatorium in Zurich. He went, but only because he had an ulterior motive: he had fallen in love with a young woman he had known since the period in Kovno. She too suffered from tuberculosis and was convalescing in the same place. He and Julia Goldman convalesced together and then passed a blissful interlude in the Swiss Alps. Her condition grew steadily worse, however, and she died in June 1904, a crushing blow for him.

Dzerzhinsky had trained in a very hard school, and it is not surprising that his thinking developed along lines similar to Vladimir Lenin's, leader of the Bolshevik faction within the Russian Social Democratic Labor Party (RSDLP). When Dzerzhinsky helped engineer the merger of his party with the RSDLP (maintaining autonomy for his group), delegates elected him to the party's Central Committee as a Polish representative. Then Dzerzhinsky and Lenin came face to face and began to forge the first link of a potent future partnership.

First, however, he returned to Poland to fight the employers of Lodz, who had declared a general offensive against the left in their city. He fought them the only way he knew—hard. He shaved his beard and mustache for the purpose of disguise. He changed his name and acquired false papers. He used invisible ink when writing to party comrades. He never slept in the same place twice and he took precautions when moving about the city. He had become a seasoned revolutionary agitator by now, and an expert at high-stakes hide-and-seek. The police caught him anyway, on April 16, 1908. They held him in prison for a year before sentencing him, mercilessly this time, to exile for life in Siberia. It took six months more before he finally arrived in the village of Taseyevo near Kansk, having traveled there under heavy guard. A week later, he escaped.

* * *

Perhaps he thought they could never keep him. Certainly, it never occurred to him to slow down, or to take a less than central part in the revolutionary movement, no matter the personal cost. But when a young party worker, Zofia Muszkat, became pregnant with his child, he married her. Almost immediately, the authorities scooped her up. She gave birth to their son Jasiek just before receiving sentence to Siberian exile. Dzerzhinsky could not take the infant; he lived on the run, but eventually he found him safe haven with friends. Then he turned his mind to rescuing his wife. He concealed a forged passport and some money in a book cover, and sent it to her, suggesting she read the book carefully "because in it you will find thoughts to raise your spirits and give you strength."[5] Zofia looked more closely at her gift, found what he had hidden inside, and made her escape. She arrived in Poland only weeks after the Tsar's police had caught up with her husband yet again.

Now commenced Dzerzhinsky's longest and harshest incarceration. For two years, he languished in isolation at the Citadel in Warsaw. Immured and alone he kept despair at bay by dreaming of his family. "I am waiting impatiently for the photo of Jasiek," he wrote to Zofia. "I long for every detail about him and I badly want to see him…to take him in my arms and caress him."[6] When she sent him photos, he fixed them to the walls of his cell with moistened prison bread and stared at them for hours. He wrote:

> Jaskiek's father turns and tosses in his dreams
> And stillness embraces his breast
> And his heart looks for his son's heart
> And tries hard to hear if from afar
> His anguished voice should cry…[7]

This is the man who only a few years later would, with a stroke of perhaps even the same pen, render countless wives into widows and children into orphans.

In April 1914, he received the sentence for his escape from exile in 1909: three years deportation at hard labor in chains. They fastened heavy fetters to his ankles and sent him to Orel provincial prison. Typhus spread among the convicts and he caught it. Still they made him work. He protested: the guards broke all his front teeth. They hit him so hard they paralyzed the muscles in his face. They put him into isolation cells for three to seven days at a time, windowless rooms with no light. Sometimes they starved him. The leg irons caused excruciating cramps and suppurating wounds. Dzerzhinsky did not yield. Often, he voiced the complaints of other prisoners, which led to further punishment. He "never laughed," said one who was there. "I can't even remember his smile."[8]

When Europe launched the cataclysm of World War I, Dzerzhinsky followed events from prison as best he could. The world conflict did not affect him, but he predicted it would lead to world revolution. In May 1916, his jailers brought him to Moscow to learn the sentence for his political activities of 1909–12. By now, he was so weak he could not stand in the dock. The judge intoned mercilessly: "three years more at hard labor." It was a death sentence, but for some reason the prison authorities removed his fetters and sent him to work in the prison tailoring shop, sewing buttons onto army uniforms. That was not so bad, and he began to recuperate. On the night of March 14, 1917, as he lay alone in his cell, there was hubbub outside, rushing footsteps, fierce shouts. His cell door burst open, and a Moscow *sans culottes* stood before him, announcing in stentorian voice: "Comrade, the revolution has begun." He tottered out into the cold; stood on the bed of a truck and delivered a speech to a crowd gathered in a city square where Lockhart, who was out that night trying to learn all he could about the situation, may have heard him; spent his first night in years in a real bed.

*   *   *

In the welter of events that followed, Dzerzhinsky played a major part. The Moscow Bolshevik Party Committee immediately accepted him as representative of the Polish and Lithuanian Social Democratic Party. A few weeks later he was elected to the Executive Committee of the Moscow Soviet. He wanted to return to Poland to speed the revolution there, but Russian events caught him up. On one side the Duma, led by Prince Lvov, the friend of Bruce Lockhart; on the other "Soviets" (councils) of workers, soldiers, sailors, and peasants: for a time, the two maintained an uneasy and temporary symbiosis called "dual power." All that spring and summer, however, the Soviets strengthened and the Provisional Government based on the Duma dithered. Prince Lvov stepped down after enormous demonstrations in July. Alexander Kerensky, a moderate socialist belonging to the right wing of the Socialist Revolutionary Party, replaced him. But Kerensky could no more control events than Lvov. Lenin, who had returned to Russia in April 1917 in the famous sealed train, discerned a revolutionary situation in the making. Dzerzhinsky agreed.

As planning for the October Revolution began, Dzerzhinsky took part in all the important meetings. When the Bolsheviks seized power on November 6 (Western calendar), his job was to take over the main post and telegraph offices. The men he commanded achieved this without firing a shot. On the following day, the Second Congress of Soviets convened and adopted a decree transferring power to itself. The day after that it elected a central government, the Council of People's Commissars (Sovnarkom) with Lenin as leader. This body, which at first comprised exclusively Bolsheviks but which was later expanded to include other socialists (e.g., left Socialist Revolutionaries), elected Dzerzhinsky to the All Russia Central Executive Committee, and to its Presidium.

The new regime faced every threat. Military cadets in Petrograd rebelled and had to be suppressed. Troops loyal to Kerensky and the Duma marched on the capital and had to be faced down. In the provinces, anti-Bolshevik army officers plotted counter-revolution. Anti-Bolshevik political parties and civil servants planned a national general strike. The Bolsheviks discovered correspondence between anti-government activists written in invisible ink, "safe houses" for counter-revolutionaries, hidden caches of arms.

The Sovnarkom met to discuss this desperate situation. It established the All-Russian Extraordinary Commission for Combating Counter-Revolution and Sabotage (or Cheka). Everyone agreed that only one man could lead it. Dzerzhinsky stepped forward unhesitatingly. The former conspirator, agitator, organizer, the former prisoner, exile, and fugitive, had attained his apotheosis. He would devote to his new role the same ceaseless, tireless, dedication that he had brought to the old one. He had become his own mirror image, a doppelganger with a reverse mission.

As 40-year-old Felix Dzerzhinsky was taking up his new mission in Moscow, 30-year-old Bruce Lockhart was meeting Prime Minister Lloyd George in London, and receiving instructions to return to Russia.

CHAPTER 5

TENDER JACOV PETERS

In 1918, Felix Dzerzhinsky's second-in-command was a young Latvian named Jacov Peters. Lockhart would come to know him well. He was "short, snub-nosed and almost stocky in build, with bristling, short, brown hair," according to the American journalist, Louise Bryant. He was "an intense, quick, nervous little chap with…an upturned nose that gave to his face the suggestion of a question-mark, and a pair of blue eyes full of human tenderness," recalled Bessie Beatty, another US journalist. She was either greener than Bryant, or more discerning.[1] Either way, it is only fair to say that in the end Jacov Peters would disappoint her; ultimately, he would be no better known for human tenderness than Felix Dzerzhinsky.

He was born in 1886, in Courland in southwestern Latvia. He told Beatty that his father had been a modestly prosperous peasant who employed farm laborers.[2] Some years later, during the Bolshevik campaign against the kulaks—so-called rich peasants, he said that his father had been a mere farm laborer.[3] In any event, Peters himself "worked in the fields" as a child. He was a sensitive boy who prayed to God to save him when there was thunder and lightning. Also, he was precociously attuned to power relationships. It bothered him that his father, "who was not nearly so clever as the workers," possessed greater political rights than they.

Figure 10. Jacov Peters

A stranger, whom he met on the road and with whom he discussed this disparity, gave him pamphlets proposing radical answers. Peters read them, brought them first to fellow students at the local gymnasium and then to his school newspaper, of which he may have been an editor. The school principal reported him to his father, who beat him. "From that moment I became a revolutionist."[4]

A "revolutionist" whose eyes were filled with human tenderness? It is not impossible. "The eyes are the window to your soul," as William Shakespeare is thought to have said. Maxim Gorky, Russia's greatest man of letters, in 1918 perceived "martyrdom crystallized" in the eyes of Felix Dzerzhinsky.[5] Why not tenderness in the eyes of Jacov Peters—in 1918 anyway, before the terrible tragedies of later years wiped it away?

At about age 15, he left the countryside for the town, Libau (today Liepaja) on the Baltic Sea, and found work on the docks, and in an oil mill. Here he came into contact with experienced revolutionists. He joined the Latvian Social Democratic Workers Party. Quickly he became a party organizer. Talented and hardworking, he rose swiftly in the party—and therefore drew attention to himself, just as he had done at school. The pattern thus far is not dissimilar from Felix Dzerzhinsky's. In 1907, police arrested him for attempting to murder a factory owner during a strike. For a year he languished in prison. He planned an escape involving a message inscribed on dry bread, which he passed to a girl by a kiss. Beatty says the girl read the message and helped him carry out the escape, but there is no corroborating evidence. Moreover, a military court in Riga acquitted him of the murder charge in 1908, which it could not have done if it had lost him. Shortly thereafter he moved to London.

We do know that the police dealt brutally with him while they had him in the Riga jail, encouraging him to confess by pulling out all his fingernails. This treatment, and what he saw done to other prisoners, shocked him. Possibly it broke him: the Okhrana compiled a list of Bolsheviks that it and its agents had turned. Peters' name appears on the list.[6] Is the list reliable? Everything else we know about him suggests he had become, and would always remain, a Bolshevik true believer. Perhaps he agreed to cooperate, but never did. Perhaps he agreed to cooperate only in order to report back to his comrades. Perhaps the Okhrana never broke him, but let it be known that it had, in order to destroy his reputation with fellow revolutionaries. The verdict on this aspect of his life must remain open.

The young revolutionist's years in London are hard to trace. At first, he barely scraped together a living, working at a Spitalfields "rag shop" for eight shillings a week. He lived at 48 Turner Street in Whitechapel, in a room he rented for three shillings per week from an anarchist. On the walls he hung photographs of various Bolshevik leaders.[7] It seems unlikely, but at this time he may have come to know Winston Churchill's cousin, Clare Sheridan, a sculptress who is said to have introduced him to May Freeman, the woman he would marry. Freeman's father may have been a banker, and she may have told him after her marriage to Peters that she and her husband "would live by their own labor and give up their [sic?] servants."[8] Certainly, Peters did somehow meet and marry May Freeman, and certainly his fortunes improved immensely thereafter. They had a daughter called Maisie. "He was a kind husband and father," May remembered. "He was never happier than when spending his evenings home with us."[9] From 1914, they lived at 18 Canonbury Street, in Islington. "He wore a frock-coat on Sundays, and walked out with his English 'missis' and his little girl in the height of order and respectability."[10] He now worked for Landau and Sons, a tailoring business in Whitechapel in the East End of London, for a respectable £4 per week.[11]

But he was "a revolutionist," "a terrorist, anarchist and communist," his putative banker father-in-law is supposed to have wailed. Long before he met May Freeman, Peters had joined the "Communist Club" which met at 107 Charlotte Street in Soho, and whose members eventually elected him secretary; and the Latvian Social Democratic Party (London branch); and the Bureau of the United Foreign Groups of the Latvian Social Democratic Workers' Party; and the British Socialist Party; and when World War I began, he joined the Russian Anti-Conscription League. All this drew the attention of Scotland Yard's Special Branch, which already in March 1914 had opened a file on him.[12]

In 1910, also before he married, Peters may have participated in an infamous robbery of a jewelry store in East London. The bandits, who were loosely termed anarchists, intended to fund their movement with the proceeds. This was a time-honored practice among Bolsheviks, one in which Stalin, among others, is said to have engaged. In this instance, however, the heist went terribly wrong. It led to a shootout in which three London bobbies and one of the thieves lost their lives. After an intense dragnet lasting nearly a week, the London police arrested Peters and two other suspects. Witnesses said they had seen him trying to assist the thief who had been shot and who would die of his wounds. A fortnight later, the police tracked two more "anarchists" to 100 Sidney Street, also in the East End, and commenced a siege which was overseen by the then Home Secretary, Winston Churchill. The two sides exchanged gunfire; somehow the house burst into flames; the two occupants perished. One of them was Peters' cousin.

At the trial of the three arrested men the prosecution could not produce evidence that Peters had shot at the bobbies when they interrupted the heist. In fact, they could not prove that he had been involved in the heist at all. He, on the other hand, produced what turned out to be a convincing alibi—that the witnesses had mistaken him for his cousin, who was now conveniently dead. In the end, at this trial the police could not produce evidence sufficient to convict anyone of anything. The judge released all three men. As in Riga in 1907, when he had been accused of attempted murder but acquitted, so now in London, Peters went free. Whether justice had been served remains an open question.[13]

The Special Branch dossier never indicates Peters' link with the Okhrana, which implies that there was none. But also, it has been suggested that London intelligence officers had been blackmailing him, threatening to say he had helped the Tsar even though he had not, and in this way had made him their instrument. In return, they secured his acquittal when he was tried for his part in the jewelry robbery.[14] The Special Branch dossier does not mention this either, however. Its agents kept tabs on Peters' continuing "anarchist" political activities, as though it believed in them.

Peters seemed to know how to cope with Special Branch agents. It is as likely he played them, as vice-versa. When one appeared on his doorstep to interview him in March 1917 about his membership in various revolutionary groups, he claimed to hold no extreme views about the war or anything else, although he opposed all wars on general principle. If he must fight, he would prefer to join the British rather than the Russian army.[15] That was rich. Only two months later, he left his wife and daughter in London, returned to Latvia, took up a position on the Central Committee of the Latvian Social Democratic Party, served on the editorial board of a local socialist newspaper, worked as a revolutionary agitator among the Latvian battalions, and participated as a Latvian peasant delegate in the Democratic Conference of September 12, 1917, convened in Petrograd by Kerensky's government. During the late summer and autumn of 1917, he traveled back and forth between Latvia and Petrograd, gaining the trust and respect of Lenin, whose hiding place he is said to have arranged, when Kerensky ordered the arrest of Bolshevik leaders. Are you "absolutely sure that Lenin is an honest revolutionist and not a pro-German?" the journalist Beatty asked him. "He raised his head with a toss of defiance and his blue eyes flashed fire." "If I wasn't sure I wouldn't [help him.]"

In October, he took a leading role in the coup that overthrew Kerensky. In December, he became, with Felix Dzerzhinsky, a founder-member of the Cheka, and then Dzerzhinsky's chief aide. He was popular with foreign correspondents "because he seemed more cultivated than the rest."[16] In February 1918, as the Germans advanced on Petrograd he told one: "If we fail now, everything is lost. In my country the business is all in my name—my throat will be the first one cut." He told Beatty, at least "the world will say that dark Russia did her best to bring peace to all the war-weary peoples."[17] Perhaps at that moment, his eyes were filled with human tenderness after all.

CHAPTER 6

THE CHEKA

Felix Dzerzhinsky intended to fashion the Cheka in his own image, but he faced difficulties. The first had to do with recruitment. Each member should possess "a burning heart, a cool head, and clean hands."[1] How many individuals drawn to police work possess those attributes? If Dzerzhinsky meant what he said, then he must cast his net into a shallow pool.

When he cast it, he faced another problem: many Russians in the pool had had enough of secret police. They would not join the Bolshevik equivalent of the Tsar's Okhrana, even if a sainted Bolshevik leader asked them to. Dzerzhinsky tried to reassure these idealists with an idealistic exhortation: "the incursion of armed men into private homes and the deprivation of the liberty of guilty people represent an evil...Our task in resorting to this evil is to root out the need for having recourse to it in future."[2] For the moment such promises persuaded few party members.

A third difficulty now arose: the government had limited resources to support the organization. Initially Dzerzhinsky's staff numbered twenty-three, including secretaries and couriers. His first budget amounted to one thousand rubles and sat in the desk drawer of his second-in-command, Jacov Peters. Meanwhile, social and economic chaos prevailed. If the Bolsheviks did not bring it under control, then a party that could do so would replace them. Equally dangerous, counter-revolutionaries, backed by foreign powers, plotted to topple the new regime. They too must be defeated.

Belatedly, hurriedly, the government found means to double Dzerzhinsky's insufficient budget, and to double it again—and then again, many times over; and to treble his staff; and to continue adding to it. Chekist branches appeared in the provincial cities and towns. Chekist military formations emerged. From humble origins grew something new and terrible in a remarkably short time. Now Dzerzhinsky could cast his recruitment net more widely. Now he really could fashion an effective sword and shield of the Revolution. "Clean hands" remained important to him, but "burning hearts" were more important still. Cold hearts and hard hearts would replace "burning hearts" soon enough.

When the Bolshevik government, fearing German occupation, fled Petrograd for Moscow in mid-March, Dzerzhinsky moved too, establishing the Cheka's national headquarters in the main offices of a former insurance agency located at Number 11, the Lubianka, convenient for Kremlin meetings. Occasionally, one of his subordinates would glimpse him early in the morning headed for work, striding up Rozhdestvenskii Boulevard from the train station, a tall, lean figure "in his simple cavalry coat, boots and a frontline sheepskin hat or a cap."[3] More often, however, he stayed overnight at the Lubianka. He had a spartan office in the building, a single room, the "plainest and smallest" there, and it looked in toward the courtyard so no sniper could fire at him through an outside window. The room contained only a bookshelf, desk, and chair, and at one side a screen that hid a thin mattress resting on a narrow iron frame. Usually he spent the night on that bed, his greatcoat serving as blanket.[4] But he scarcely slept: Chekists reported seeing his light burning hours after midnight when they finally went home exhausted from a long day's labors, and they would find him at his desk the next morning no matter how early they arrived. He would be hard at work already, drinking endless cups of mint tea, smoking his own rolled cigarettes of rough Russian tobacco. Because he genuinely preferred doing so, although also to make a point, he ate in the Cheka canteen with the men and women who served under him, although often they received only half a tin of meat each, per day.

The Revolution changed Dzerzhinsky's circumstances, and enabled him to change his appearance to a degree, but never his overall outlook or work habits. He grew a mustache and from his chin a straggly brown beard, but he remained as always tall and gaunt, although no longer skeletally so, with a long aristocratic nose, hooded eyes, delicate hands with tapered fingers. He could not smile properly, because he never completely healed from the beating inflicted by his jailers at Orel provincial prison. As for his

Figure 11. Felix Dzerzhinsky in about 1918

psychology: if anything, it had grown more austere. "Have you no shame," he chastised Chekists who put in for a salary hike despite their country's desperate plight. (They withdrew the request.)[5] "I will not eat it," he told his sister when she prepared him a pancake with flour she had purchased from a private trader. Then he flung the offending morsel out the window.[6] His general approach too remained unaltered. He continued to risk his health by working harder, longer—and better—than anyone. His terrifying intensity and burning, not to say masochistic, commitment to the cause of socialism, still defined him.

The Bolshevik government gave him new and awful powers. It made him the Revolution's chief inquisitor. He was a saint with authority to "hammer the heretics" as Torquemada had done during the Spanish Inquisition. Did he hesitate? Yes, but not for long. He overcame scruples about employing agents provocateurs.[7] "His face [was] deadly white and in torment," but he signed a death warrant anyway—and then another, and another after that.[8] He would not shrink from what he conceived to be his duty, no matter how awful, no matter the cost. He wrote to his wife: "My thought forces me to be merciless and I have the firm will to follow my thoughts to the end."[9]

(Significantly, Jacov Peters underwent a like evolution. "I wasn't made for this work," he told Bessie Beattie shortly after he joined the Cheka. "I detest jails so that I can't bear to put anyone into them." Then he told her: "We will never restore the death sentence in Russia."[10] He said the same to Louise Bryant: "His face was white and stern; he appeared on the verge of collapse."[11] But only a year later, he would be described by a British journalist who had known him, and to whom he had "always been kindly and considerate" as "signing away daily the lives of scores of men he never saw." "We are fighting for our lives," he explained.[12])

Under the lead of these two men, Dzerzhinsky at the fore, the Cheka made short shrift of people who engaged in criminal behavior.[13] Something like order began to reappear in Russia's major cities. Counter-revolutionaries posed a more difficult problem, however. During the winter and early spring of 1917–18, the Cheka suppressed a strike of government employees receiving support from bankers and industrialists.[14] It blocked another strike by bank officials. It crushed "Black Dot" and "White Cross" counter-revolutionary organizations.[15] It destroyed a "Landowners Union" working with the White Generals Kornilov and Kaledin in the Don region, and broke up organizations recruiting and transporting counter-revolutionaries to the Generals' armies.[16] It seized the printing presses of illegal political parties and groups. Dzerzhinsky directed most of these operations. Sometimes he took part in them. He drew upon his own experience to teach his agents everything. Peters wrote of his chief: "The Cheka workers learned from him how, when deciphering various scraps of paper, to unravel threads leading to counter-revolutionary conspiracies."[17] Often Dzerzhinsky conducted the interrogations that followed arrests.

At first, the Cheka dealt relatively mildly with detainees. During its first six months, it carried out twenty-two executions.[18] Dzerzhinsky quickly concluded, however, that desperate times demanded a ruthless response. The Cheka began executing suspects without trial. "Iron Felix" saw "no other way to combat counterrevolutionaries, spies, speculators, house-breakers, hooligans, saboteurs and other parasites."[19] One dissident, who experienced an unexpectedly mild interrogation led by him, nevertheless said correctly, when it was over, "There was something terrible in him."[20]

In mid-April, the Cheka conducted a major operation that demonstrated its growing strength, confidence, prowess, and importance to the regime. Oddly enough, Raymond Robins provoked it—and, even more oddly, in doing so he became responsible for bringing Felix Dzerzhinsky and Jacov Peters together with Bruce Lockhart for the first time.

* * *

Every morning, Robins' chauffeur would drive him to a government telegraph office from which he could dispatch cyphered messages. On April 9, when he emerged from the office, he found his automobile surrounded by ten armed men. They did not wear uniforms. "Requisition & anarchist: two words," the American wrote afterwards in his diary. The leader of the group indicated that Robins should get into the car. Four bandits sat next to him, two on either side. Six stood on the running boards, their bayonets fixed, their rifles cocked. They made his interpreter, another American, called Alexander Gumberg, stand on the running board with them. The leader spoke to Robins' driver. He wanted to be taken to Number 9 Povarskaya Street. This was one of the most prosperous and handsome boulevards in the city; number 9 was the address of a grand house that had been taken over by anarchists calling themselves "Immediate Socialists."[21] Robins realized his life was in danger. As the car began to move, he told Gumberg to instruct the chauffeur to drive slowly. The chauffeur did so. Robins jumped from the moving automobile, Gumberg following. An anarchist aimed his rifle at Robins' chest. He had his finger on the trigger but he did not pull it. The car disappeared down the road. Shaken, the two Americans returned to their rooms at the Hotel Elite. Then, "We go after power," Robins wrote in his diary. He meant that he and Gumberg went to see Felix Dzerzhinsky.[22]

The head of the Cheka knew about the anarchists already. Before the October Revolution, their movement had made a marriage of convenience with Bolshevism. Ideological anarchists had wanted to overthrow Kerensky's provisional government just as much as Bolsheviks did. This meant their representatives, of whom a handful sat in the Petrograd and Moscow Soviets, often voted with Bolsheviks, and their followers of whom there were thousands, took part with them in demonstrations and street fighting. Ideological anarchists believed in direct action. They shrank neither from violence nor even from terrorism. Plagued by internal disagreements, conflicting egos, and bombastic leadership, their movement never attracted a mass following, but nor did it have merely negligible support.[23] At one point, Lockhart advised the Foreign Office: "Many people [see] in their ranks the elements of a successful counter-revolution."[24]

By April 1918, ideological anarchists published two newspapers in Moscow, one of them daily. Their followers had seized the Merchant Club, a luxuriously appointed mansion, with library and theater, and made it their headquarters. This was only one of twenty-six houses they "requisitioned," most of them big, lavishly furnished and in the best neighborhoods. While living in them in comfort, the anarchists held meetings, and printed pamphlets and journals. They invited poor working-class families to join them. They fortified these houses with machine guns and artillery. Different ideological anarchist groups took romantic names such as "Sandstorm," or "Hurricane."[25]

It did not take long for the anarchist honeymoon with Bolshevism to end. Normally ideological anarchists abhorred "the straitjacket of Marxism." They wanted no central government at all, let alone a dictatorship of the proletariat. They thought present Bolshevik domination of the Soviets meant boss rule. They opposed formation of a secret police and hated the Treaty of Brest-Litovsk, which they deemed a capitulation to German imperialism. Bolsheviks had the Red Guard to protect them; ideological anarchists organized a Black Guard. One faction began to plan an anti-Bolshevik uprising, but predictably, another faction opposed the plan. Still, German intelligence learned about the planners and contacted them, as subsequent events would disclose.

Ideological anarchists believed in immediate redistribution not just of mansions and fancy automobiles like the one they took from Robins, but of all forms of wealth. This attracted men and women with no interest in anarchist theory. Gangs of thugs who called themselves anarchists roamed the streets. They held up individuals, and plundered private homes, shops, and warehouses. In Petrograd one "anarchist" gang stopped the sleigh of the chief of the city's branch of the Cheka, stealing all his belongings and his clothing.[26] Ideological anarchist leaders disavowed such acts, but the confiscations continued.[27] As a result, long before they stole Robins' vehicle, "anarchists" had alienated the vast majority of Russians, Muscovites in particular.

Finally, counter-revolutionaries, who had no interest in ideological anarchism whatever, discovered that no one questioned them when they sought accommodation in the anarchist houses. They stayed because libertarian scruples inhibited their hosts from inquiring into the origins and motives of their guests. In this manner, White Guard officers and others active in counter-revolutionary scheming secured lodgings only minutes from the Kremlin.[28] Some had German connections. Now a new marriage of convenience began to take shape: some White Guards began to think they could use Black Guards to hammer the Bolsheviks; some anarchists began to think they could hammer Bolsheviks with White Guards. The Germans intended to use them all as hammers.

After the appropriation of his auto, Robins asked the Bolsheviks, "Who really rules?" They would show him. Dzerzhinsky instructed his agents to scout the twenty-six houses, and learn their approaches, escape routes, and defenses. Two days later, April 11, he had the necessary information, and a characteristically thorough and canny plan. He summoned representatives of Red

Figure 12. Captain Eduard Berzin, Latvian Rifle Brigade

Army units, of the newly formed Cheka military detachments, and of the Latvian Rifle Brigade, which had a deserved reputation for reliability, anti-German fervor and heroism under fire. The Latvian Rifle Brigade had become Bolshevism's Praetorian Guard. Captain Eduard Petrovich Berzin, a music lover who had trained as a painter before the war at the Berlin Academy of Fine Arts, "a tall, powerfully built man with clear-cut features and hard, steely eyes," a war hero, twice wounded in the struggle with Germany, represented it at the meeting.[29] As it happens, he and Bruce Lockhart would have important dealings in the months to come too.

Dzerzhinsky instructed them all to wait until midnight, then to order their men to cordon off and surround the twenty-six buildings, demand surrender within five minutes, and commence firing when five minutes had elapsed. Five minutes is not many: the aim, it seems clear, was to destroy the anarchist forces once and for all.[30]

They did it, taking their opponents completely by surprise. Nevertheless, some houses put up fierce resistance. In the fighting, Captain Berzin and his riflemen distinguished themselves. Robins wrote in his diary, "Shooting last night. Again, and again, from the window of Hotel Elite we saw the Bolshevik vs. Anarchist combat. Talk and shoot and run to cover."[31] On April 13, he sent an account of the operation to the American ambassador. It concluded: "Soviet used four-inch cannon where resistance lasted beyond ten minutes. One big house blown pieces. Anarchists fighting from cellar until dislodged by smoke bombs. Five hundred twenty-two arrests, forty killed, wounded anarchists. Soviet three killed, fourteen wounded…Soviet government has now destroyed bandit organization."[32]

The next morning, Robins called upon Dzerzhinsky, and brought Arthur Ransome and Bruce Lockhart with him. This was the first time the British agent met the man who would become his nemesis. Lockhart wrote in his memoir that he initially met Dzerzhinsky in July, but his diary and a dispatch he sent on April 13 to London prove otherwise. In the memoir, he recorded his "first" impression of the Cheka chief: "a man of correct manners and quiet speech but without a ray of humor in his character. The most remarkable thing about him was his eyes. Deeply sunk, they blazed with a steady fire of fanaticism. They never twitched. His eyelids seemed paralyzed."[33] Dzerzhinsky promised to return Robins' car the next day. In the meantime, he lent the trio a different motor to tour the battlefields of the previous night. He sent Jacov Peters as their escort.

The probable jewel thief, possible murderer, conceivable turn-coat—but more likely dedicated revolutionary whose heart probably was hardening daily by now—brought Lockhart, Ransome, and Robins to Number 9 Povarskaya, captured from the anarchists the previous night by Captain Berzin's Latvians. What they saw there might have been anarchy, but it was not the ideological kind. "The filth was indescribable," Lockhart recalled. "Broken bottles littered the floor...wine stains and human excrement blotched the Aubusson carpets." The corpse of a young woman lay face down on the floor. Callously, "Peters shrugged his shoulders. 'Prostitutka' he said." Other bodies lay where they had fallen as well, including "officers in [White] Guard's uniform." Bullet holes pocked the walls and ceiling, evidence of the firefight the previous night. Amidst the rubble, the Cheka claimed to have discovered machine guns of German manufacture. They were so new no one recognized them. The Bolsheviks interpreted this as confirmation of the anarchist–White Guard–German axis, an inherently improbable combination that nevertheless may have been in an early stage of formation.

* * *

The Cheka had dealt with one threat, but it could not rest upon its laurels. During the spring and summer of 1918, counter-revolutionary conspirators more formidable than ideological anarchists would plot moves, procure weapons, move pawns and more powerful pieces into place, and launch them into action. Bruce Lockhart would circulate among these conspirators and eventually develop a plot of his own. He did not know it on April 12, in the aftermath of the operation against the anarchists (at that date he still hoped for a modus vivendi with the Bolsheviks), but Raymond Robins had just introduced him to the men who would become his chief antagonists: Felix Dzerzhinsky and Jacov Peters. And Captain Berzin, whom he had not yet met, but who would also play a prominent role in his undoing, remained just behind the curtain, waiting in the wings.

PART III

TOWARD THE FALL

CHAPTER 7

THE "ACE OF SPIES"

Sidney Reilly may have been Ian Fleming's model for James Bond. He is known to history as the "Ace of Spies," and remains, as he would have wished, an enigmatic figure. He attempted to shroud even his origins in mystery; for example, his wife believed that "his father was an Irish merchant sea captain and his mother a Russian."[1] In fact, his best biographers have traced him to a Jewish family in Russian Poland, where he was born in 1874.[2] His name at the start probably was Shlomo ben Hersh Rozenbluim. Twenty years later, he appeared in England with knowledge of chemistry almost certainly gained in Vienna, and certainly not gained, as he sometimes claimed, at Cambridge University. Already he had mastered English, Russian, German, French and, one suspects, Hebrew and Yiddish as well, aside from his native Polish. Evidence suggests that while still in Russia he had informed on socialist comrades to the Tsar's Okhrana.[3] Once he arrived in London, this history, combined with his linguistic skills, made possible work as a paid informant for Scotland Yard's Special Branch émigré intelligence network. In 1899, a friend at the Yard expedited his successful application for a British passport in the name of Sidney George Reilly.

The man married four times; he never divorced. Eventually he had two wives in England, one in St. Petersburg and one in New

York City. He may have arranged the murder of his first wife's husband. He kept a string of mistresses all his life (and not seriatim) but never became emotionally involved with any of them. Most of his biographers think he never became emotionally involved with anyone at all, that he only used and discarded people, that he was a compulsive conman, a sociopath. He had defenders, however. One with whom he would work closely in Russia recalled: "He was an extraordinarily good friend and generous to a fault to those whom he liked. From my experience he was essentially a man of great integrity."[4]

His first marriage made him wealthy. He severed the formal connection with Scotland Yard, but established one with British Intelligence, although what he did for it remains unclear. Possibly he was instrumental in gaining valuable oil concessions for Britain from Persia. In 1904 he traveled to the Far East as representative of a trading firm, arriving in Port Arthur just in time for the Russo-Japanese War, just in time, also, to make a great deal more money as a war profiteer, and then to make still more by selling information to both sides. What he did after the war is, again, unclear. He may have stolen German armaments plans for Britain. He may have committed murder to do so. At any rate, he lived primarily in Russia for more than a half a decade before 1914 and established himself as a general contractor with an interest in the arms trade. The wide range of political, social, and business contacts he developed during these years served him well when he returned to Russia as a British agent during World War I.

Before that, however, he had gone to New York City. When war broke out, he positioned himself there as a contractor for Russian armaments and supplies. His sharp business practice made him enemies, but also yet more money. By now he had a fortune, part

Figure 13. Dangerous Sidney Reilly

of which he spent on Napoleonic memorabilia. As for espionage, he appears to have performed services during the early years of the war for Russian, British and German intelligence agencies, never to satisfy his own convictions, always to further his own interests. Stories he later cultivated, however, about having infiltrated wartime Germany to steal important military documents, are probably without foundation.

During the early part of World War I, he met and impressed Sir William Wiseman, head of the British Secret Service in New York City. "Complexion swarthy," recorded Wiseman's assistant, who met Reilly at the same time, "a long straight nose, piercing eyes, black hair brushed back from a forehead suggesting keen intelligence, a large mouth, figure slight, of medium height, always clothed immaculately, he was a man that impressed one with a sense of power."[5]

In September 1917, Wiseman arranged Reilly's return to Russia to work for MI1c, the British intelligence service, gathering information on the country's land and naval forces before Germany took them all. By now Reilly had, or soon would have, a commission as a second lieutenant in the British Army's Royal Flying Corps (predecessor of the RAF). This would be his cover. Back in the land of his birth, he renewed acquaintance with military men and secret policemen, with businessmen and spies, and with women, plenty of them (although apparently not with the wife who lived in Petrograd). He made important new connections too. He may at this time have met George Alexander Hill, Britain's chief military intelligence officer in Moscow. The latter would become significant because he had established already a network of couriers who would be able to get important information to British authorities once they landed in north Russia. At whatever time they met, the two spies got along and "agreed to cooperate whenever possible."[6] Reilly began to lay the groundwork for his later clandestine operations, establishing aliases, arranging safe houses, and so on. He left the country for London, not New York, sometime in December 1917.

In fact, Sidney Reilly did sincerely hold one political conviction: anti-communism. When the Bolsheviks took power, he believed their creed represented a greater threat to Britain and the world than Prussian militarism. He would do his best to destroy it. Hence his return to Russia yet again, in early April 1918, this time as MI1c's agent ST1.[7] He entered Petrograd, now under Bolshevik rule, and thought: "Something like this...Hell must be: paved with desolation, filth, squalor, fiendish cruelty, abject terror, blood, lust, starvation."[8] Reilly would devote the rest of his life to defeating the movement he believed was responsible for all that.

In April 1918, in Moscow, he wore the Royal Flying Corps uniform, and posed before the Bolshevik authorities as an officer attached to the British military mission. In fact, he did more than pose; he strutted—right up to the Kremlin, where he demanded an audience with Lenin, and actually received one with a high-ranking official. Then, kitted out in Flying Corps uniform, for months he ostentatiously wined and dined former Russian contacts, some of whom held important positions in the new government, others of whom already had begun contemplating or already were involved in underground anti-Bolshevik plotting. He spoke openly, as a British officer, of his distaste for the new regime.

Simultaneously he engaged in surreptitious work. In Moscow he established a second identity as Mr. Constantine, a Greek businessman, sharing an apartment with two young actresses, with one of whom he began an affair. In Petrograd he slipped into a pre-established alias, Konstantine Massino, Turkish businessman. There he took up with a former mistress, Elena Boguzhevskaia, whom he persuaded to pose as his wife. He renewed acquaintance with Alexander Orlov, a former Tsarist prosecutor, now chief of Petrograd's Criminal Investigation Commission. Orlov provided him with a third false character: Sidnei Georgievich Reilinski, detective. Orlov was an active counter-revolutionary with links to Captain Cromie, whom Reilly also quickly came to know. Through another old contact, he arranged his fourth nom de guerre: K. P. Vasil'ev, Soviet official, dealing in automobile parts. This brought him a pass for unrestricted travel on government trains. Perhaps most extraordinary of all, somehow Reilly managed to obtain a fifth alias: Georgii Repinski, an officer of the Cheka.

And the women: in his guise as Konstantine Massino he took a lover, Olga Starzhevskaia, who served as a staffer at the Soviet All-Russian Central Executive Committee. He set her up in a separate love nest from Elena Boguzhevskaia, his "wife." Starzhevskaia supplied him with the agendas, and even the minutes, of those Executive Committee meetings. These found their way back to

Whitehall via George Hill's courier service. He employed three women more, all dancers or actors; with one of them, Yelizaveta Otten, he formed yet another sexual attachment. One of the others, Maria Fride had a brother, Lieutenant Colonel Alexander, of the Latvian Rifle Brigade, with whom Reilly may have crossed paths in New York City during the early years of the war. Alexander Fride was an anti-Bolshevik Latvian nationalist who nevertheless held an important position on the staff of the Russian Army's military communications unit. Soon, through his sister, he was supplying Reilly with secret dispatches from various fronts, and Reilly was using Hill to send them back to Whitehall too.

Through the Frides, brother and sister, Reilly renewed acquaintance with another New York City contact, the exotically named Xenophon Dmitrievich Kalamatiano, brought up in America and an American citizen, although born in Vienna to a Greek father and Russian mother. Kalamatiano was a former businessman who now ran in Russia an "Information Bureau" supported by the American Consulate. Its thirty agents collected the sort of information Bolsheviks did not wish foreigners to have, for example delicate or secret military, political, and economic intelligence. Reilly and Kalamatiano worked out a system for sharing it: Kalamatiano's sub-agents—military men, businessmen, academics—scoured the country gathering data, which they conveyed to Alexander Fride. He edited their gleanings for Kalamatiano's use—but also passed them along to his sister, who gave them to Yelizaveta Otten, who carried them to yet another cut-out called "Vi," who gave them finally to George Hill. And Hill, of course, gave them to the couriers in his pay, who brought them to British authorities.

This is important because it shows that British and American intelligence agents had begun cooperating months before

Lockhart conceived his plot. Soon they would be cooperating with French intelligence agents as well. The three Allied Powers would all have more or less to do with the plot once Lockhart conceived it and began to move it forward.

Meanwhile Reilly: he attended a lecture by Trotsky and sent Whitehall a summary.[9] He developed a relationship with Mikhail Dmitriyevich Bonch-Bruyevich, Military Director of the Supreme Military Council, where, Reilly reported, "he is the brain-center of the whole organization, originating reforms and new schemes for military organization." Lieutenant Reilly of the Royal Air Force, as the Royal Flying Corps had just become, interviewed Bonch-Bruyevich regularly, and sent a steady stream of reports back to London on the state of Russia's army. They were good ones. "I have seen several reports from Reilly," noted one mandarin, "and have always found them quite satisfactory."[10]

No matter the evolution of policy in London, Reilly's aim in Russia remained constant: it was to eradicate Bolshevism. He sought an alternative to Marxism–Leninism, a more compelling dogma with which to woo the nation's masses. He found it in Christianity.

"It is necessary to adopt a concrete program of Church schools all over Russia," Reilly lectured Whitehall. "The widest participation of the clergy in educational work outside the schools and the Church; direct influence upon the people through propaganda by means of flooding the villages with appropriate literature; the organization of personal spiritual propaganda and agitation over the whole country; these are the necessary steps." Such an ambitious program would take cash, he acknowledged: '20–25 million R[uble]s (at the present exchange) [about £18–£23 million today] and spread over the period of one year." The reward, however, would be more than commensurate: "imperishable ties between the Russian people and the Allied nations." These would enable the Allies to win the war and to overthrow Bolshevism. Then, the Church would repay the money.[11]

Whatever Bruce Lockhart's initial impression of this fantastic figure, a meeting of minds soon took place. The young Scot was looking for a way to ingratiate himself with his masters in London who, as he now correctly judged, largely shared Reilly's outlook, not Robins' and Ransome's. Moreover, he too likely had already a connection with the Russian Church, through the Patriarch Tikhon, its senior figure, "an ardent absolute monarchist" and convinced counter-revolutionary.[12] "Church will soon gather healthy forces of nation round her...Russia will once more take part in war," someone, and the style is Lockhart's, reported the Patriarch telling him.[13] If the "Ace of Spies" wanted money to channel to the Church for counter-revolutionary purposes, Lockhart would find it. He did: £200,000 (about 12 million rubles). Tikhon may have been "under the closest observation," but Reilly and George Hill packed the banknotes into suitcases and delivered them to him anyway.[14]

It was only the beginning of the Lockhart–Reilly collaboration, for the Russian Orthodox Church would need military partners if it were to play the part for which they had cast it. But when Allied soldiers occupied the three ports and began to march south, even Russian churchgoers would deem them to be invaders, as bad as the Germans—unless Russian soldiers marched alongside them. Where could those soldiers be found? How recruited and mobilized? Eventually, Lockhart and Reilly thought they knew. And then they concocted a daring scheme.

CHAPTER 8

FIRST STEPS TOWARD THE COUNTER-REVOLUTION

During the late winter and early spring of 1918, the Allies' ambitious, improbable plan for occupying the three ports (Vladivostok, Murmansk, and Archangel) and for reconstituting an Eastern Front matured. Firstly, Japanese and Allied soldiers would seize Vladivostok (which in fact they did on April 5, against Bolshevik wishes and Lockhart's advice) and then head west along the Siberian Railway. Secondly, British and Allied troops would occupy Murmansk (which Admiral T. W. Kemp and a small detachment of British troops already had done in late March, again against Lockhart's counsel), and then travel south to take Archangel, led by General Frederick Cuthbert Poole who would command all Allied forces in northwest Russia. From Archangel they would head for Vologda to meet the Japanese advancing along the Siberian Railway. Allied planners fondly predicted that as the two columns converged on the town, figuratively beating drums and flying flags, they would rally many thousands of Russian fighting men, former deserters from the Tsarist army, to the anti-German, pro-Allied, cause. Finally, from Vologda, coordinating with the White Volunteer Army of Generals Kornilov and Alexeyev, far to the south, they would present the Germans with daunting forces on two sides, a refashioned Eastern Front.

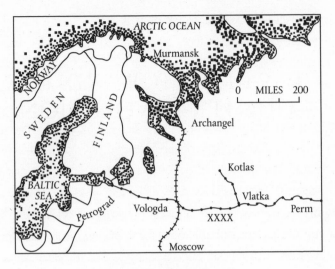

Map 5. Northwest Russia

There were several flies in the ointment, however, and the name of the first one was Woodrow Wilson. The American president did not want Japanese troops on the Russian mainland. He feared Japanese imperialist ambitions all along the Pacific Rim, where America too had economic interests and aspirations. Reluctantly, he acquiesced in Japanese occupation of Vladivostok, but he would not accept the further Japanese component of the plan. Nor would he agree to substitute US troops for Japanese. The Anglo-French scheme of intervention foundered, therefore, against the rock of President Wilson's initial refusal to accept one of its crucial elements.

Anglo-French planners responded by seeking an alternative to Japanese troops marching west from Vladivostok, and for a while, they thought they had one. Tsarist generals had formed a Czechoslovak Legion from prisoners taken after Russian victories over Austro-Hungarian forces early in the war. Forty thousand strong, well-led, well-disciplined, well-armed, and completely independent of the Russian Army (such as it was at this point), the Legionnaires wanted to go to France (there no longer being an Eastern Front) to help defeat Austria-Hungary and form from part of it a Czech sovereign nation. To get to France they would take the long way around, sailing from Vladivostok across the Pacific and Atlantic Oceans. First, however, they must reach Vladivostok. Lenin and Trotsky agreed to let them to do it, via the Siberian Railway, and various detachments of the Legion entrained. By mid-May, a few of them had reached the far eastern port already. Other Czech detachments dotted the railway line. The Allies intended to divert some of them to Vologda, in place of the Japanese.

One fly taken care of then, perhaps, but a second fly proved more difficult. The White Volunteer Army in the region of the Don, from which the Allies expected much, was not prospering. Its leaders, Generals Alexeyev and Kornilov, loathed each other. Its officers tended to sympathize with the old elites in most matters, including crucially the matter of returning to its former owners land expropriated by the peasants. This hardly lent it mass appeal. Moreover, White nationalist insistence upon "Russia one and indivisible" alienated the minorities in the former Russian Empire who longed for autonomy. Most particularly in this instance this Russian nationalism alienated a second fighting force in the region, the Don Cossacks, with whom the Whites needed to unite if they were to prove successful.

Furthermore, the leaders of both forces were unlucky. Poorly-trained Red Guards defeated the Don Cossacks at Taganrog. The mortified Don Cossack commander, General Kaledin, committed suicide. Shortly thereafter, General Kornilov perished when a single Red Army shell struck the house in which he quartered. He was the only casualty. Not much later, General Alexeyev, founder of the Volunteer Army, died of a heart attack. Eventually, the White Army did rally under General Denikin and succeeded in gaining control of much of the Caucasus. Ultimately, it would manage to form an uneasy alliance with the Don Cossacks—but too late to help the Allies win World War I, and therefore too late for the Allies to help them overthrow Bolshevism. At any rate, even if it had wanted to, the Volunteer Army was not ready, in late winter/early spring 1918, to march west against the Germans and help to reopen the Eastern Front.[1]

And finally, there was a third obstacle in the way of the Allied plan. As the months passed, Allied resistance stiffened to General Ludendorff's last great offensive on the Western Front. Germany had her hands absolutely full there; certainly, she no longer had the strength to continue advancing into Russia. When the Bolsheviks grasped this, they ceased to contemplate even the possibility of inviting the Allies to occupy the three ports. The third fly in the ointment therefore, was the now full-fledged and non-negotiable opposition of the Bolsheviks to Allied occupation of any part of their country.

That third fly led inevitably to the following questions: If the Bolsheviks opposed Allied intervention, but the Allies thought intervention necessary in order to reorganize an Eastern Front and defeat Germany, then must not the Allies oppose the Bolsheviks? Must not they do what they could to aid Russia's anti-Bolsheviks? For men in London and Paris who had no sympathy with Bolshevism to begin with, the answers were obvious.[2]

* * *

When the Bolsheviks changed their minds about scuttling Russia's Baltic fleet, and the Allies changed their minds about waiting for an invitation to occupy the three ports and invaded anyway (in Vladivostok and Murmansk—not yet in Archangel), it cut the ground beneath the feet of Bruce Lockhart and his circle, and it split them. Robins and Ransome always had opposed uninvited Allied intervention, and continued to do so. They opposed even more strongly Allied intervention intended to overthrow Bolshevism. They believed Russia should be allowed to work out her own destiny; that Bolshevism, for all its faults, represented the only viable path forward for Russia, and should be encouraged by the Allies into more moderate paths; that therefore Allied opposition to Lenin and Trotsky would be counterproductive and, moreover, would throw the Bolshevik leaders into Germany's arms. In his heart of hearts Lockhart believed these arguments too, but as we have seen, he had begun to waver. Garstin, who had written the previous year that "England needs Russia just as much as Russia needs England"; who in February 1918 had found the Bolshevik feminist Alexandra Kollentai "charming...she bowled me over"; and who still judged Lenin to be "the biggest force I've ever felt in my life," nevertheless, had begun to waver too: "If you look at what the Bolsheviks want to do you feel sympathetic," he wrote, "but if you look at what they've done, you're dead against them."[3] Cromie, of course, had abandoned the Bolsheviks long ago.

Given these disagreements within the once collegial circle, it is not surprising that Robins decided to return to the USA and continue the struggle there. He no longer felt himself a member of a compatible band of companionable rebels advocating a correct but unpopular policy. Rather, he felt he could be more useful at home. The likeminded Ransome summarized their argument in a pamphlet which he wrote at white-hot speed for the Red Cross colonel to bring with him: *On Behalf of Russia: An Open Letter to America*.[4]

On May 14, Robins set out from Moscow via the Siberian Railway, with the pamphlet, Lenin's blessing, and the Bolshevik leader's signed *laissez-passer* to speed his train.[5] He carried, too, Lenin's invitation to the American government to dispatch an Economic Commission to his country to explore trade possibilities. He reached Vladivostok in good time and in good spirits, although noting the Allied occupation of the port with disapproval, and sailed for home on June 2. "The headlands of Asia fade from view," he wrote in his diary that night; "the only sound is the sweep of the surging sea, the stars shine out, the way ahead is blue-black, and the Russian tale is told and I have had my day!!!"

When the Red Cross colonel arrived in America he met with senators, cabinet ministers, labor leaders and other leading figures—and experienced a rude shock. Almost everyone in the US disapproved of his message. The president, upon whom he pinned his hopes, remained inaccessible and silent while advocates of intervention in Russia worked on him. Finally, on August 4, Wilson let it be known that Japanese forces could march east after all, so long as US troops accompanied them. He made no mention of Lenin's invitation concerning Russo-American trade. "The long trail is ended," a bitter Robins finally admitted to himself in his diary. "So finishes the great adventure."[6]

As for Lockhart and the remainder of his group back in Russia, it was full speed ahead for intervention now. Garstin first put into words to Whitehall the plan they had begun to contemplate. On May 10, the young captain reported by cable that he had just "been approached secretly by two large organizations of old army." They promised to mobilize near Nizhnii Novgorod, east of Moscow as soon as the Allies took Vologda and secured the railheads of the Archangel and Siberian Railways. Then they would launch the counter-revolution. That he and Lockhart had weighed and decided they approved of the offer before sending it seems evident, since Garstin recommended that London dispatch the same number of Allied troops from Archangel to Vologda as Lockhart had suggested in earlier telegrams: "at least two divisions."[7]

Garstin was dabbling in counter-revolution here.[8] So was Captain Cromie, the man once celebrated for his ability to reconcile Bolshevik sailors and their Tsarist officers and now scheming to destroy Russia's Baltic fleet. And so too was Britain's previous leading champion of Anglo-Bolshevik cooperation, Robert Bruce Lockhart. No doubt they both shared Garstin's reservations about the Bolsheviks. But the truth is that, also, all three of them believed that in conspiring against the regime they were doing what the British government wanted them to do. And this was decisive. Not one would stand up to Whitehall. In the end, despite occasional heartburning, not one could resist the temptations offered to participants in the counter-revolutionary movement: accolades from their British masters and the dizzying prospect of the rewards that success would bring; the opportunity to exercise a decisive influence in Russian and world affairs; the sheer thrill of wielding power in a chaotic situation. Instead of the dovish, more sober Robins and Ransome, they consulted with men who had been in the counter-revolutionary camp all along.

Of these, three Allied diplomats would become most influential with them. One was the American Consul General in Moscow, DeWitt Clinton Poole (no relation to the British General Poole).

Figure 14. American Consul General in Russia, DeWitt Clinton Poole

Laconic and dry, thin and middle-aged, flinty and duplicitous, this New Englander had established contact with anti-Bolsheviks shortly after the October Revolution. He now oversaw the spy ring, which he disarmingly termed an information gathering service, run by his chief lieutenant, Xenophon Kalamatiano.[9] Poole had no reservations about what he and Kalamatiano were up to. Like Sidney Reilly, he perceived the struggle with the Bolsheviks in Manichean terms: "we who were on the spot saw clearly that they were anti-civilization."[10]

Another consular official with whom Lockhart, Garstin, and Cromie began now to come into increasing contact was the Frenchman, Fernand Grenard (whose real name was Joseph Fernand). As a young man, Grenard had gained a reputation for daring. Most famously he had endured extreme hardship trekking across the wilderness of Tibet in an unsuccessful attempt to penetrate Lhasa, where foreigners were forbidden. He had survived running gun battles with Chinese bandits on the way back, although the leader of his expedition did not. A French commercial company memorialized his exploits on an educational playing card.

After these exploits, Grenard may have been seeking a comparatively tame existence when he joined the French consular

Figure 15. French Consul in Moscow, Fernand Grenard

service in 1899. He did not have one now as French Consul General in Moscow but, after what he had been through, Bolshevik hard men did not intimidate him. One suspects that Lockhart rather admired this man. They would work closely together.

The third anti-Bolshevik with whom Lockhart and the remnants of his circle also now established close relations was the French ambassador to Russia, Josef Noulens. He dominated the community of foreign diplomats still in Russia.[11] And he shared the visceral anti-communism of the Quai d'Orsay in Paris (the French Foreign Office). Although in March he once had encouraged Trotsky to resist German invasion by promising French support, in reality he had always hated the Bolsheviks and never really believed France could find common ground with them, not even against Germany. Bolshevism threatened French business and financial interests in Russia. But, said Noulens, "We shall not be allowing any further socialist experiments in Russia," said Noulens.[12] From

Figure 16. French ambassador to
Russia, Josef Noulens

April 1918 onward, following directions from Paris with which he
completely agreed, he did his best to help nearly every anti-
Bolshevik schemer who approached him. In the past, Lockhart
had ridiculed him for his reactionary views. Now the British agent
followed in the Frenchman's footsteps. Noulens, he acknowledged,
"commenced to finance and support these [counter-revolutionary]
organizations before I did."[13]

But Lockhart was primed now to collaborate with Noulens and
the others. Recall that he first met Sidney Reilly on May 9, and sent
Garstin's telegram on May 10. On May 14, he bade farewell to
Raymond Robins at a Moscow railway station. Then, on May 15,
the day after seeing off his erstwhile friend and ally, he met "an
agent sent to me by Boris Savinkoff [sic]."

* * *

One might write of Boris Savinkov that he was the Scarlet
Pimpernel of the Russian Revolution, had he not also been a
stone-cold killer. Of hair's breadth escapes, bold-faced impos-
tures, and general derring-do, this extraordinary man was a

Figure 17. Boris Savinkov, the great conspirator

master. "Small in stature; moving as little as possible and that noiselessly and with deliberation; [displaying] remarkable gray-green eyes in a face of almost deathly pallor," Savinkov was a dandy who always wore yellow spats—even when otherwise disguised. This son of a judge was a poet, a novelist, a chain-smoking morphine addict, and the former head of the prewar Socialist Revolutionary Party's "Fighting Organization."[14] He had been a terrorist during the Tsarist period. The Tsar's courts convicted him of complicity in the 1904 assassination of Russia's Minister of the Interior, Vyacheslav Plehve, but as with so many of their prisoners, failed to hold him after they caught him. Free to follow his ruthless inclinations, Savinkov had planned or taken part in thirty-two additional killings, or at least so rumor had it.

In 1917, this great conspirator served for a brief period as Kerensky's Assistant Minister of War, but then supported General Kornilov's abortive right-wing uprising against him. When the Bolsheviks took power, he fled to the Don region, to contact the counter-revolutionary Volunteer Army of Generals Alexeyev and

Kornilov. The latter two despised each other, as noted above, but they despised Savinkov more. Alexeyev wrote to Lockhart that he would rather cooperate with Lenin and Trotsky.[15] No sooner had Savinkov arrived in the White Army camp than someone tried to assassinate him. Not surprisingly, he returned to Moscow, dove underground and, independent of Alexeyev, with whom despite everything he nevertheless remained in touch, began to plan an anti-Bolshevik rising.

Moscow was by then an anti-Bolshevik hothouse, as Lockhart was beginning to appreciate. A "Right Center," of counter-revolutionary monarchists, right-wing Kadets and other conservatives, had pro-German leanings. A counter-revolutionary "Left Center" of liberal Kadets and various anti-Bolshevik socialists favored the Allies. Savinkov entered neither body but encouraged them to combine in a "National Center," which eventually they did, although without ever relinquishing their distrust for each other. The great conspirator refused to join but recruited from this body, and promised to cooperate with it. Meantime he was organizing his own Union for Defense of the Motherland and Freedom (UDMF). When he contacted Lockhart, he had between two thousand and five thousand men under his command.[16] He had spies shadowing Lenin and Trotsky, preparing to assassinate them. And he had begun to plan a rising in three towns north of Moscow to coincide with the Allied intervention "on a large scale" that Lockhart's new ally, ambassador Noulens, already had encouraged him to believe would take place in late June or early July.[17]

Lockhart reported to London on his meeting with Savinkov's representative, and added: "With your approval I propose to continue to maintain an informal connection with [him] through third parties." The Foreign Office did approve. Lockhart would be safe enough: he is "so much identified with Bolsheviks that he is hardly likely to be suspect," noted one mandarin. Sir George Russell Clerk, a more senior and experienced official, added more cagily still: "I believe that the Bolsheviks know pretty well everything that goes on. I am not quite sure of our cyphers, and I am confident that unless Mr. Lockhart gets direct instructions to the contrary he will continue to keep in touch with Savinkoff [sic]. I should therefore leave this unanswered for the present."[18]

Cagey, yes; but Clerk had set a precedent that would have significant consequences. At the end of May, Lockhart took note that the Foreign Office remained silent on Savinkov, and understood, quite correctly, that it meant for him to maintain the connection. In the middle of August, at a crossroads again, and with the Foreign Office again incommunicado, he not unreasonably drew a similar conclusion and plunged into even deeper waters, this time with fatal results.

Now, self-confident and determined as ever, although pursuing a program diametrically opposed to his initial one, he embarked upon a series of dangerous, clandestine meetings, often accompanied by the equally fearless Grenard. "I am in touch with practically everyone," he reported to London on May 23.[19] Through Lieutenant Laurence Webster, an intelligence agent acting as Passport Control Officer in Moscow, he engineered a series of meetings with two leaders of the Moscow Center, Professor Peter Struve, a former Kadet, and Michael Feodoroff, a former Tsarist minister, both now supporters of General Alexeyev.[20] He also established links with counter-revolutionary right Socialist Revolutionaries, to whom he gave money.[21] Quickly he realized that the Moscow hothouse was planning something big. Where previously he would have talked things over with Robins and

Ransome (who might have acted as restraining influences), now he talked to Reilly, Garstin, and Cromie, and to Noulens, and Grenard and DeWitt Clinton Poole. They all favored the forward policy.

Lockhart engaged Captain Cromie in discussions about destruction of Russia's fleet in the Baltic Sea. Britain's naval attaché lived in the Petrograd hothouse rather than the Moscow one and, as soon became apparent, he was doing more than dabble in counter-revolution there. Where first Cromie had wanted to destroy Russia's Baltic fleet so Germany could not have additional ships, now he wanted to destroy Bolshevism so Germany could not have Russia. Already he was "the moving spirit" among a group of Petrograd anti-Bolshevik activists, including other Allied officials and members of Savinkov's UDMF. They often met near the docks not far from the British embassy at a Latvian social club (of which more later) that catered to sailors and their officers.[22] These Petrograd conspirators had a pipeline funneling White volunteers north to Archangel. They had Russian and British agents already *in situ* planning to overthrow its Bolshevik-dominated Soviet with the help of those volunteers, just as Poole's occupying forces ("not less than two divisions," Cromie also stipulated, no doubt after consultation with Lockhart)[23] arrived from Murmansk.[24] Then they would establish a White counter-revolutionary Volunteer Army in Archangel to accompany Poole's troops when these marched upon Vologda, and onward to aid Savinkov when he launched his insurrection. In other words, Cromie and the Petrograd hothouse knew what the Moscow hothouse was planning and intended to help.[25] Lockhart decided to help too.

First, he requested that London supply additional funds for Cromie to bribe the Russian naval officers he had charged with destroying the Baltic fleet.[26] Whitehall cabled its Petrograd consul: "Please hold at immediate disposal of Captain Cromie 1,500,000 rubles [then approximately £25,000; today approximately £1,375,000][27] from Embassy or any other available accounts. Lockhart has been asked to facilitate in any way possible your operating on above accounts."[28] Lockhart tried to spur Whitehall to additional commitments: "Desirable to make destruction [of the Russian Baltic fleet] coincide with Allied intervention...most important we should be informed in good time when action will take place." He added, "I shall probably go to Petrograd tonight Saturday for 24 hours and will telegraph again when have seen Naval Attaché."[29] Whitehall cautioned him: "You would do well to leave... [destruction of the fleet] in the hands of the Naval Attaché, so that at least you may be able to disclaim being a party to any action that may be taken."[30] Lockhart met with Cromie anyway.

On the 26th, he met with another of Savinkov's representatives as well, from whom he learned that plans for an uprising were nearly complete. He reported to London: "Savinkov proposes to murder all Bolshevik leaders on night of allies landing, and to form a Government which will be in reality a military dictatorship....He...is quite prepared to act."[31] The young Scot thought events were approaching a climax. "My work here is coming to an end."[32] He did not yet appreciate, as London was starting to, that manpower demands on the Western Front meant Britain did not have the troops necessary to occupy the northern ports, any more than Germany did—let alone to send an additional "two divisions" from Archangel to Vologda to aid Savinkov, and that therefore the downfall of Bolshevism was not so imminent after all.

Whitehall also had begun to realize that the Czech Legionnaires wanted to get to Vladivostok and to sail across oceans, and to fight

Austrians; not to travel by rail in the opposite direction from Vladivostok, and fight Bolsheviks. Or, if they could be persuaded to travel to Vologda after all, it was only because they saw it as a way-station on a shorter route to the Western Front. True, when Trotsky placed obstacles in their way in order to satisfy the Germans who did not want additional enemies in France, the Legion and the Bolsheviks came into conflict, with the Czechs invariably victorious. They took control of several nodal points along the Siberian Railway, made alliances with local anti-Bolsheviks, gave them money supplied by France, and even helped establish anti-communist local soviets. The Bolsheviks now perceived the Czechoslovak Legion as one of their most dangerous enemies. Nevertheless, the British finally had begun to understand that the Czechs' ultimate goal was not to destroy the Bolshevik regime, but rather to return to France and destroy the Austro-Hungarian Empire. And therefore, because British officials could not say when the Czechs would arrive in Vologda, or what they would do if they ever got there, they could not tell Lockhart when their own landing would take place. Consequently, they feared that Savinkov was jumping the gun. His "methods are drastic, though if success-ful probably effective," mused the mandarin George Clerk about murder and dictatorship, "but we cannot say or do anything until intervention has been definitely decided upon."[33]

Savinkov's drastic methods did not faze Lockhart either. The energy and intelligence he once had devoted to advocating Anglo-Bolshevik cooperation he lavished now upon speeding Bolshevik destruction. He channeled money to the great conspirator, although the latter always said he received his funds mainly from France.[34] He tried to get the Foreign Office to plan with Savinkov in mind: "Intervention from Archangel would be very stimulating," to Savinkov's rebellion, he wired. "Whatever help Allies can give [to Savinkov] will be supported out of all proportion."[35]

These messages worried wily George Clerk. He saw that Britain's man on the spot was getting ahead of the game. He was putting himself into danger after all, and not only himself but also Savinkov's entire conspiracy, by cabling enthusiastic reports about counter-revolution that the Bolsheviks, if indeed they had cracked the British cypher, might read. Clerk had taken Lockhart's measure by now. Britain's agent in Russia was brash, capable—and flexible, as his political volte face demonstrated. Clerk thought that Lockhart was subtle too: he could read between the lines; could find meaning in silence; could understand nuance and misdirection. Clerk sent a note to the Foreign Secretary: "I think we should caution Mr. Lockhart to have nothing whatever to do with Savinkoff's [sic] plans, & to avoid enquiring further into them."[36] Balfour duly repeated these words to Lockhart in a cable—no doubt for Bolsheviks to read as well. It has mystified historians who did not piece together Clerk's logic or the preceding chain of telegrams that makes the prohibition's meaning clear.[37] Lockhart's masters in London now knew their agent would understand the cable to be a blinking yellow light, not the red one it appeared to be.

Moreover, Lockhart would have noted that the Foreign Office did not disavow, or even question, Savinkov's ruthless program. Not surprisingly then, his next step, more dangerous than any so far, was to meet with Savinkov in person. The latter came to see him at the Hotel Elite wearing a French uniform and dark-tinted glasses as a disguise, but also his trademark yellow spats.[38] Lockhart gave him money.

Thus, the month of June 1918 passed in a welter of confusion, falsehood, and misdirection. Raymond Robins had embarked upon an epic, ultimately unsuccessful, journey home to persuade President Wilson against intervening in Russia. Lockhart, now firmly in the interventionist camp along with the remnants of his circle and his new anti-Bolshevik allies, was barraging the Foreign Office with cables exhorting intervention in Russia as soon as possible and asking for the date. But London was prevaricating: it realized intervention would be beyond Britain's power until she could find additional troops. Meanwhile, Cromie was secretly preparing to destroy Russia's Baltic fleet and funneling White officers north to launch a coup in Archangel. The French ambassador was falsely assuring Russian counter-revolutionaries that Allied assistance was imminent and, as a result, Boris Savinkov was honing his plans for a rising. The Czechs occupied one town after another as they continued along the Siberian Railway, in the wrong direction from Britain's point of view. The last page of the monthly calendar turned and July dawned, hot and humid, storms brewing.

CHAPTER 9

THE QUESTION OF MOURA

Lockhart had reversed his outlook when he realized the Bolsheviks no longer feared German invasion, and therefore no longer needed an Anglo-French counterweight. Also, he had reversed it in order to save his career, and to avoid offending friends and relatives, and to have a chance to exercise real power by helping to overthrow a regime which he continued to think represented Russia's most likely path forward. He had reversed it too as the brutality and ruthlessness of the regime became more apparent to him. There was more to it even than this, however. He was a man whom beautiful women found attractive, a man who could not resist beautiful women, no matter how dangerous or inappropriate they might be. He should have stuck to the policy in which he believed or, even better, resigned his position and returned home in protest of the British anti-Bolshevik policy. But, in addition to all else: "I was unable to leave Russia because of Moura."[1]

She had stayed with him in Moscow for ten days after appearing at his hotel with the sun in her hair in late April. From his diary, we know they went to the ballet on her first night in town. That was when Raymond Robins wrote that he found Lockhart "too gay." The second night they went to hear Trotsky speak—and it is telling that they did so. Lockhart would not have brought Moura with him if politics had meant little to her. Afterwards they would have shared impressions, and it is fair to wonder how discreet he would have been with a woman with whom he was head over heels in love. On Wednesday, they attended the ballet again, *Don Quixote*. On Sunday evening, April 28, she must have been present when Robins (with less than three weeks left in Russia) delivered at the dinner table an extempore homage to one of his great heroes, the South African capitalist and British imperialist, Cecil Rhodes. Lockhart recorded in his diary that it had been "a wonderful and really theatrical account." As for what else the couple did, it seems clear enough.

Within twenty-four hours of returning to Petrograd, Moura received two telegrams from the British agent. She replied: "You know I care for you very very much, or all that has happened wouldn't have happened." During her stay, he must have told her something of his past affairs, for she also wrote: "Do not class me with the rest, will you, with the rest who trifle—and with whom you trifle." She need not have worried. Neither of them was trifling.

And she wrote to him about politics, which again suggests they had discussed them in Moscow, and indeed that common interest in them helped bring them together. Like her lover she was a shrewd commentator, even in her first letter to him since their parting. She observed of Petrograd, where political pluralism was not yet dead: "as for political orientation, one might as well be in another country [from Moscow]." She warned him: "One expects all kinds of things on the 1st [May Day]—and the Germans…No resistance will be offered by Petrograd if they come, which they will do from the sea."[2] From whom had she learned that?

"I hope to be able to come [to see you again] sometime during Easter Week," she concluded—and she realized her wish, appearing for another ten-day stint at the Hotel Elite on Ascension Day, May 9, the same day that Lockhart first met Sidney Reilly. She was in Moscow when he sent Garstin's cable; when he saw off Robins at the railway station; when he met Savinkov's agent, when, in short, he reversed his political position. Could he have kept all this from her? Is it likely that he did? Did their romance, which now blossomed and deepened, provide merely a backdrop to his increasingly dangerous counter-revolutionary activities, or did it and Moura provide something more, perhaps a sounding board, possibly a helpmeet? We cannot know; there is no written record.

One night they attended the opera again.[3] On Saturday, May 18, he took her to Archangelskoye, twenty kilometers west of Moscow, where a magnificent palace, former country retreat of the Yusupov princes, sits in wonderful grounds at a bend in the Moskva River. That day he snapped her photograph.[4] They returned the next day, but it rained.[5] With Moura still visiting, he received an unexpected letter from the Foreign Office about his wife: "She has been moving heaven and earth to get out to you."[6] This cannot have been welcome news. Immediately he cabled back with instructions: tell Jean "it is really out of the question for any English woman to think of going to Russia in the present condition of confusion and uncertainty."[7] This was true, but also convenient.

Perhaps he felt guilty. On another night, he brought Moura to Streilna, a restaurant-cabaret run by a famous woman gypsy performer whom the Bolsheviks still tolerated. Bon vivant that he was, Lockhart knew the place from previous years. He loved the kerosene lanterns that lit the place, the vodka and champagne that all who entered must drink. He loved gypsy music and to watch the beautiful gypsy men and women who performed it and danced to it. There was one song in particular that "in those days was in tune with my own turbulent soul":

They say my heart is like the wind
That to one maid I can't be true;
But why do I forget the rest,
And still remember only you?

That night, he demanded that the singer repeat this song over and over.[8]

It did not stop him courting Moura, however, and if she felt guilty about betraying Djon, that did not stop her either. They knew tongues would wag, and they did not care. He would have to return to Britain when his mission in Russia ended, but they would try not to think about that. When it was time for her to go back to Petrograd, he brought her to the railway station. She wanted to tell him how deeply he had stirred her, but he hushed her. She must not say "foolish things." She said them in a letter instead, the instant she got home: "My little Baby Boy, Here I am back in the old place." His past affairs continued to worry her: "There is nothing I fear more than you should think of me in the same way as you have probably often done with many others." Over and above that, however, "Baby boy, I love you … I am caught at last and for good … I am so childishly happy … I am just living in the thought of coming back and seeing you again … I kiss you very tenderly."[9]

*　*　*

Recall Moura's Ukrainian origins, for they had a bearing on what followed. In January 1918, a Ukrainian Republic led by anti-Bolshevik, moderate socialists declared independence from Russia. When the Bolsheviks sent troops to crush it, the Ukrainians asked Germany for help. This the Kaiser provided since he coveted

Ukraine's rich supply of grain. His soldiers routed the Bolshevik troops, but when the fledgling socialist Republic failed to make timely deliveries, he directed his army to install a new regime that would be more efficient. Pavlo Skoropadsky, a wealthy Ukrainian landowner, assumed dictatorial power on April 29, backed by German bayonets.

Skoropadsky, who took the title Hetman (head of state), was a conservative traditionalist. He preferred the Germans to the Bolsheviks, but hoped that someday Ukraine would rejoin a restored Russian Empire under a restored monarchy. During his six-month stint in power (he fell in November and fled to Germany), he reversed the liberal and progressive reforms of his socialist predecessors. For example, his government returned to its former owners the land that the socialists had distributed to peasants. The Bolsheviks condemned such measures, and did what they could to undermine him. Throughout his six-month rule, the Hetman and his German backers faced guerrilla and terrorist opposition.

Meanwhile, most anomalously given the general state of relations between their two countries, a few British experts and their Russian Bolshevik counterparts continued to cooperate in the one area where their interests still coincided, namely in trying to undermine German occupation of the former Russian Empire. Spying against the Germans and the puppet government in Ukraine fell into this category.

It is not inconceivable that now a British intelligence officer with a channel to the Cheka thought of Moura. Perhaps he had personal knowledge of her extraordinary charm, courage, presence, and intelligence. Perhaps he knew she had reported on German sympathizers attending her Petrograd salon (if she ever did that) and so had some experience of intelligence work. Perhaps he thought the Cheka could send her to Ukraine, governed as it now was by men who would welcome her as a daughter of one of their own. She need not do anything dangerous there; only keep eyes and ears open, and then report, not only to the Bolsheviks but to the British as well. Or, slightly riskier, she might offer to keep eyes and ears open for the Ukrainians too. Then she could travel back and forth, ostensibly to spy on Bolsheviks, but really to gather more information in Ukraine. Perhaps then, a Cheka agent, prompted by his British equivalent, approached her with such a scheme in mind. Or perhaps a Cheka agent approached her without having been prompted by a Briton.

On May 29, Moura wired Lockhart in Russian: "Imperative I see you."[10] A day or two later she pressed him again, this time in English: "I may have to go away for a short time and would like to see you before I go."[11] On Saturday, June 1, Lockhart went. He took the night train to Petrograd. Two days later, he wrote in his diary about the visit: "Went out for a drive to the Islands, dined at Contant's [one of Petrograd's most elegant restaurants] and to Bi-Ba-Bo [a cabaret] afterwards." He told the Foreign Office that he made this trip to discuss demolition of Russia's Baltic fleet with Cromie. Surely, however, he drove to the islands and supped at Contants and went to Bi-Ba-Bo not with Cromie but with Moura, and surely, at some point that day she mentioned the Cheka approach—if there had been one—and the secret reason for her pending journey—if there was a secret reason. On Tuesday, Lockhart returned to Moscow.[12]

There followed a month of silence, which ended on July 4, when Lockhart recorded in his diary that "Mme. Benckendorff left for Petrograd," which means that she had been to see him again in

Moscow. What had happened between the beginning of June, when he went to Petrograd to see her, and late June/early July when she journeyed to Moscow to visit him?

Perhaps she spied in Ukraine. The period in question was precisely when the Bolsheviks and the Hetmanate engaged in negotiations. Both sides wanted to know what the other was thinking. In 1929 in Berlin, Kirill Zinoviev, scion of an aristocratic émigré Russian family, lunched with the deposed Hetman. Zinoviev, who knew Moura, asked Skoropadsky if he knew her too. The old man reflected for a moment. "Yes, I remember now," he replied. During his period in power, he had thought she worked for his intelligence department, but realized later that she worked for the Bolsheviks.[13] There are at present two documents supporting this charge. The first, from 1921, is located in files kept by the French Ministry of War. The translated relevant portion simply states that in 1918: "the Countess [sic] was a member of the Petrograd Cheka…" No proof is offered, and it does not stipulate when during 1918 she started working for it.[14]

A second, undated, document, this one located in a British MI5 file devoted to Moura, is more detailed—but inconclusive. Translated from Russian, it reads:

> In 1918, she travelled to Kiev during the Hetman Government from Petrograd…and offered her reconnaissance services in the territories seized by the Bolshevik government to the Prime Minister, Lizogub. Lizogub, who was himself a Poltava landowner, knew the family of the baroness's father, who was also a big Poltava landowner, placed credit in the baroness's story and ordered the reconnaissance organization of the Ukrainian Government to utilize the services of the baroness. Under various pretexts, the baroness then began to travel to the USSR [sic] and on her return to convey information.

After this paragraph there follows an independent line, perhaps written by someone else: "The impression was that the baroness was working on two fronts."[15]

But there is contradictory evidence as well. In the MI5 file another "officer in this department" wrote of Skoropadsky that to him "all 'independent' Russian émigrés were 'Bolshevist spies' and [he] consistently denounced quite innocent people."[16] Perhaps the Hetman slandered Moura eleven years after the fact.

Perhaps he did not. She moved in British circles where such a scheme might have occurred to someone with power to introduce her into a still surprisingly permeable Cheka. Or it may not have been a Briton who introduced her. Either way, if that body made a proposal to her, she might have found it appealing: after all, she knew she had the courage, poise, and nerve to do what they asked, and she relished knowing important people and being at the center of events. Or, perhaps that is condescending: perhaps she sincerely wanted to help her country; perhaps the proposal appealed to her sense of patriotism. Another possibility: perhaps she calculated that agreeing to the proposition would please her lover, since it would afford him a window, however opaque, into the workings of the Bolshevik secret service. She could have summoned him from Moscow to tell him about this.

More plausibly, however, she summoned him for the reason lovers usually call to each other. And she went to Ukraine to see family and friends, met high-ranking officials, of the same background as herself, who questioned her about conditions in Russia, and then upon returning to Petrograd received a summons to be interviewed by high-ranking officials there. That does not qualify as espionage. Moura's daughter said she did not believe her mother ever had been a spy, but that she liked to embellish and exaggerate in order to feel important. In lieu of conclusive evidence, it is safest to conclude provisionally that both Ukrainian and Bolshevik intelligence officers felt the need to speak with Moura, but not necessarily to employ her.

Either way, by June 1918 not only had Lockhart and Dzerzhinsky finally crossed paths, and not only had Lockhart and Moura embarked upon their mad, passionate, love affair, but also, Moura probably had established some kind of connection with the Bolshevik secret police, either because they just questioned her after her trip to the Ukraine, or because they actually employed her. Had she crossed paths with Iron Felix, or with his second-in-command, Jacov Peters? If not, then she soon would.

CHAPTER 10

WHY LOCKHART TURNED TO THE LATVIANS

The British government never directly instructed Lockhart to rid it of the Bolshevik regime in Russia, at least not in a surviving Foreign Office telegram. But like the four knights who murdered Thomas Becket in 1170 because they thought, correctly, that was what their king, Henry II, wanted them to do, so Lockhart thought he knew now what Lloyd George and Arthur Balfour wanted from him. Shortly after Raymond Robins' departure for the United States, he began working to undermine and uproot Russia's revolutionary government. He operated on a wide front, for many counter-revolutionaries needed his support. Meanwhile, on the other side, the Bolsheviks knew that they were engaged in a life or death struggle. They fought on many fronts too.

* * *

Shortly after taking power, Lenin's regime had outlawed non-socialist political parties, but not all socialist ones. In fact, during the summer of 1918, the Bolsheviks still shared power with a rival socialist party, the left Socialist Revolutionaries, on various Soviets, and in the central government. Left SRs also held important positions on diverse official bodies, including even Dzerzhinsky's Cheka.

Left SRs differed with Bolsheviks on certain fundamentals.[1] They opposed the Bolshevik tendency toward single-party rule both on principled grounds and from self-interest, and Bolshevik suppression of the bourgeois press, and the notion of state sponsored terror, although members of the left SRs had committed individual terroristic acts and would commit them again. Although they had cooperated with the Bolsheviks in implementing a revolutionary policy of egalitarian land redistribution, they opposed Bolshevik establishment of "Committees of the Village Poor," tasked, among other things, with seizing grain from wealthy peasants (kulaks), so that it could be shipped to the starving cities. They charged, quite correctly, that the committees were brutal, needlessly divisive, and counterproductive. Perhaps most importantly at this moment, however, they believed the Bolsheviks had abandoned their revolutionary principles by surrendering to German imperialism and signing the Brest-Litovsk Treaty; more specifically, they accused the Bolsheviks of having betrayed Ukrainian peasants who now suffered at the hands of German occupier overlords.

On July 4, 1918, a Wednesday, 1,164 delegates chosen by an electorate from which the aristocratic and middle classes had been largely purged, convened in Moscow to attend the Fifth All-Russian Congress of Soviets, and to fashion new policies for the revolutionary nation. In a country the majority of whose citizens were peasants, the left SRs had expected to win a majority of delegates. They did not; the Bolsheviks did, by a large margin, with left SRs at about half the Bolshevik strength, and an assortment of other socialist parties bringing up the rear, none with more than half a dozen deputies, except for seventeen Maximalists, whose party had broken off from the SRs in 1906. Most historians conclude, as the left SRs did at the time, that the Bolsheviks had fixed the process. They probably did not expect what followed, however. The left SRs, already deeply alienated, finally despaired of influencing government policy in the usual way. What we might term an unusual way beckoned; only it was not unusual for them.

Moscow was "very hot and sultry" during that first week of July 1918.[2] The Congress took place at Moscow's Bolshoi Theater, "the third finest [auditorium] in the world...where I used to go to see the ballets," remembered Denis Garstin,[3] but to Lockhart, who also attended as an observer, the close and sticky atmosphere reminded him more than anything else of a Turkish bath.[4] Imagine eleven hundred delegates milling about the vast, elegant, stifling hall. Imagine a high stage at the front, on which sat about one hundred members of the Central Executive Council of the Congress, and at the front of the stage a long table around which gathered the most prominent Bolsheviks and left SRs. Imagine packed balconies rising in tiers above and around them. Imagine that everybody present was hot, sweaty, and irritable.

"We were in a large box on [the] right hand side of the stage," Lockhart recorded in his diary,[5] "with the Boche above us," Garstin recalled. It was one of the oddities of their situation that representatives of two nations at death grips with each other in France occasionally found themselves sharing the same space in Russia. Now the agents of the Allies, and ten feet above them the agents of the Central Powers, including Germany's newly appointed ambassador to Russia, Wilhelm von Mirbach, gazed down upon Lenin and Trotsky, and the left SR leader, Maria Spiridonova, and all the others.

Figure 18. Maria Spiridonova

Maria Spiridonova had assassinated a Russian government official in 1905, had been convicted as a terrorist, had spent eleven
years in tsarist prisons, and had survived torture at the hands of
her jailers that prematurely aged a formerly beautiful young
woman. She had been a supporter of Lenin in 1917, as a Socialist
Revolutionary, never as a Bolshevik, but she supported him no
longer. "It is painful," she told assembled delegates, "to realize that
the Bolsheviks with whom until now I worked side by side, with
whom I fought behind the same barricade and with whom I hoped
to fight the glorious battle to the end...have taken over the policies of the Kerensky government." She meant that they had sold
out the peasants of Ukraine. As she spoke she kept making a hacking motion with her arm, in time to the cadence of her speech.
Perhaps in her mind she was hacking Bolsheviks. "Do you know
that...in the occupied regions there is not a peasant whose back is
not scarred [by German whips]?...You Bolsheviks have betrayed
the cause of the peasants....Dictatorship of the proletariat in an
agricultural country! You are bound to fail...We call for a dictatorship of the proletariat *and* the peasantry."[6] Then she demanded

resumption of the war—to liberate Ukraine. Communist delegates booed and jeered. Left SR delegates roared their approval.

A little later Boris Kamkov, another left SR leader, stood before the podium. He too raged against Bolshevism, which he considered now to be Germany's handmaiden. He too hinted at what was to come. "The Soviet is nothing but the dictatorship of Mirbach," he charged. Then he strode wrathfully across the stage to stand beneath the box of the German ambassador. He pointed his finger at the impassive, imperious figure seated above, and in a voice of thunder denounced him as a murderer and barbarian. Four hundred SR delegates, and probably not a few Bolsheviks, stood and stamped their feet and shook their fists, and cried: "Down with the tyrant! Drive him out of Moscow!" For ten minutes pandemonium reigned.[7]

That was Thursday afternoon, the second day of the Congress. Perhaps people should have foreseen what was coming. Friday, shortly after lunchtime, in a different part of Moscow, at the German embassy, members of staff gathered in shock over Count von Mirbach's corpse. The ambassador lay at the end of a room whose window at the other side had been blown out by a grenade. The grenade was not what had killed him, however. Two left SRs had shot him down in cold blood. At precisely 2:15 that afternoon, Mirbach had agreed reluctantly to see them, because they belonged to the Cheka and claimed to have important business to discuss. Indeed, they presented a letter of introduction signed, ostensibly, by Felix Dzerzhinsky. Mirbach sat with them at a table accompanied by an interpreter and the embassy first secretary. He appeared to be bored. Then, suddenly the two Cheka men stood up. "This is a matter of life and death," said one. "I will show you," said the other. They pulled out their pistols and opened fire, first missing their target who tried to run from the room, then finding the range, shooting him from behind, killing him. The grenade shattered the first-floor window. As they leapt from it into a waiting car, one of them tossed a second grenade for good measure.[8]

Here was left SR terrorism all right: its aim was to cause an irreparable breach between Russia and Germany, to force a resumption of war between them that would lead to liberation of the Ukraine, and revolution across Europe. Spiridonova, who had helped plan the operation days earlier, returned to the Opera House that afternoon to make a speech justifying it, and appealing to Bolshevik delegates to renounce Brest-Litovsk. Her aim, the aim of her party, was not to overthrow the Bolsheviks but to force them to change course.[9]

Meanwhile, probably (but not certainly) unaware of the mayhem that had taken place not far away, Bruce Lockhart was working in his rooms at the Hotel Elite. A knock at the door interrupted him. Britain's agent opened it to discover Karl Radek, a leading Bolshevik whom he had met through Ransome and with whom he was on good terms, standing before him, visibly excited. Radek told him what had just happened. "I received this news at 4 o'clock and went immediately to Congress," Lockhart cabled to Whitehall.[10] Returning to his box, he noticed that many seats on the stage remained vacant. Delegates milled in the hall, realizing something had happened, not knowing what it was. Lockhart could see Maria Spiridonova looking "calm and composed."[11] Someone ushered the remaining Bolshevik delegates outside. No one else could leave.

In his memoir, Lockhart wrote that Sidney Reilly appeared at about 6 p.m., to report that troops had surrounded the building and that there had been fighting in the streets. Then he and a French agent in the box began pulling what Lockhart recognized as "compromising documents" from their pockets. They tore them into pieces and swallowed them.[12] But why would Reilly have entered a building surrounded by soldiers to swallow documents he could more easily have disposed of elsewhere, and why at such a late hour, and why did the soldiers admit him? Likely it went the other way: Lockhart entered the building because he had a pass from Karl Radek, appeared in the box, told his party, including Reilly and the Frenchman who were there already, what had happened, and warned them to destroy incriminating evidence. This cannot be proved, but given what we know of Lockhart's recent activities and schedule that day, it seems to be the logical deduction.

And what was the evidence that the two agents felt obliged to destroy? There is no proof that Lockhart, or Reilly or his French counterpart (who remains nameless) knew the SR plans, but it seems likely that the Frenchman did, for French agents, directed by Noulens, had supplied the bombs used in the assassination.[13] It is not impossible that Reilly and Lockhart knew them as well. The former was cooperating with French agents by this point, and was in touch with left SRs. The latter already was supporting SRs with hard cash. Conceivably all three men had incriminating documents to destroy that afternoon.

There is even an indication, albeit nothing more, because elicited by the Bolsheviks while conducting a show trial of SRs in 1922, and we do not know by what means they obtained it, that Lockhart was no more opposed to murder as a political tool during wartime than Monsieur Noulens. At the show trial a witness testified that in 1918 the British agent had passed money to an SR operative, Boris Donskoy, who shortly thereafter murdered the German General Herman von Eichhorn in Ukraine. Perhaps Lockhart knew nothing of SR plans, either in Ukraine or in Moscow, but gave them money for general purposes only. It is fair to wonder, however, whether some of his money might have helped to fund one assassination or the other—and fair to point out as well that in July 1918, with his country and Germany still at war, he would have had every reason to consider it money well spent.

By 2 p.m. Saturday, what the Bolsheviks already were calling the left SR "uprising" had been suppressed, chiefly by Captain Berzin and his Latvian Rifle Brigade. The Bolsheviks arrested Spiridonova and the rest of the left SR delegates and executed several whom they supposed to be ringleaders. (They spared Spiridonova.) And they launched a furious attack upon the "Anglo-French imperialists" whom they judged to have inspired and funded the assassination. Once again, Lockhart thought the climax approached. "As this may be last telegram I may be able to send I would once more impress on you vital necessity for immediate action [by which he meant occupation of the ports]. I would also beg you to give me power immediately to spend up to 10 million rubles [worth approximately £125,000 then, the equivalent of nearly £6,875,000 today] in supporting those organizations which may be useful to us in event of intervention."[14]

*   *   *

Whatever Lockhart may have known about SR intentions, it seems impossible that he did not know what Boris Savinkov meant to do now. He would have discussed and coordinated with Cromie in Petrograd, and with Savinkov's agents, whom he continued to meet in Moscow. Apparently, Savinkov had not known precisely what the left SRs were planning. He believed, because of talks with ambassador Noulens, and because of Lockhart's encouragement and money, however, that the Allies would occupy Archangel that very week aided by an uprising from within, and that then, aided by Czech Legionnaires, they would take Vologda, from which point they could menace both Moscow and Petrograd. "Bountiful promises of both men and money were held out" to Savinkov, Lockhart later confessed.[15] The great conspirator did not know, and neither did Bruce Lockhart, that British General Frederick Cuthbert Poole, who arrived in Murmansk from Britain late in May, had despaired of the Czechs reaching Vologda in time. Poole judged his own numbers too few to proceed without them. He had nothing like the two divisions that Lockhart, Cromie, and Garstin all had fixed upon as necessary for a successful invasion. He could not contact Savinkov to tell him, or Bruce Lockhart either, however, for British telegraphic traffic from Moscow to Murmansk had been temporarily interrupted (to this day no one knows why or by whom). Nor did the French, whose lines of communication remained intact, tell Savinkov that the Allies had postponed action. The great conspirator later suspected that Noulens kept the information from him because he had been "trying to time our operation with the [left SR] revolt in Moscow."[16] Surely, he was right.[17]

Mistakenly assuming, then, that Allied reinforcements were in the offing, and just as the left SR's were detonating their bomb in Moscow, Savinkov launched a three-pronged insurrection in Yaroslavl, Rybinsk, and Murom. Had he taken those towns, and had the Allies taken Vologda, then Moscow would have faced from northwest to northeast, a partially encircling belt. The belt might have tightened, if sympathetic uprisings had broken out in the south, and if the White Army of General Alexeyev in the South Don region likewise had taken action. Then the belt would have formed a circle and might have choked the Revolution to death—without regard to the success or failure of the left SR action in Moscow.

In Yaroslavl, the rebels took the city center, began cold-bloodedly executing leading local Bolsheviks, and issued a proclamation: "Bolshevik rule in Yaroslav Gubernia has been overthrown.... Events similar...have taken place in other cities along the Volga.... Only a few more efforts are needed and the Bolsheviks...will be wiped off the face of the earth."[18] But in Rybinsk, after ferocious street fighting the rebels fled; in Murom the insurrectionists seized a few buildings, came under fire, and bolted; and in Archangel and Vologda—nothing. Nor did the White Army of the south stir. Isolated and surrounded, the Yaroslavl men held on, hoping for Allied assistance that never came.

Back in Moscow, Lockhart wrote despairingly in his diary on July 10, "I know what we ought to do, but God knows what we shall do." For the moment, the Allies and Whites did nothing, but the Red Army advanced upon Yaroslavl. Once more, fierce fighting, and then the UDMF men scattered. Boris Savinkov and his chief aides went into hiding once again.

*   *   *

In the wake of these twin disasters, Britain's agent in Russia embarked upon a series of increasingly dangerous, clandestine meetings. It is wrong to think of him as a playboy dilettante blithely swimming out of his depth in shark-infested waters as some historians have depicted him. Determined, competitive, hardnosed, capable, and supremely confident, he set out to recoup the situation. This, he was sure, was what Whitehall expected of him. He must have suspected that the Bolsheviks were watching him closely, but it did not deter him. He commenced a game of wits against the Cheka, which meant, therefore, against Felix Dzerzhinsky and Jacov Peters.

The British agent met with the leader of the National Center on July 13, which is to say shortly after the suppression of Savinkov's revolt.[19] Three days later, this time accompanied by Fernand Grenard, he attended another clandestine meeting and, on his own authority, gave the organization one million rubles (worth approximately £12,500 then, £687,000 today). The Frenchman made a like contribution. And the two planned to combine forces to find for it the astonishing additional sums of eighty-one million rubles (a little over a million pounds then, or £57 million today), and ten million rubles more for General Alexeyev who now proposed to join forces with the Czechs if some of them would turn back toward Vologda after all, and half a million yet again for Savinkov, hiding underground.[20] Lockhart had devised a method for transferring his share of these vast amounts: writing Foreign Office checks in pounds to a British firm in Moscow, Camber-Higgs and Company, which cashed them in rubles and submitted them to London for repayment.[21]

The recent twin debacles had led him to rethink the interventionist scheme, however. Previously he had believed the Czechs were key to a successful intervention, because, as they traveled west to confront the Bolsheviks, they would be establishing Allied control, symbolically planting the Allied flag, all along the Siberian Railway. "The man who controls central Siberia will be economic master of Russia," he had coached the Foreign Office.[22] But the Czechs, who were focused upon their nationalist goals as always,

Figure 19. Soldiers of the Latvian Rifle Brigade

had let down Boris Savinkov as badly as the Allies had done. If they would not play the role for which the anti-Bolsheviks had cast them, who would? Then Bruce Lockhart thought of the Latvian Rifle Brigade.

On the surface, this appears odd. As the historian Geoffrey Swain has shown in a series of deeply researched articles, the Riflemen, numbering about twenty thousand, played a crucial role in the October Revolution. They had purged their regiments of anti-Bolshevik officers and defeated the campaigns of early counter-revolutionaries. They provided leadership to the new Red Army that Trotsky had just begun to build. They saved the Bolsheviks by overwhelming the anarchists and left SRs in separate, equally ruthless, operations. Sent to confront the Czechs, they almost alone proved an effective fighting force against them. They suppressed disorder in Pskov Province, Novgorod Province, Velikiye Luki Province, Staraya Russa, and Saratov. To quote Swain on the Latvian Rifle Brigade during the revolutionary period: "Clearly the presence of Latvian Riflemen was crucial for Bolshevik survival in times of crisis."[23]

Why the Brigades had proved so comparatively effective and dependable is not easily explained. Perhaps it was because, since they were so far from home, they could not throw down their weapons and desert the army, as many Russian soldiers had done. Perhaps it was because, as relative strangers in Russia, they felt more reliant on the government that paid and fed and housed them, no matter what government it was. Nevertheless, they viewed the occupation of Latvia by Germany as many Ukrainians viewed German occupation of their country—it was an affront to nationality. Likewise, patriotic Latvians viewed the Treaty of Brest-Litovsk as the Ukrainians did, and the anarchists and the left SRs as well—it was a humiliating Bolshevik surrender to German imperialism.[24]

It is unclear when Lockhart first began to think the Latvians might be ripe for recruitment into the counter-revolutionary movement. In June, as part of the British effort to support local opposition to German occupiers everywhere, he had wanted to channel funds to the Latvian Provisional National Council, which intended to raise a brigade to expel the invaders from their country.[25] Perhaps this planted the idea in his mind.[26] Or perhaps the seed took root a month later, in July, when General Poole in Murmansk grew impatient of Czechs, and began trying to enlist Latvians to help him fight Bolsheviks in the north.[27] Because he was in close touch with Captain Cromie it is likely he knew that the naval attaché was recruiting Latvian sailors to help him scuttle Russia's Baltic fleet. He must have known by then too that that several of Savinkov's chief lieutenants had served previously as officers in the Latvian Rifle Brigade. And surely, he discussed the matter with Sidney Reilly, who claimed to have understood from his first moment in Bolshevik Russia that: "If I could buy the Letts, my task would be easy."[28]

Everyone knew that Lenin would send the Latvian Rifle Brigade to stem the Allies when they marched south from Archangel. At some time during that summer Lockhart asked himself the following questions: What if the Latvians did not stem the Allies? What if they stood aside and let them pass, because the Allies had won them over with bribes and inducements—such as a promise to help establish an independent Latvia? The Latvian Rifle Brigade came to occupy in Lockhart's mind the space previously taken by Czechs.

Felix Dzerzhinsky's sensitive antennae picked up some of this. "Rumors about the attempt of the Anglo-French to bribe the command staff of [the Latvian Rifle] division," reached him even before Savinkov mounted his abortive insurrection at the beginning of July.[29] If the rumors were true, if the Latvian Riflemen did prove susceptible to Allied bribes, the results could be fatal for Bolshevism. How could the Cheka stymie this latest gambit of the Allies? Could they even turn it to advantage? Felix Dzerzhinsky began to devise a plan.

CHAPTER 11

DZERZHINSKY COUNTERS

B ut Felix Dzerzhinsky's situation was complicated. Mirbach's two assassins had belonged to the Cheka. They had presented the German ambassador with a letter of introduction displaying Dzerzhinsky's signature. To this day historians differ as to whether it was genuine.[1] At the time the Germans had no doubt. They thought Dzerzhinsky had authorized Mirbach's murder (which is unlikely), and then had failed to apprehend the killers (which is indisputable). Moreover, he had failed to arrest the left SR committee that had given the assassins their orders. Rather, that committee had arrested him when he arrived to question them, and held him until Captain Berzin's Brigade came to the rescue. To appease the Germans, Lenin accepted Dzerzhinsky's resignation. Jacov Peters replaced him. In fact, Dzerzhinsky remained the Cheka's invisible head. He played a central role in ensuing events from behind the scenes, and he would resume the lead position on August 25.

Those ensuing events originated in Dzerzhinsky's musings during the weeks before the July insurrections along the Upper Volga and in Moscow. "We knew already," remembered Jacov Peters, that "Allied consulates in Soviet Russia were the headquarters of counterrevolutionary organizations."[2] Now those same consuls were trying to bribe the Latvian Rifle Brigade. What could Dzerzhinsky do about it?

In mid-June 1918, a Cheka head of department asked one of his young subordinates, Jan Avotin, formerly an officer in the Latvian Brigade, if he "had two free commissars available for traveling to Petrograd on an important assignment." Avotin immediately suggested two friends, Latvian front-line ex-military men like himself: Jan Buikis and Jan Sprogis, with whom he shared lodgings. Of Sprogis, Avotin would write that he was in those days "not tall, thin, collected, artful, self-confident, with a penchant for inventions and pranks." As for Buikis, Avotin wrote that he was "a bit larger, simpler, more modest, mild mannered, disciplined, less independent." These two Jans, both Latvians, would play leading roles in the drama about to unfold.[3]

The day after Avotin supplied their names to his superior, the pair received a summons from Dzerzhinsky. When they entered his famously spartan office, the head of the Cheka was conferring with Jacov Peters. Dzerzhinsky, "very gaunt, with bloodshot eyes," said to them: "We called you for an important, very important, task." He rehearsed various counter-revolutionary outrages performed by Savinkov, the Czechs, others, "links of one enemy chain," he said. "Our task is to uncover it and destroy it. For this we need to infiltrate the enemy underground." He thought that "For you former [Latvian] officers of the czarist army it will be easier than for anyone else to pose as enemies of Soviet power and to enter into the anti-Soviet milieu that interests us."[4]

Dzerzhinsky intended to send them to Petrograd, "a major hotspot of counterrevolutionary organizations," but not by themselves. With them, he would send a more senior figure, Alexander Engel'gardt. "An imposing man, about forty," he was likewise a Latvian, but from a wealthy aristocratic family from Riga, a former black marketeer who had been caught smuggling provisions

Figure 20. The three Jans:
Sprogis, Buikis, Avotin

into Finland, and whom Dzerzhinsky had recruited personally. Dzerzhinsky thought this elegant and compelling agent could smooth the way for his younger, less polished colleagues in the high White social circles they were about to enter.[5]

Note that Dzerzhinsky and Peters (himself a Lett) had chosen three Latvians to undertake this crucial mission. They well understood that the triumvirate represented especially inviting bait to dangle before the British and French at this juncture. Note, too, that they sent them to Petrograd: that was where Francis Cromie sat plotting destruction of the Russian Baltic fleet. Cromie, as much as Lockhart, had long been interested in Latvians, not only because he knew that many of them were disillusioned with Bolshevism, but also because many of them served as sailors and officers on ships docked in Petrograd harbor.[6] Whom among them might he bribe when it came time to sink those vessels? He had been conferring secretly with one Latvian in particular to find out. But it was not so secret: Dzerzhinsky knew all about it, as will become apparent. That must be why he assigned the three Latvians to Petrograd and not to Moscow. Dzerzhinsky already knew that Cromie wanted to speak to people such as they would purport to be.

The first goal of the Cheka trio, once arrived in Petrograd, then, would be to make contact with the British naval attaché. The second would be to infiltrate his organization. The third would be to divert him, to lead him away from genuinely disillusioned Latvians who really might help overthrow Bolshevism, by dangling all sorts of possibilities before him, and promising that they were the Latvians to deliver them. Eventually, the Cheka could roll up Cromie's organization altogether, and Cromie with it.

Dzerzhinsky's three designees took pseudonyms: Buikis became "Bredis," Sprogis became "Shmidken," and Engel'gardt became "Shtegel'man." Arrived in Petrograd, they spent several weeks "getting to know former officers, inviting them to restaurants, getting them to be intimate with us." None, however, provided an introduction to Cromie.[7] Then, one day, as the trio strolled along the bank of the Neva River, they passed a Latvian Club, across from the Russian admiralty building. A poster in the window announced a dance that evening, with orchestra, refreshments and open bar. Free food and drink at a time of such dearth: "We ought to visit this 'oasis of culture,'" one of them said.

They did, appearing at the appointed hour in suits, white shirts with starched collars, neckties, and officers' peaked caps. "We were young and sociable," recalled Buikis/Bredis. A waitress told them that the dance was one of a continuing series. Most of the men present were sailors and officers from a guard ship nearby. The captain of the guard ship paid for these extravaganzas. He regularly attended, but rarely danced. Rather he and important looking men would sit, and eat, and drink, and consult at the back of the room.

That was enough to interest the three intelligence officers from Moscow. They returned to the Latvian Club whenever a dance took place. They came to know the Latvian captain of the guard ship and his officers well enough to find "a common language." The common language was anti-Bolshevism. "In two-months' time," Buikis/Bredis exulted, "we had so entered into the trust of the enemy organization that its chiefs suggested we meet—Cromie."[8]

This remembrance, which caused a stir when published during the 1960s, and brought Jan Buikis from obscurity into the Russian limelight as an early Soviet hero, must be taken with a grain of salt, however. Most egregiously, Buikis claimed for himself the role actually played by his friend, Jan Sprogis, who was posing as Shmidkhen. That is why he did not mention that early during the stint in Petrograd he, Jan Buikis, was "recognized...by some fleeting acquaintance who exclaimed: 'Who did you bring here? This is a Chekist!'" At which point, thinking fast, the young agent had spun on his heel in a military manner and walked out "in a silence that had frozen the confused guests."[9] Jan Sprogis, posing as Shmidkhen, and Engel'gardt, posing as Shtegel'man carried on the mission in Petrograd without the third member of the original trio.

At this point, it becomes necessary to investigate a parallel and related set of wheels set spinning by Felix Dzerzhinsky.

Figure 21. Colonel Friedrich Briedis

Sometime before he conceived the operation against Cromie, interrogation of captured anti-Bolsheviks had produced a nugget of useful information. Colonel Friedrich Andreevich Briedis, war hero, and former commander of the 1st Latvian Rifles Regiment who worked currently for Soviet military intelligence against the Germans, was in fact a double agent. Briedis (not to be confused with Bredis, the *nom de guerre* employed by the ill-starred Buikis), had co-founded Savinkov's underground UDMF, and continued to serve as head of its intelligence and counter-intelligence departments.[10] Moreover, he had dealings in Petrograd with Captain Cromie and Sidney Reilly. At the very Latvian Club discovered by the trio from Moscow, they had discussed blowing up Russia's Baltic fleet to facilitate the occupation of Archangel and an ensuing counter-revolution.

Dzerzhinsky took in this revelation—probably he would have smiled, had he been able to. He could use the Latvian colonel. Briedis may have been a counter-revolutionary but, because he was a Latvian nationalist, he wanted the Germans out of his country as much as any Bolshevik did. So long as he devoted himself to undermining German interests, the Cheka could employ him, keep him under strict surveillance, and possibly discover additional counter-revolutionaries. Perhaps not amazingly, one of the agents Dzerzhinsky assigned to watch the colonel was none other than Jan Sprogis, operating under the same Shmidkhen pseudonym he would use a month later in the mission against Cromie.[11] (This suggests that he had more experience as a counter-intelligence officer than his friends ever knew.) Shmidkhen did not merely watch Colonel Briedis, however—he befriended him.

Perhaps it was through Sprogis/Shmidkhen then that the Cheka learned the colonel maintained a friendship based upon shared early wartime heroics and hardships, and Latvian nationality, with none other than Captain Berzin of the Latvian Rifle Brigade. Indeed, Briedis had recruited his old friend into his anti-German intelligence unit. Berzin had no idea that his comrade worked also for Savinkov. Sometime in "May/June," probably just before the trawling expedition in Petrograd began, Briedis introduced Berzin to his new friend, Shmidkhen, another fellow Latvian. Berzin had no idea that Shmidkhen's real name was Jan Sprogis, and that he worked for the Cheka, keeping an eye on Colonel Briedis.[12]

In early July, with the Petrograd trawling expedition well underway, but not yet netting anything, Colonel Briedis took part in Savinkov's rebellion in Yaroslavl. He had expected French and British support, but it never arrived. The Red Army captured him. Then came punishment. Dzerzhinsky sent the colonel to Butyrka Prison, the very place where he himself had undergone such torment before February 1917. Immured in his cell, knowing he would soon face the executioner, doubtless grinding his teeth whenever he remembered the Allies' failure to help at Yaroslavl as promised, the colonel obsessed over the fate of his country, trampled under the boot heel of German occupiers, and of his fellow Latvians in the Rifle Brigades, cannon fodder for the Bolsheviks—and he, powerless to help them.

But Dzerzhinsky and Peters were not done with him. When it came to cat and mouse, when it came to games of wit, few could best Felix Dzerzhinsky. Now he realized that Briedis' patriotic fixation, and crucially, his connection with Captain Cromie, could be turned to advantage; could expedite the ongoing operation in Petrograd; that is to say, could facilitate the Cheka trio's introduction to the British naval attaché. And that was not all it could do.

That Jacov Peters was himself a Lett made things easier. Sometime toward the end of July, Peters, no doubt after many careful conferences with Dzerzhinsky, summoned the prisoner, his countryman, to his office at the Lubianka. He placed a loaded revolver on his desk, but spoke disarmingly, in Latvian. Though himself a steadfast Bolshevik internationalist, he too retained a soft spot for his native land—or so he stated. He knew that Briedis had contact with Captain Cromie in Petrograd, and as it happened that connection could be useful to them both.

Peters told Briedis that he realized the Latvians of Moscow, by which he meant the Latvian Riflemen, had had enough of Revolution and wanted to go home and that they certainly did not want to get into a shooting war with British troops if the latter should march south from Murmansk and Archangel. Yet, if the British ever did that, then inevitably the Bolshevik government would send the Brigade to stop them. He would like to spare them that; Lenin could find other troops.

Peters told Briedis that he had opposed signing the Brest-Litovsk Treaty, and remained anti-German. He could truthfully have said the same of Dzerzhinsky, and probably he did. Then he would have explained that the plan he was proposing would not hurt Russia, but only Germany, Russia's and Latvia's common enemy. He was offering Briedis a chance to perform one last act on behalf of his people.

Here was the crux of Peters' proposal to poor, doomed Colonel Briedis. He should give to Peters a letter of introduction to Captain Cromie which he, Peters, would pass on to a trusted agent. The latter, accompanied by someone whom Briedis could designate, would take the letter to Cromie. They would ask him for a second note, this one addressed to General Poole in Archangel. When the pair met the general, they would make him a promise: that the Latvian Riflemen, at any rate, would stand aside when Allied troops marched through Russia to re-form the Eastern Front—if he promised in return that the Allies would help the men of the Brigades return to their home country.

No doubt Colonel Briedis kept a poker face as he listened to this proposition, but no doubt also he thought it offered him something approaching resurrection. He was doomed, but now he could reach from beyond the grave on behalf of his countrymen. He immediately wrote the letter. He named his friend Captain Berzin as his proxy.

This new scheme reveals Dzerzhinsky's and Peters' ruthless cunning and ambition, and the latter's remarkable ability to act a part. Initially their aim had been to bring down Cromie. Now the goal was bigger, grander. Of course, they had no intention of arranging for the Latvian Riflemen to stand aside when the Allied invaders came. Now they sought to defeat not merely Cromie, but General Poole as well. They would lure the general and his men into a trap south of Archangel, and decimate them—with the very Latvian soldiers who had promised to step aside.

For his part, the hapless colonel probably entertained a separate and contradictory dream, which likewise remained unspoken. He thought he was tricking Dzerzhinsky and Peters. He must have thought that the Allies, having defeated Germany without first having to fight the Latvian Riflemen, would feel obliged to reward them not merely by repatriating them, but also by supporting creation of an independent Latvian state. So, the two parties to the negotiation kept their own counsel, nourished their own mutually exclusive goals—and made their agreement.

There is another plausible interpretation of what took place at this meeting, however. Conceivably Dzerzhinsky and Peters were more direct with Colonel Briedis. Conceivably they played upon his resentment of the Allies for failing to appear at Yaroslavl. Conceivably, they explained to him the true aim of the plan, and Briedis approved it as a means of squaring accounts with the men who had betrayed him and his comrades several months earlier.[13]

Either way, the Cheka got what it wanted from Colonel Briedis, the letter to Captain Cromie, and either way, the discussion lasted long into the night. At its conclusion Peters, whose revolver still lay upon the desk, closed those famously suggestive eyes and fell asleep. He would have been well satisfied. Or, he seemed to fall asleep: it may have been a ruse designed to lull Colonel Briedis.[14]

*   *   *

To recapitulate in order to render an exceedingly complicated and murky situation more comprehensible: during late spring and early summer 1918, Felix Dzerzhinsky and his second-in-command, Jacov Peters, set two related counter-espionage operations in motion. The first was to send three operatives, Sprogis/Shmidkhen,

Buikis/Bredis and Engel'gardt/Shtegel'man to Petrograd in hopes of making contact with Captain Cromie, in order to penetrate and then to destroy his organization. The second operation was more complex. On one level, it was meant to facilitate the first: Colonel Briedis would either be tricked or persuaded to ease the Chekists' way to Cromie. If all went well, that introduction would lead to a meeting with General Poole. The Chekists would gain his confidence too, learn his plans, and lure him and his army to destruction every bit as complete as that intended for Britain's naval attaché.

Felix Dzerzhinsky and Jacov Peters intended to use Colonel Briedis, then to deceive Captain Cromie and after him General Poole. Then it became necessary to deceive their own agents as well.

* * *

Dzerzhinsky chose Engel'gardt to carry Briedis' letter. In late July or early August, the Latvian aristocrat, disguised as Shtegel'man, and Sprogis disguised as Shmidkhen—(not Berzin as Briedis had wanted, possibly because Briedis deemed Shmidkhen an acceptable substitute for Berzin since he knew him too)—met Cromie, either at the French Hotel in St. Petersburg, or at the embassy itself. Anyway, the pair had not only the letter composed by Colonel Briedis, but also references from the officers in the Latvian Club. Thus, they finally established their bona fides with the former submarine commander.

At this initial meeting, the Chekists also met Sidney Reilly, elegant and dangerous. Additional meetings followed, during which both sides tried to gauge the other. It would seem that the Russians had the better of it, for eventually Cromie told them that "the secret struggle against the new government was taking on a broad and active character, and they might render in this struggle a great help." Sprogis/Shmidkhen crowed later that he had not had to recruit anyone to counter-revolution, but rather had been "welcomed...and himself recruited."[15]

Yet Cromie did not offer to act as intermediary between the disaffected Latvians and General Poole as Peters and Dzerzhinsky had hoped he would. Possibly, he was exercising caution. Possibly, he judged that Bruce Lockhart had assumed the mantle of leadership among British conspirators, and should make the most important decisions. Possibly, he was following Reilly's advice to send the Latvians to Lockhart, which is what Lockhart's son Robin, believed.[16] At any rate, Cromie composed a letter for the two to take not to General Poole in Archangel, but rather to Lockhart in Moscow. He sealed it, so the two could not read it. But then he gave to Sprogis/Shmidkhen his card with a note on the back: "Talk over mutual interests with Goppers." He meant the card for Lockhart, and had just incriminated them both beyond repair, for Karlis Goppers, another hero commander of the Latvian Rifle Brigade was a well-known counter-revolutionary. He had resigned his post in protest when the Bolsheviks took power. He was a founding member of the UDMF, and had fought with Savinkov in the abortive uprising at Yaroslavl right alongside the imprisoned Colonel Briedis.

Although Buikis was not there, his description of what followed is probably true, since he must have been repeating what his friend Sprogis reported to him. Sprogis and Engel'gardt shared a room at the Petrograd Hotel Select. The morning after they accepted the card and letter from Cromie, Sidney Reilly knocked at their door. He wanted to make sure they had the letter, had not given it to anyone else; in short, that they really were about to deliver it as instructed. Of course, the Chekists had the letter, but only because they had not yet carried it to Felix Dzerzhinsky and Jacov Peters back in Moscow.

The two agents realized now if they had not already, that the Anglo-French were monitoring them. They left Petrograd on a train bound for Moscow later that day. Disembarking at the Moscow station, they did their best to throw off track anyone who might be following: "we walked on foot...opting for quiet little streets and passageways."[17] Eventually they reached the Lubianka. Felix Dzerzhinsky and Jacov Peters steamed open the envelope. They read that Cromie was arranging his exit from Russia, and planned "to bang the door" when he left, an obvious reference to his plan to blow up Russia's Baltic fleet.[18] They would follow that up in due course, but first they would exploit the possibilities opened by the introduction to Bruce Lockhart. If not Cromie, then perhaps he could be induced to provide a letter of introduction to General Poole.

Dzerzhinsky and Peters needed Engel'gardt/Shtegel'man to maintain the link to Cromie. They sent him back to Petrograd. But they needed another senior figure to accompany Sprogis/ Shmidkhen when he brought Cromie's letter, now restored to its envelope, to Bruce Lockhart. They chose Colonel Briedis' nominee, Captain Berzin. After all, he knew Shmidkhen already. Peters and Dzerzhinsky instructed Sprogis to recruit Berzin into Briedis' counter-revolutionary organization. Then they instructed Berzin's commanding officer to tell him to expect an approach from an agent of the imperialists, an anti-Bolshevik Latvian nationalist. Berzin should convince this man that he sympathized. He should allow himself to be recruited.

Here were wheels within wheels within wheels, mirrors reflecting mirrors reflecting mirrors. Here were Dzerzhinsky and Peters tricking not only the British enemy but their own agents as well. They worried about Latvian loyalty. Now they would have two Latvian agents working together in the field, each unaware of the other's status, each reporting back to their chiefs about the other. Should one waver, the other would know—and tell.

(The reinsurance policy was a wise one. The Latvian Riflemen really were ripe for subordination, as Lockhart had perceived. At this very moment, Kurt Reizler, former chief aide to the murdered German ambassador, von Mirbach, *also* was negotiating with Latvian officers about a *German* anti-Bolshevik coup, and offering them the same kind of bribe as Lockhart's. But he abandoned the scheme when the tide of war turned against his country.)[19]

Anyway, Sprogis/Shmidkhen dutifully sprang what he conceived to be a trap. "The Bolsheviks are ruining Russia, have sold her and Latvia in particular to the Germans," he told Berzin sometime between August 8 and 10. "Only an external force in the form of the Allies can bring freedom from the German yoke…Every honest citizen should aid the Allies…and the Czechoslovaks." Although warned to expect the approach, Berzin reported it to the Cheka anyway. This proved to Dzerzhinsky and Peters that they could trust him.[20]

Sprogis reported to Peters and Dzerzhinsky that he had Berzin under control. Berzin reported to Peters and Dzerzhinsky that he had young Shmidkhen (that is to say, Sprogis) under control. On August 14, the two Latvians, one a Cheka agent carrying the letter of introduction to Bruce Lockhart given him by Cromie, and posing as a Latvian nationalist, the other a Latvian army officer, posing as an anti-Bolshevik but in reality working now for the Cheka too, neither understanding the other, each thinking him a traitor, knocked at the door of Britain's special agent in Russia.

CHAPTER 12

INTRIGUE AND ROMANCE IN REVOLUTIONARY RUSSIA

On July 24, three weeks before the Latvians knocked at Lockhart's door, the Allied diplomats who had sought refuge at Vologda suddenly entrained for Archangel from which port they intended to leave the country. Bolsheviks could not help scenting danger, and they were right to do so. On August 2, General Poole, accompanied by a force of about 400 men, arrived from Murmansk in Archangel. A telephone call from one of the newly arrived diplomats predicting the momentary and much anticipated White uprising against the local Soviet prompted his move but, in fact, no insurrection occurred. Allied warships had to enter the port with guns blazing. Supported by seaplanes, they swiftly reduced its modest defenses to rubble. Twenty-four hours after Poole arrived, the White conspirators belatedly issued an invitation to occupy. Douglas Young, the British consul in Archangel who had opposed an uninvited intervention all along, and who had passed to Whitehall Bruce Lockhart's inconstant telegrams (which he had read with mounting alarm) felt shame and disgust. "Such at any rate were not the methods which won victories, and accepted reverses, upon the playing fields of that unpretentious institution in which I received my early education, and I had supposed that such things were not done by English gentlemen."[1]

In Moscow, news of the invasion at Archangel confirmed Bolshevik fears. No one realized how small the occupying force was. Everyone thought its appearance marked the advent of Allied sponsored counter-revolution. Everyone assumed that Allied soldiers would march on Vologda, and perhaps then on Moscow or Petrograd. That was, in fact, the Allied plan. Rumors swept the two cities: that Trotsky had gone missing; that Lenin was preparing to flee to Sweden aboard a boat docked in Petrograd harbor, and that other leading Bolsheviks likewise were putting into motion long-held plans of escape.[2]

In fact, the Bolsheviks meant to fight. They rounded up thousands of former Tsarist officers who might welcome the Allied incursion, and sent them into prison. They arrested the few remaining Allied officials they could find, although still not those, like Lockhart, who could claim diplomatic immunity. They came one evening for Captain Cromie, but he escaped from an upper story window, fled over rooftops, and began spending nights in a secret attic room at the home of Petrograd's British chaplain, Bousfield Swan Lombard.[3] The captain continued plotting during the day, but now he looked "thin and worried."[4] Lenin declared that a state of war existed between his country and the Allied powers. His government would cease to recognize passports belonging to Allied nationals in Russia so that they could not leave the country, effectively making them all hostages. Even when the Bolshevik government rescinded the state of war, the ban on travel remained. Bruce Lockhart assumed that now, really, his days in Russia were winding down. He expected to be detained and eventually deported, and made plans with that in mind.

Meanwhile, in Archangel, General Poole was considering his next move. He sent out mapping expeditions.[5] The Bolsheviks had squeezed shut the pipeline of White officers from Petrograd by arresting all they could lay hands on, but Allied reinforcements began to arrive: 600 British marines, 900 French colonials, 1,200 Serbians.[6] Some of these Poole sent south, which is to say up the Dvina River; others he sent south along the railway: the target for both columns was Vologda. Poole still hoped the Czechs might get there eventually. He also continued to imagine that many thousand "loyal Russians" would greet his soldiers as a liberating force and join it, but instead Red Guards blew up tracks and bridges, the crowds stayed away, and his army stuck about seventy-five miles from its departure point.[7] Belatedly the Bolsheviks realized that General Poole had only a small army at his disposal.

* * *

As for Lockhart and Moura: before the occupation of Archangel and even after, in fact all that spring and summer, they indulged their passion for each other. Of plot and counterplot, spy and counterspy, assassination and insurrection, and their participation in or knowledge of such doings we have gleanings already. Beyond all that, beyond the great events of the day, stood their romantic love: fervent and perfect. At this chaotic moment in Russia's history, they lived dangerously, but also, they found time to walk "hand in hand…day dreaming and happy," with "trees and grass and a blue sky and the air sunny and warm,"[8] and "no one, except you and me in the whole world."[9] He was enraptured as he had been with Amai, and his wife Jean before he married her, an unhappy portent had Moura but known it. She did not. She was enthralled too. Blissfully unaware, she fantasized about the future: "We will start life—just you and I—on just and kind principles—and be happy, so happy."[10]

Figure 22. "Happy-go-lucky" Moura von Benckendorff

When earlier in the spring they had been apart, they wrote each other daily. When Moura visited him in Moscow, she stayed with him in his suite at the Hotel Elite. When the hotel turned him out and all the other foreign diplomats as well, to make room for Bolshevik officials, he managed to rent the same spacious, well-appointed flat in which he had lived with Jean just a year ago in the western Arbat region, not far from what today is called Povarskaya Street: 19 Khlebnyi pereulok (which is to say Bread, or Grain, or Baker's Alley), Apartment 24.[11] Once again, he shared rooms with Hicks, but also this time Moura moved in immediately.

If Lockhart suffered from ghosts in this place, he did not mention them. If the thought of her husband and children troubled Moura, it did not stop her. She described herself at this stage as a "big, strapping, noisy, gay creature...[who] used to pretend to run things in our ménage-a-trois."[12] Despite everything else going on in the world, Lockhart thought her "happy-go-lucky" in those days.[13]

During working hours, the flat became his office. She recalled with affection the typists he employed there, and "Hicklet" (as Hicks had now become to her) "and dear, dear Garstino [as she called Denis Garstin]—and you backing in now and then—walking about like a little tin god. The nice happy times."[14] At night they would attend the opera, or the ballet, or return to the gypsy café, Streilna (until finally the Bolsheviks shut it down), or they might host a small party. DeWitt Clinton Poole thought they provided "a very pleasant haven. We went there Saturday nights from time to time and played poker." He judged Lockhart "a very brilliant fellow," and "a great hand with the girls." As for Moura, she was "one of the most charming women I ever knew."[15]

All that spring and summer they flaunted their love; they would not dissemble. That meant everyone knew about it, including the Foreign Office in London, although a file devoted to the affair of which Lockhart claimed to know, has never surfaced. "We had flouted all conventions," he would recall wistfully, almost proudly.[16] Inviting scrutiny, however, meant they could not object when they got it, nor be surprised by the ironic twist that came with it. Given the double standards of the time, Moura's supposed racy past—not his—caused them trouble.

She had worried that Lockhart would class her with all the other women with whom he had dallied. Now she learned if she did not know already, that she had a reputation for having dallied too, and that people who wished them ill would use this against them both. Captain Cromie, who may have heard of Lockhart's relationship the previous year with "Madame Vermelle," and who needed him as a strong and active partner in their various clandestine enterprises, tried to persuade her to end the affair:

> "You are friends with Lockhart and don't wish him any harm?"
> "Of course not. Why should I?"
> "Then don't go to Moscow again. It might harm him. He has many old enemies in Moscow."[17]

He meant that Lockhart's enemies could use her reputation to blacken Lockhart's. Cromie remained a friend to them both, however. When he realized that they would not, could not, end the affair, he left off asking her to. Perhaps he sympathized because he was engaged in a passionate extramarital affair too, with Princess Sophie Gagarin.

Lieutenant Colonel Cudbert Thornhill, formerly Britain's chief of military intelligence in Russia, and now chief of intelligence to General Poole who was still at that moment in Murmansk awaiting the signal to enter Archangel, had no sympathy or restraining bond of friendship with either of them. A ferocious interventionist, he coordinated with Lockhart now, but disliked him for his belated conversion to anti-Bolshevism. He thought he knew something of Moura and he disliked her too. "If he comes here and suspects something between you and me," Moura worried, "he will be sure to try and blame me in your eyes. There is nothing I deserve less."[18] She may have feared that Thornhill suspected she had spied for Germany, and would use that knowledge to poison Lockhart against her. Another of her letters suggests something different: she feared Thornhill knew of and would tell Lockhart about her previous flirtations and liaisons. "What I should give to be able to wipe out all the useless frivolities, all the trifling in the past—which have made me such bitter enemies as Thornhill, and led people to believe me to be something which I am not."[19]

She also worried that Lieutenant Ernest Boyce, head of British Secret Service's Moscow Section, the man to whom Reilly and George Hill reported and who conveyed their information to an SIS man in Stockholm, believed the rumors too. She invited Boyce to lunch, and then wrote to Lockhart, "I was very head up in the air like—I think it impressed him, at least he saw, I think [that] it really was unfair."[20] Whether they judged her a scarlet woman or a Mata Hari, here is further testimony to her powers of persuasion. One of the files in her MI5 dossier notes that, "In 1922, she applied for a visa for the UK," giving two referees. They were Commander Boyce and Colonel Thornhill.[21]

*　*　*

Sometime in late June, Moura discovered she was pregnant. She could not have been more delighted, even though her condition meant they must face up to the reality of their situation and make concrete plans. This they did at the end of the month, after her return from Ukraine, when she visited him again in Moscow.

Lockhart acted the way a gentleman should. He acknowledged that he had placed her in a false position, and said he would understand if she chose to return to her husband and later claim the baby was Djon's. Then she would not have to leave her children or increasingly frail mother, or even her husband. Could he have secretly thought that her pregnancy provided an excuse to end their affair? Probably not, and anyway Moura would have none of it. "I might as well think of giving up light—air." His second proposal suggests that he remained very much in love, although it proved to be an equal non-starter: that they leave Russia together through Murmansk which British forces controlled, before the Bolsheviks interned him in the wake of Allied invasion. Moura answered his "dear letter" with common sense. "Of course, it would be unheard of joy for me to leave with you." But she needed time to deal with family, and to organize financial matters. She instructed Lockhart to use his contacts at the Russian Foreign Ministry to procure her a passport, and his influence with the British ambassador in Sweden to make things easy for her when she arrived there. She thought it would take "about 1 month to settle things and go to Stockholm where I will wait."[22] He should return to England via Murmansk to deal with his own affairs and meet her there.

An additional complication soon occurred to them: because they could not marry until they had each divorced, and because that would take many months, their child would face the social stigma of having been born out of wedlock. Their solution: Moura would journey one last time to Yendel, not to tell her husband that she intended to leave him for another man, but to take him to bed, so that when the infant was born, Djon and all the world would think it his. "I wonder if you realize all what this voyage means to me in every way," Moura wrote Lockhart. "But I will be brave for your sake, baby."[23]

She had to be. "I am writing you this from Yendel," she scribbled on July 20. "Babykins, it is still worse than I thought." German officers, part of the conquering army occupying Estonia, had made themselves at home in her home. "They took over the estate house without standing on ceremony," Moura's son Paul would recall. They "ate in our dining room, while we had to be content with some little back room in which to have our meals." In general, they behaved with cavalier indifference.[24] Moura felt great anger. "It is torture…unfair…I want to scream and say I am not going to bear it."

If her husband, Djon, felt as she did he did not say so, which only aggravated Moura further. He may have resented Germany's intrusion, but not the anti-Bolshevik reasons for it. Worse still, he had not seen his wife for many months. Who knows what he expected from her? Moura knew the main purpose of her visit, but "I cannot refrain from shrinking at his touch."

In that enormous house, she would snatch a moment, find an empty room, and dash off a secret note to her lover: "Sunday: I am miserable. I want you. Good night. Moura." "Monday: I cannot write. I feel an utter blankness. I feel lost. I only know I love you more than all the world. Your Moura." "Tuesday: Five days since I heard your voice on the telephone. I keep thinking and wondering how you are getting on and praying that I should see you again before you have to go. I love you baby. I am miserable, miserable. Moura."[25]

Eventually she left the place. Presumably, she had accomplished her purpose, at what personal private cost who can say? Servants would have brought her from the manor house to the nearest major town, Narva. From there she set out for the border, which she crossed on foot. In Moscow, Lockhart sat playing endless hands of patience, steeped in nervous expectation. He thought he would soon be leaving Russia one way or another. He had not heard from her in ten days and feared that he might not hear from her before he had to go. Then, on July 29, the telephone rang and it was she, finally returned to Petrograd. She would take the first train to Moscow to see him.

Did he love her now as fervently as she loved him? He did—for the moment. Would he make difficult sacrifices as she had just done to maintain their love? It seemed that he would. But Amai, in far-off Malaya, could have provided evidence to the contrary. So could have his wife, in distant Britain. So, much closer to home, could have "Madame Vermelle."

* * *

Now we come to the crux of the matter regarding their relationship: Did Moura know about the anti-Bolshevik conspiracies in which her lover engaged? If she did know, did she report them to the Cheka? Such evidence as exists suggests that while she knew what Lockhart meant to do, at least in a general sense, and at least during the period before his undertakings reached a climax, she did not report to anyone about them.

She tried to be useful to him. In her letters from Petrograd, always delivered by hand by friends and therefore written without fear of prying eyes, she would forward information that might not have reached him in Moscow. For example, "Swedes say the Germans have taken new poison gas to the Ukraine stronger than everything used before." And she tried to keep him abreast of the mood in Russia's former capital: for example, "There is strong feeling against the Allies."[26]

Any woman might send letters to her lover containing information to help him in his job. In Moura's case, however, the letters reveal intimate knowledge of, and sympathy for, her lover's point of view. They suggest that he had confided it to her. Thus, in late May, just as he was coaching the Foreign Office to muzzle the British press in order to keep news of the planned intervention in Russia secret, she wrote to him: "news of intervention has suddenly burst out [in Petrograd]...It is such a pity."[27] Another example: Cromie appears to have warned her that their correspondence might not be as private as they thought, and asked her what it contained. She reported this to Lockhart on the telephone and he grew worried. As soon as they hung up, she wrote to reassure him: "You funny boy…getting anxious when I spoke of letters being searched. What did you think? That I had put Cromie in the confidence or what?"[28] Since Cromie, and everyone else, knew of their affair already, she must have meant she had kept from him political secrets that Lockhart didn't want even Britain's naval attaché to know.

In fact, "I cultivate him," she explained to Lockhart. "He is a kind of gramophone…That's why…"[29] She lunched with Cromie in early July in Petrograd, right after she had returned from her post-Ukraine visit to Lockhart in Moscow and just before Savinkov's uprising in Yaroslavl. It was also shortly after she had realized she was pregnant, shortly before she left for Yendel. Cromie told her, "this is…very confidential: Everybody is laughing at Poole [who had recently arrived at Murmansk]. Everyone knows he is here and on an 'arctic expedition' [headed for Archangel]…He considers he is placed above everybody, you [Lockhart] included."[30]

In the same letter, Moura told Lockhart: "Noulens and the Vologda people are rather set against you…and your chief mistake they say is that strong desire to be independent of them." Was it true? Did Lockhart chafe against the domineering Noulens? Certainly, the tone is not fond when he mentions the French ambassador in his memoir. But who told her about Noulens' attitude anyway? Cromie perhaps, but it could have been Arthur Ransome. He had recently returned from visiting the diplomats in Vologda. Moura describes him rushing into her house in Petrograd at about this time, and "stagger[ing] my mother with his Bolshevik appearance."[31] She may have had other sources of information, however, because she knew everyone.

When she was in Moscow, Lockhart would remember: "We [went] everywhere together."[32] He cannot have brought her to covert meetings with counter-revolutionaries and representatives of illegal political parties. Probably he asked her to leave the room, or even the flat, when such people came there to him. He also wrote, however, "We…shared our dangers."[33] This suggests that he shared sensitive information with her even if he did not take her literally every place. At that moment, he was too much in love not to confide his hopes and dreams.

She was too much in love to reveal them. She would have died for him. This is the inescapable conclusion for anyone who reads her letters. Everyone writes love letters; they are not always true. Moura's must have been. Their intensity and scope is almost overwhelming. She writes: "Thinking of your dear hands touching these sheets, your beloved eyes reading of my love to you," and breaks into tears. Almost every letter contains something similar. Whether Lockhart might eventually find the sheer force of her passion constraining or even intimidating was another matter. The point is that whether she had a connection with the Cheka yet or not, Moura would never have betrayed a love so fierce.

CHAPTER 13

THE LOCKHART PLOT
TAKES SHAPE

Once General Poole landed in Archangel, no one thought he would stop there; everyone thought he would march south—and no one believed any longer that he would then march west to reopen the Eastern Front and fight Germans. Everyone assumed the Allies intended to overthrow the Bolsheviks, whatever Allied leaders might say to the contrary. That included Bruce Lockhart in Moscow. He took it as given that the Allies would be successful. They must not think they could install a liberal democracy to replace Bolshevism, however. Perhaps remembering the plan formulated by Boris Savinkov, he tutored the mandarins in Whitehall: "a military administration will be essential for some months to come."[1] Gone was the man who believed that Russians should work out their own destiny even if it meant Bolshevism, and who had wanted his government to reassure them that the Allies had no desire to interfere with any regime they supported.

He did not realize how numerically insignificant Poole's invading force really was. When he did, it left him aghast. For months, he had warned that London must send an impressive contingent, and that a positive Russian response would be proportional to the size of the entering army. As things now stood, Poole was a damp squib, and so would be the reaction of the Russians to whom the general hoped to appeal. It was half past noon on August 14, and Lockhart was sitting disconsolately at the dining table in his flat picking at his lunch. He no longer believed the intervention would be successful.

A month earlier one of the Foreign Office mandarins had scribbled of Lockhart that he was "courageous and tenacious," and "might run personal risks" leading to "politically undesirable" consequences.[2] It was a fair assessment—and prediction. The two Latvians, Sprogis/Shmidkhen and Captain Berzin, knocked at Lockhart's door. When they told him why they had come, it must have seemed to him like an answer to prayer. Suddenly he thought he saw the way forward. It would take courage; it would be risky if the Bolsheviks found out, in which case it certainly could have politically undesirable consequences. None of this deterred him.

Historians have termed the Lockhart Plot, which from this point forward he began to devise, a minor matter in the great sweep of the revolutionary period, because it was unsuccessful. They have judged its chief architect naïve and inexperienced, and therefore doomed to fail; and his chief lieutenant, Reilly, megalomaniacal and unrealistic, even zany.[3] These judgements are mistaken. In the summer of 1918, Bolshevism hung by a thread and the Bolsheviks knew it, just as Lockhart and Reilly did. The new government had failed to end famine, disease, and general breakdown. It depended upon increasingly brutal measures to maintain power. No wonder it had grown unpopular. Moreover, it chiefly relied for defense upon a military element, namely the Latvian Rifle Brigade, that was shot through with pessimism and defeatism, and wanted above all else to return to an independent homeland. All this Lockhart already knew. What he did not know was how to make a connection with anti-Bolshevik Latvian officers to take advantage of their disillusionment. When Berzin and Sprogis/Shmidkhen came to him, therefore, he must have thought them heaven sent. The tragedy from his point of view was that they had not come from heaven or even from Captain Cromie, but from the supremely cunning Felix Dzerzhinsky. Lockhart had his Latvians now, but they were the wrong Latvians.

He knew that Whitehall wanted him to facilitate General Poole's march south from Archangel, which he understood to be intended as a first step in overthrowing Bolshevism, not a staging ground for an assault on Germany's eastern flank. This entire project, of which he had despaired because Poole had so few soldiers, he instantly perceived the Latvians could save. Lockhart did not have carte blanche to plan a counter-revolution, but he must have remembered when the Foreign Office remained conspicuously silent about his connection with Boris Savinkov. He had interpreted that silence correctly—it had been tacit approval of their continuing relationship. He must have recalled, too, that the Foreign Office later had prohibited, ostensibly, further contacts with Savinkov—when in reality it meant for him to maintain them. Now there could be no communication with Whitehall because British cyphers had been compromised, and telegraphic communication interrupted. But Lockhart thought he knew what Whitehall wanted from him, even if the mandarins could not tell him.

Research suggests that London never specifically endorsed the Lockhart Plot; it never knew its details. But research also suggests that Lockhart would not have tried to use the Latvians to overthrow Bolshevism unless he believed that was what London wanted him to do. He thought London would applaud him, as surely it would have—if he proved successful. Probably he did not think much about the possibility of failure.

But it is hard to uncover precisely what Bruce Lockhart did during the last two weeks of August 1918. They marked the climax of his work in Russia, and of his life, although he would live another half century, and do other important work. But, during that fortnight, he and a few co-conspirators attempted nothing less than to wrench the world onto a different path. There is hardly a record of it. Lockhart reported to no one. He already had destroyed his most important papers as a precaution. He sent no cables to Whitehall for reasons adduced above. When he returned to London a few months later, he understood that the British government wanted no mention of a failed plot to overthrow the Russian regime, and so in his report, written immediately after his homecoming, he carefully refrained from referring to one. In 1932, he wrote a self-exculpatory account of "the fairytale" plot uncovered by the Bolsheviks. In it he claimed to have done little more during those two weeks than continue to try to arrange his departure and to play bridge, poker, and football.[4] Significantly and suggestively, his diary, located at the House of Lords Records Office, from which was drawn a published version in 1973, is blank from August 10 to 30, precisely the days during which the plot took final shape.[5]

Did he confide in Moura? One can imagine him doing so—he trusted her implicitly, they were so close, they "shared their dangers"; indeed, there is some evidence that he may have done so (for which see Chapter 16). But the evidence is not conclusive, and so one also can imagine him not confiding in her, at least in detail—he was engaged in more perilous behavior than ever before, would have wanted to spare her from worrying, would have wanted to protect her in case things went wrong. At one point in her life, Moura began to write an autobiography. That might have told us a lot about the Lockhart Plot. Then she destroyed it.

*　*　*

Captain Berzin, tall, powerfully built, formidable, and Jan Sprogis/Shmidkhen, short, pale, and clever, but also brash, decisive, and adventurous, stood in Lockhart's dining room. Each Latvian mistakenly thought the other to be a traitor. Both correctly deemed Lockhart to be a counter-revolutionary—and hated him for it. They saw before them "a strong athletic man, about thirty years of age. He did not look like an Englishman, there was something Russian about his appearance. He comported himself politely, attentively, spoke Russian without the slightest accent."[6]

Was Moura present? If so, no one mentioned it, and anyway surely Lockhart would have asked her to leave when his guests indicated the nature of their visit. This they did by showing him their package. Sprogis/Shmidkhen handed it to Lockhart. "He took a long time reading over Cromie's recommendation letter."[7] "I scrutinized the letter carefully," Lockhart confirmed in his memoir. "It was unmistakably from ... that gallant officer."[8]

The British agent asked his guests what they wanted. As he remembered fifteen years later, Berzin did most of the talking:

> While the Latvians had supported the Bolshevik revolution, they could not fight the Bolsheviks' battles indefinitely. Their one ambition was to return to their own country. As long as Germany was powerful this was impossible. On the other hand, if the Allies, as now seemed likely, were to win the war, it was clear that the Allies and not Germany would have the final word regarding the future of Latvia. They were therefore determined not to put themselves wrong with the Allies. They had no intention of fighting against General Poole's forces at Archangel. If they were sent to that front, they would surrender. Could I arrange matters with

General Poole so that they would not be shot down by the Allied troops?

It was a paraphrase of the report he wrote for the Foreign Office in 1918. He wrote both times also that he responded sympathetically, but deferred a decision. He would consult his colleagues. The two Latvians should return tomorrow evening.

The Bolsheviks recalled the conversation differently. Berzin wrote a report of the entire affair during the first week of September, almost immediately after the plot had been defeated. According to him, at this initial meeting, once Lockhart ascertained their bona fides and realized why they had approached him, he mainly wanted to know "the mood of the Latvian units and whether it is possible to count on them in the event of a coup." The Scot stressed the crucial role the Latvians could play in such an action, and "*emphasized, strongly and multiple times that money is no object* [an interested reader underlined the phrase in Berzin's account]." Berzin and Sprogis/Shmidkhen must have told him that their comrades in the Brigades were near breaking point. Cold-bloodedly, Lockhart then suggested their estrangement from the Bolsheviks would increase "if they are not given provisions."[9]

If Sprogis/Shmidkhen wrote an account of the fateful meeting, it has not turned up. Thus, there are only Lockhart's two descriptions and Berzin's. There is contemporary supplemental material, however. Berzin reported to both K. A. Peterson, commissar of the Latvian Rifle Soviet Division, and to Jacov Peters. They each summarized the meeting in writings of their own, either nearly immediately or within months of the event. Both repeated Berzin's claim that Lockhart suggested starving the Riflemen in order to undermine their loyalty to the regime, and that he offered money to bring the Latvians on board, including money for the two with whom he was talking.[10] Peterson added proudly that Berzin explained to Lockhart that his men were patriots, not mercenaries, and would never accept British funds. "The old diplomat of 'the most cultured' country failed the exam miserably," wrote Peterson, "while comrade Berzin, having come into contact with 'diplomacy' for the first time in his life, passed the exam with an 'A'."

There is additional, troubling, material about the meeting, but it is inadmissible. During the purges of 1937–8, both Berzin and Peters fell foul of the Stalin regime, which accused them of having harbored Latvian nationalist sentiments all along, and of having worked against the Soviet state even in 1918.[11] They both "confessed" to this crime, but it did not save them. Both died at the hands of executioners. Three leading historians of Stalin's Great Terror unanimously advised the author not to trust these "confessions."[12] Vladimir Khaustov, former head of the History Faculty at the Federal Security Service (FSB) Academy in Moscow, and himself an FSB colonel, agreed: "These testimonials must not be believed."[13]

Discounting testimony extracted in dubious circumstances and possibly by abhorrent means, which version of the initial meeting, the British or the Russian, is more trustworthy? Lockhart would admit repeatedly in later years that his various accounts of the plot were less than complete and true.[14] On the other side of the ledger, it is possible that the Bolsheviks, writing in the immediate aftermath of the event, wanted to trump up their case against him. After all, they had just arrested and intended to try him in court. The reader should proceed with all this in mind.

The day after the initial meeting in Lockhart's flat, London received a cable from General Poole: "In order to take over all duties in towns such as Murmansk and Archangel could you spare me a garrison battalion and so relieve active troops with dependable personnel? I find it very necessary already, and when I occupy Kotlas, Vologda and Viatka shall want it very much more." Viatka (present day Kirov) is more than 500 kilometers southeast of Kotlas and about double that distance east of Vologda, which is to say not remotely on the way to Germany—which is odd if the general intended to reopen an Eastern Front. He added, "a brass band should accompany it, as this is invaluable for recruiting."[15] Lockhart, meeting with his French counterparts on the afternoon of August 15, however, was trying to render additional troops dispatched from Britain, or even musicians, completely unnecessary. He wanted Latvians. "I thrashed out the whole matter with General Lavergne [French military attaché] and M. Grenard, the French Consul General."[16] Presumably, while he was doing that, Berzin and Sprogis/Shmidkhen were thrashing out matters too, with Peters and Dzerzhinsky.

That evening, Berzin and Sprogis/Shmidkhen returned to Lockhart's apartment at "19:30 o'clock," as the punctilious Berzin recorded. There they met Grenard and Sidney Reilly, whom Lockhart introduced as Mr. Constantine (and whom Sprogis/Shmidkhen must have known already from the meetings in Petrograd with Captain Cromie). There is no mention of Moura. As for what then transpired, Grenard never wrote about it, nor, as far as can be told, did Sprogis/Shmidkhen, nor even Reilly in his "autobiography" (much of which was edited and polished by his widow—or rather, by one of them, his fourth wife). Lockhart wrote in his memoir only that, "I saw the two Latvians, gave them a paper saying 'please admit bearer, who has an important communication for General Poole, through the English lines,' and put them in touch with Reilly."[17] In the 1918 report he added that he quoted to them President Wilson on the rights of small nations "and self-definition," and that "Berzin expressed himself satisfied with this statement." Also, that Berzin dwelt upon the need to protect Latvian prisoners of war held by the Allies or Russians, and therefore practically insisted that he and his colleagues discuss the matter with General Poole in Archangel, which is why Lockhart provided him with the "paper" that would serve as introduction.

But this is clearly insufficient. In reality, Lockhart must have judged this meeting to be a climacteric in his months-long clandestine operations against Bolshevism. Without consulting London, because he could not, but also because he believed that he need not, he took irrevocable steps that night: he wound up the spring. From now on, the plot would move forward—until the Cheka put an end to it.

For a more detailed account of what transpired, we turn again to Captain Berzin. He wrote that Lockhart acted as interpreter for Grenard when the latter addressed him and Sprogis/Shmidkhen: "Judging by your conversation yesterday with the ambassador [sic Lockhart] the fate of Latvia greatly concerns you. If we, the Allies, succeed in wresting it from the Germans, we although lacking specific authority from our governments, nonetheless can promise you a reward for your cooperation—self-determination in the complete sense of that word." Berzin repeated Grenard's statement verbatim in his report, and Peters reiterated it in his.

As for other issues mentioned that night: Berzin expressed concern "lest…we will be wholly dependent upon the Allies." The two diplomats tried to reassure him: We "will do everything [we] can so as to satisfy all the demands of the Latvians." They suggested that Berzin recruit within the Rifle Brigade to help organize a nationalist Latvian political party. They asked how many Latvian soldiers were stationed in Moscow. They reiterated that these should not fight against General Poole. They again brought up money, and this time Berzin estimated that it would take between four and five million rubles (between £2.75 million and nearly £3.5 million in today's values) to make all arrangements. This suggests the experienced hand of Dzerzhinsky or Peters in the background, for in agreeing to provide the sum, which they did immediately, Lockhart and Grenard implicated themselves beyond denial in counter-revolution. There is evidence that they were prepared to find ten million rubles.[18]

Then the fatal step: Lockhart provided not a single piece of paper, as he wrote in the memoir, but three passes so that the Latvians could consult with General Poole: one for Shmidkhen, another for an imaginary officer whose name Berzin made up on the spot, "Krysz Krankl," and the third for Jan Buikis, recommended to Lockhart by Sprogis/Shmidkhen. This is how Buikis got back into the game, and is why he could write convincingly about later aspects of the plot nearly fifty years afterward.

At the meeting's end, Lockhart instructed the two Latvians: "Don't come here anymore."[19] It was not a matter of cowardice, he never shrank from personal danger, and he intended to monitor the plot from the shadows and to pull its strings for as long as he could, but he was not an active espionage agent. That is one reason why he instructed Berzin to communicate with him henceforth indirectly, via Reilly.

There was another reason. He expected to be detained and expatriated shortly, as did consul General Grenard. That too explains the presence of Reilly. "If on the departure of the Diplomatic Corps all the money had not been handed over, drafts would be left with Lt. Riley [sic], to enable us to carry out the scheme." This is the voice of George Hill, with whom Reilly had remained in close contact.[20]

Previously Hill had operated above ground, as an RAF officer advising Trotsky on the creation of a Russian air force and even helping to establish a Bolshevik secret service, while organizing his networks of spies, couriers, and sabotage units. They had worked against the Germans in Ukraine and south Russia, sometimes in concert with the Bolsheviks. But also, he had set up eight Moscow safe houses, as well as disguises and false identities, anticipating the time when he would have to go underground to work against the present Russian government. That time had come at the beginning of August when General Poole arrived in Archangel and the Bolsheviks began making things difficult for all Allied nationals in the country. Reilly too had dived underground then, hence his identification by Lockhart as Mr. Constantine. Hill and Reilly would now work together on the conspiracy Lockhart had set in motion. Reilly led the way. Hill thought that he "knew the situation better than any other British officer in Russia, and as also he had the more delicate threads in his hand, I therefore agreed to cooperate with him and leave the political control and our policy in his hands."[21]

It is worth quoting Hill's report again: "The proposed turning of the Lettish troops to our cause...could not be achieved without very seriously affecting the Moscow and Petrograd centres. The simultaneous change on the fronts and at Moscow and Petrograd would have destroyed the Soviet Government."[22] Precisely so: whatever disclaimers Whitehall might produce at the time or later about invading Russia only to protect supplies from the Germans and to reconstitute an Eastern Front, in fact they aimed to destroy Soviet power from the moment Poole embarked from Murmansk, if not from long before.

As for Bruce Lockhart: that was his aim too, beyond the shadow of a doubt. Once he thought he had grasped the increment of strength to the counter-revolution that his Latvian visitors represented, he did not hesitate. He would be the expediter, as he knew London wished him to be; he would put the Latvians in touch with General Poole who, with their assistance, could march on and capture Vologda after all. Everything would follow from that, because Vologda was the last important stop on the Siberian Railway before Petrograd to the west and Moscow to the south. Whoever controlled Vologda could threaten either of those cities militarily; and also control Russia's access to Siberia's rich granaries. Bruce Lockhart, not Sidney Reilly, was the originator of the "Lockhart Plot," and its aim was to destroy Bolshevism. Having set the clock ticking, he intended now to step back and let the true undercover men take over. Only, neither he nor they realized that the Latvians belonged not to them, but to the Cheka.

PART IV

THE FALL

CHAPTER 14

THE LOCKHART PLOT

O n Saturday afternoon, August 17, Jan Sprogis returned to the flat he shared with Jan Buikis and Jan Avotin. "I'm going to a secret rendezvous tonight," he told them. "Lockhart will be buying the Latvian Rifles from Berzin." Avotin did not take his friend seriously, but he should have.[1] At seven o'clock that evening, Lieutenant "Shmidkhen" (as he had now again become) met Reilly and Berzin (whom he still thought a traitor), at the Café Tramblais on Tsvetnoi Boulevard. Almost immediately Reilly handed over 700,000 rubles (worth approximately £481,250 today) for suborning Latvian Rifles. It was merely a first installment, he promised. Of that sum, half a million came from the French, and the remainder from the Americans. The gift of 200,000 rubles exactly "matched a large special advance to Kalamatiano in this period."[2] Lockhart must have spoken that day with Consul-General DeWitt Clinton Poole, who authorized the expenditure—in which case, the plot had American as well as French backing.

Then, there at the cafe, and later walking along the street past its famous flower stalls and market, Reilly explained the rest of the plan. Of course, it was not his plan only; Lockhart and his French colleagues had shaped it as much as he; perhaps they had shaped it more, having only brought him into it when they realized that one way or another they would be leaving Russia while he would be staying. This seems probable, as Reilly practically discounted ownership of the plan right away, an important point given that later he would assume, and also be saddled with, full responsibility for it: "the plan of action … was developed by one French general, whose surname he did not tell me," Berzin reported to the Cheka only a few days later.[3] It is reasonable to suppose that Grenard, with whom Lockhart had consulted on the 15th, brought in the head of the French military mission in Russia, General Lavergne, who supplied the necessary military expertise.

Whoever designed it, the plan was audacious and ruthless, and reflected the realization that bread riots had helped to spark the February Revolution and could spark yet another. Thus, Allied agents, who previously had deployed their skills as saboteurs against the Germans in occupied regions of Russia, would deploy them now against the Bolsheviks. Reilly may not have known that General Lavergne had just requested from the Deuxième Bureau in Paris "poison for livestock and rot for cereals and potatoes [sent in] reduced packets, by preference boxes of conserves,"[4] but he told the two Latvians of plans to destroy bridges and rail lines to interrupt food supplies. The hungry people of Petrograd and Moscow, including the Latvian Riflemen, would understand only that the present regime could not feed them. Meanwhile, Reilly claimed, other Allied agents would be stockpiling food in depots close to the big cities. It would be released, and people fed, immediately after the counter-revolution.

That was the backdrop, the precondition for revolt. As for the main outlines: Reilly wanted Berzin to arrange the transfer of two Latvian regiments from Moscow to Vologda. There they would perform the job originally intended for the Czech Legion: capture the city and turn it over to General Poole and his forces when they arrived. Then there would be an uprising in Moscow, either at a meeting of the Sovnarkom (Council of People's Commissars), or at a joint plenary session of the TsIK (Central Executive Committee) and the Moscow Soviet. Lenin, Trotsky, and other important Bolsheviks would be present on both occasions. A small group of desperados, led by Reilly himself, but backed by another brigade of Latvians ostensibly guarding the event, would arrest them all. "In case there was any hitch in the proceedings," Reilly promised, "the other conspirators and myself would carry grenades."[5] Simultaneously, additional Latvian regiments would be capturing the Moscow state bank, telephone and telegraph offices, and main rail stations. Then the leaders of the coup would declare a military dictatorship, pending the arrival of Allied troops from Vologda.

The conspirators did not rely entirely upon the Latvians. As we know, Lockhart and Reilly already had links with the underground White Guards of the Moscow National Center. In his "autobiography" Reilly claimed that 60,000 of them, led by a former Tsarist officer, General Yudenich, would emerge from hiding as soon as the coup began. In fact, Yudenich was involved with the Petrograd plotters at this time. Later, he would organize the White forces in the Baltic provinces against the Bolsheviks. Probably, he would have played no role in Moscow events, but the Moscow White Guards most certainly would have. Reilly said they would form up in pre-arranged units to patrol the city and maintain order in working-class districts where resistance might be expected.[6]

Lockhart and Reilly also had established links with the Russian Orthodox Church, as we know. The Patriarch Tikhon, to whom they had delivered a suitcase of money earlier in the summer, had arranged for public prayers and sermons supporting the coup.

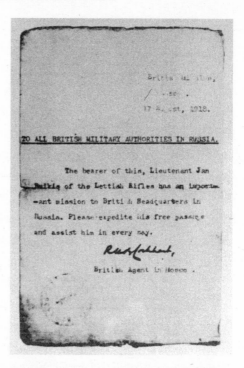

Briti h M son,
/ .so .
17 A st, 1918.

TO ALL BRITISH MILITARY AUTHORITIES IN RUSSIA.

The bearer of this, Lieutenant Jan
Buikis of the Lettish Rifles has an import-
-ant mission to Briti h Headquarters in
Russia. Please expedite his free passage
and assist him in every way.

British Agent in Moscow .

Figure 23. One of the laissez-passers signed by Lockhart

The Patriarch himself would announce a prayer of thanksgiving on the morrow of the uprising.

Reilly handed over the three passes to General Poole's headquarters in Archangel promised by Lockhart two nights ago. They bore that day's date, August 17. He gave the Latvians a cyphered message also from Lockhart, to General Poole, another sign that the Scot had been busy that day, remained involved with the plot, wished it to go forward.

At the close of the meeting the three men went their separate ways. Berzin brought the message and the three passes directly to the Cheka. They were never used, except as evidence against the plotters. The ciphered message to General Poole must likewise have landed in Cheka files, although no historian has ever cited it.

Perhaps it was an anodyne message merely introducing the three Letts to the British general. Or perhaps the Cheka never decoded it. At any rate, after reporting to Peters, Sprogis/Shmidkhen returned to the flat he shared with the two other Ians. Given what we know of him, probably he was crowing. And Reilly reported to Bruce Lockhart.

It must have been late at night by now, yet Lockhart had with him both General Lavergne and Consul-General Grenard. Moura, too, must have been present since she lived there. Did Lockhart ask her to leave the room when the "Ace of Spies" appeared? He makes no mention of her in his account of the evening, but as will become apparent later she almost certainly knew something of Reilly's role in the affair. In fact, in his memoir, Lockhart minimized the significance of the rendezvous altogether, while nevertheless making an important point about it. He wrote only that Reilly returned from meeting Sprogis/Shmidkhen and Berzin to say that "he might be able, with Lettish help, to stage a counterrevolution in Moscow. This suggestion was categorically turned down both by General Lavergne, Grenard and myself."[7]

Do not believe it. Firstly, Latvian help for counter-revolution had been the subject of the previous meeting in Lockhart's flat, and moreover Lockhart and his colleagues had been thinking and plotting about how to involve the Latvians in counter-revolution for a while now. Why would they categorically turn down the Latvian offer conveyed by Reilly at this critical moment? They would not have. Secondly, a few days later, Lockhart told the American ambassador's secretary, Norman Amour, who had stayed behind when the ambassador fled to Archangel, that he had "the opportunity to buy off Lettish troops [and] that the scheme was known to and approved by French and American consuls."[8]

Thirdly, after both of them cheated death and returned safely to England, Reilly presented Lockhart with a silver box "from his faithful lieutenant, in remembrance of events in Moscow in August & September" 1918.[9] "Faithful?" "Lieutenant?" These are not the words of a man who launched a plot to overthrow the Bolsheviks with Latvian help against his chief's wishes—and that Lockhart was, indeed, his chief in Russia and Reilly his lieutenant is made clear by another Foreign Office document that describes the young Scot "using" the older man "for some political purpose."[10] Fourthly, at the end of his life, Lockhart confided to his son that in reality, "he worked much more closely with Reilly than he had publicly indicated."[11] And finally, Reilly had just told the two Latvians that a French general designed the plot in the first place; why then would General Lavergne (probably the French general to whom Reilly had referred) now categorically reject it? Reilly cannot have been introducing the subject of Latvian help for counter-revolution to Lockhart, Lavergne, and Grenard for the first time as Lockhart implied in the memoir, and therefore it is impossible to accept Lockhart's claim that the three of them summarily turned it down. Surely, he and the two Frenchmen blessed Reilly's work and instructed him to continue.

None of them realized they had been tricked, but in fact Bolshevik knowledge of the plot would soon reach the very top. As soon as Berzin's commanding officer learned "of the diabolical plans of the malefactors," he warned Lenin personally. The Bolshevik leader "was merely amused...laughed heartily and exclaimed: 'just like in the novels.'"[12] That did not stop his lieutenants from taking precautions. Dzerzhinsky and Peters kept close watch over the entire affair. They debriefed Sprogis/Shmidkhen and Berzin after every meeting with Reilly. The Cheka also assigned men to keep Lockhart's flat under constant surveillance because, as Peters explained, "all suspicious individuals and individuals about whom has already been established that they are active members of the counterrevolutionary-espionage organization…frequently visited this apartment."[13] According to Jan Buikis, the Cheka had yet another way to fool the plotters. It knew Lockhart would want to keep tabs on the Latvians—not by following them himself, but by having someone he trusted following them, so Dzerzhinsky instructed them to tell the Scot whenever they were going to meet: "usually at the Olen'yi Ponds and the territory of the amusement rides at the Sokol'niki Park."[14] It sounds like a scene from the great Orson Welles film, *The Third Man*, in which a giant Ferris wheel figures, except that in this case British surveillance of the amusement park "only confirmed our reliability and further reinforced [Lockhart's] trust in us."[15]

* * *

The second time Reilly, Berzin, and Sprogis/Shmidkhen met alone (there is no mention of Buikis in these or subsequent meetings) was August 19, two days after the meeting at Café Tremblais. This time they convened at 4 Griboedou Alley, a safe house taken by Berzin at Reilly's suggestion. This time, Reilly had discrete tasks for his Latvian co-conspirators (as he deemed them) in addition to the broad ones he had outlined previously. He wanted to know about guns situated along a main east–west railway line between Rogozhno, which is far to the west of Moscow nearly all the way to Latvia, and Cherkizovo, which is practically a western Moscow suburb: there were nine artillery batteries of five-inch guns, and two batteries of British-made eight-inch guns along this route. "It would be desirable to learn about the condition in which these batteries now are." Conceivably Reilly wanted to know the military obstacles along the railway, should British-subsidized units, secretly formed in Latvia, head east to help their brethren in the anti-Bolshevik movement. Or, he may have thought the guns could be stolen and brought to Moscow and used in the insurrection.

Reilly also wanted information about a railway station at Mitkino, just west of Moscow, where informants told him 700 Latvian soldiers guarded several carloads of the Tsarist regime's gold and banknotes. These must be seized when the coup began; they could help to finance the new government. Then he turned to the issue of propaganda among the Brigades. His Latvian colleagues should gain access to a printing press; should arrange publication of anti-Bolshevik, Latvian nationalist pamphlets and proclamations; should "obtain people from among their milieu who could take it upon themselves to read the appeals." They should form a Latvian patriotic anti-communist committee.[16]

Reilly would meet with the pair several times more during the coming days. He continued to give them money, between 1.2 and 1.4 million rubles in all (that is to say, up to the equivalent of £962,500 in today's values). He and Berzin discussed Jacov Peters: "only a bullet would cure him of his Bolshevism," Reilly opined. They also discussed what to do with Lenin and Trotsky after they had been arrested. Later, all the British principals, including Reilly, said the plan had been to hold them up to ridicule by parading them through the streets of Moscow in their underwear. This is not to be taken seriously. According to Buikis, Lockhart told him, "with Lenin alive our undertaking will be a failure."[17] According to Berzin, Reilly said: "it would be better to shoot Lenin and Trotsky on the day of the coup." Surely, this was the intention. Lockhart had not blinked when he learned of Savinkov's plan to shoot Bolshevik leaders earlier that year, nor had the Foreign Office: it is naïve to think that he or any of the others would have blinked now. Conceivably the plotters would have humiliated the two communists first—and then directed that they be shot.

There is another reason to believe that the conspirators would not have shrunk from murder. Both Hill and Reilly kept in touch with Lieutenant Ernest Boyce, the man whom Moura thought suspected her of having spied for Germany. Apparently, Boyce had asked another agent, "G," probably a Russian, "if he was prepared to do away with one or two prominent members of the Soviet Government." Whether this was in connection with Lockhart's larger plot is uncertain. But "G" was threatening to make this information public, and Boyce's superior, Lieutenant Webster, ostensibly a passport control officer, "felt it was advisable to pay up rather than having anything fresh brought up against us."[18]

Reilly often discussed with the two Latvians what should be the date of the Moscow coup. He learned that the Bolshevik principals would not all meet together until September 6, a week later than originally scheduled. At this, a warning bell should have sounded in his ear because changing the date would give the authorities more time to prepare to defeat him. He did not hear the bell. He thought the postponement gave him and his colleagues more time to arrange the defeat of Bolshevism.

Did Reilly report to the progenitors of the plot, as the two Latvians reported to Dzerzhinsky and Peters? In their memoirs both Lockhart and Reilly claimed that he did not, but that cannot be taken as definitive either. Berzin, in his coerced testimony of 1938, said that Reilly occasionally consulted with Lockhart before deciding what he, Berzin, should do next. Given the circumstances under which this statement was obtained the reader may accept or reject it. But Lockhart, in his "Secret and Confidential Memorandum on the Alleged Allied Conspiracy in Russia," written shortly after he got home, said: "I saw Reilly as rarely as possible," and then admitted to meeting him at least twice during the two-week period after August 15. On the first occasion Reilly "expressed great confidence in Berzin—a confidence I frankly admit which we all shared." Then on "about the 25th August," Lockhart saw Reilly to arrange a meeting for him with "the American and French consuls and General Lavergne."

This last is a curious and significant admission, for a crucial meeting did take place on the evening of that date. It may have been held so the men in the field could report to their superiors. Most of the Allied conspirators attended. American Consul General DeWitt Clinton Poole hosted the gathering at the American consulate, which was considered safer than any venue the British or French could provide. Yet the total number attending cannot be determined. Grenard presided, even though the meeting convened under American auspices. Lavergne was there, also the chief French undercover agent and saboteur in Russia, Colonel Henri de Verthamon who, previously, had engaged in "destructive work" against the Germans in Ukraine.[19] Poole made sure to bring Kalamatiano. Reilly and his close colleague in espionage, George Hill, represented Britain. According to Peters, Lockhart attended too; according to every other account he did not—but the sentence in Lockhart's own report cited above suggests that he may have, and is accepted by Robert Service, one of the most reliable, knowledgeable, and sophisticated historians of the subject.[20] One of the Latvians (we do not know which) attended as well, and an additional Frenchman, René Marchand, a journalist working for the French newspaper *Le Figaro*. Somehow Grenard had obtained the impression that journalism was his cover, and that, really, he worked for French intelligence, but Grenard was mistaken. He had invited a cuckoo into the nest.

Two weeks previously, Poole had brought together the underground men, Kalamatiano, Verthamon, and Reilly, to tell them they must be ready to cooperate when the aboveground men, the consuls and officials such as himself, Grenard, and Lockhart, left Russia.[21] The three had taken him at his word, as René Marchand was about to discover. What he heard horrified him.

"I learnt that an English agent was arranging to destroy the railway bridge across the river Volkoff, before the station of Zvanka," Marchand wrote. "Now, it requires but a glance at the map to see that the destruction of this bridge would mean *the complete starvation* of Petrograd [emphasis in the original]." The English agent to whom he referred was Sidney Reilly. Then, as the journalist remembered: "A French agent added to this that he had already attempted to blow up the bridge of Tcherepovetz, which as far as the provisioning of Petrograd is concerned, would have the same effect as the destruction of the bridge of Zvanka." This time the speaker must have been Verthamon, who went on to sketch out his plans for derailing and destroying rolling stock on various lines. "Not for a moment," Marchand was to write subsequently, "did [any of this] disturb the equanimity of Poole or Grenard, to whom the plan, it seemed, was no novelty."[22]

Obviously, such measures would not hurt Germany, with whom Britain, France, and America were at war, but only the "inoffensive and toiling Russian population."[23] As a French patriot, Marchand thought that such measures could be condoned, perhaps, if the Russian government intended to side with Germany against the Allies and resume the war, but he could see no evidence that it had or would. To the contrary, German occupation of various parts of the country only magnified Russian hatred of her. The actions of the Allied agents were not merely immoral then, he concluded, but also counterproductive.

At one point during the evening, the Latvian representative "raised the question of Latvian autonomy." Afterward, he would report to Jacov Peters that several present had mocked him, "as if now is [not] the time to be occupied with such a trifle."[24]

Eventually, Consul General Grenard took the floor. "It is of the utmost importance that Bolshevism be compromised in the eyes of Western Socialists," he lectured. "Unquestionably there is some kind of agreement between the Bolsheviks and the Germans...A telegram from the Bolshevik military commissariat, or some similar document, confirming the above supposition would be of enormous value. It should, I think, be possible to get hold of something of the kind..." He meant that a document demonstrating that Lenin and Trotsky worked for Germany could be fabricated if necessary. It would lend credence to the old charge that Lenin had accepted German gold to return to Russia, that his Bolsheviks had been bought.

Marchand would write about Grenard's role at the meeting only after the war, but he wished to put an end to the Allies' anti-Bolshevik machinations now. Thus, the form of his initial protest: a letter of remonstration addressed to French president, Henri Poincaré, in which he condemned rogue agents, but not accredited representatives of the Allied governments who instructed them. This also allowed him to maintain his reputation as a loyal Frenchman and independent reporter. He did not wish to be seen as Bolshevism's tame journalist. Nor did the Bolsheviks wish him to be seen that way. When the shocked Frenchman came to them with news of the meeting, Lenin and Dzerzhinsky suggested his course of action. He should write to the French president and leave the letter in his flat where Cheka searchers could pretend surprise when they found it. They would bring it to their masters who would know how best to make use of it. This is what happened, but nobody has ever believed Marchand did not intend for his letter to be discovered.

We can imagine Dzerzhinsky, at this point, alone in his room at the Lubianka late at night, reading and rereading reports from Berzin and Sprogis/Shmidkhen and Buikis and Peters, and planning what to do once he had the letter by Marchand, and satisfaction shining from his hooded, bloodshot eyes. It cannot be accident that he reassumed the reins of the Cheka on this very day, August 25.

* * *

Denis Garstin had died ten days earlier, on August 15, the day after Lockhart first met the Latvians. His position in Moscow had grown increasingly difficult during the late spring and early summer as the Bolsheviks grew ever warier of Allied intentions, and placed ever more onerous restrictions upon Allied citizens and officials in their country. Many who no longer could carry out their duties, or who had no pressing reason to stay, and who could do so, began planning to get out. Once the Bolshevik regime decided to no longer recognize their passports this became more difficult.

Garstin had turned from being an admirer of Bolshevik idealism in January and February to being an enemy of Bolshevik excess in May, as we have seen. He certainly approved and may have participated in Lockhart's counter-revolutionary activities during June and July. By the end of that month, however, he had begun looking for a way out of Moscow. British authorities summoned him to Archangel, where he could continue his mission under General Poole, who arrived there on August 2. But the Bolsheviks had forbidden officers attached to the Allied military missions to move about the country.

It appears that Garstin set out from the Russian capital for Petrograd on foot,[25] then somehow made his way to Kem on the western side of the White Sea,[26] and finally sailed across, arriving in Archangel in the first week of August "after many perilous escapes and adventures."[27] Better they had caught him. By now British and Russian forces were clashing bloodily. General Poole's troops had pushed Bolshevik soldiers back on Lake Onega. Garstin "greatly distinguished himself" in the continuing southern military thrust. On August 11, in what he thought would be "a nice quiet expedition," he led a squad that captured an armored car from the enemy (as the Bolsheviks had now become for British soldiers in northwest Russia), and then attempted to capture another. Bullets flew once more—and this time one of them killed Captain Denis Garstin. He had with him when he died a wristwatch with strap, a map of the region, a pocket diary, tobacco pouch and fifty-six rubles in various denominations. He was 28 years old.[28]

His friend, Arthur Ransome, likewise managed to get out of Moscow—on August 2 in his case—just as General Poole was arriving in Archangel. The reasons for his leaving were complicated. He told his editor in London that he did it because "'an interned correspondent, or one who un-interned is unable to telegraph freely, is no use to anyone."[29] That would have been part of it, but there was a lot more.

Ransome thought that when the Bolsheviks clamped down on Allied citizens they were only doing what they had to do to survive. Nevertheless, he did not think they would survive: if the Germans did not succeed in overthrowing them, as had seemed likely in February and March, then the Allies would, as began to seem likely in May and June. The Bolsheviks read these tea leaves too. They would resist as long and as fiercely as possible, but they wanted to establish an international press bureau in Stockholm to serve their interests whether they remained in power or not. They thought Ransome could help them do it.

The job appealed to Ransome for more than one reason. From Stockholm he could send independent-minded articles about Russia to Britain as he always had been doing, now based upon exclusive access to documents provided by the Bolsheviks to the bureau; he could continue helping his Bolshevik friends by making the bureau work; and he could continue providing intelligence, likewise based upon information given the bureau, to the British Foreign Office. He could have his cake and eat it. But there was more going on even than that. His relationship with Evgenia Petrovna Shelypina, "the big girl," had deepened over the course of the spring and summer. He wanted her to come with him to Stockholm. On June 19 she agreed to do so.

It was not clear the Bolsheviks would let her go, but the British controlled ingress and egress at Murmansk. Ransome asked Bruce Lockhart for a passport listing Evgenia as his wife. Lockhart knew that Ransome had a wife at home already, but then so did he; and he had a lover in Russia, just as Ransome did; and he too was thinking about how to get her out. Lockhart had betrayed Ransome on a political level, but he proved to be a loyal friend. Again, however, wheels within wheels: Lockhart also knew, or thought he did, that there would be counter-revolution soon in Moscow. Ransome would probably be safe even if vengeful Whites went prowling through the city streets looking for Reds, but what of Ransome's lover who happened to be Leon Trotsky's secretary? Lockhart wanted to protect her, albeit without saying why particularly. He wrote to the Foreign Office: "A very useful lady who has worked here in extremely confidential position in a Government Office, desires to give up her present position. She has been of the greatest service to me...I wish to have authority to put her to Mr. Ransome's passport as his wife and facilitate her departure via Murmansk."[30]

Possibly there was more to it even than that. It is not inconceivable that Ransome's best friend among the Bolshevik leadership, Karl Radek, a puckish, sardonic hard man, warned him that he should leave Russia while he still could. Ransome certainly appears to have left Moscow in a hurry, "without saying a word to the Members of the [British] Mission" even though he knew "there was a party in the Soviet, headed by Radek, which wished to go to extreme lengths with the Mission on account of the British landing at Archangel."[31] Thus, if Lockhart earlier had betrayed Arthur Ransome by turning away from him politically without saying so, then perhaps Ransome paid him back now by getting out of Moscow in the nick of time, and leaving his friend to face the consequences of his pro-interventionist actions. In the end, Ransome traveled not on the British passport provided by Lockhart (issued without permission of the Foreign Office), but with papers provided by Radek. Evgenia did not take advantage of Lockhart's help either, but accompanied a Bolshevik delegation to Berlin and made her way to Sweden after.

*　　*　　*

On Tuesday, August 27, Reilly met the Latvians at the safe house on Griboedou Alley for what proved to be the last time. He wanted Berzin to meet the counter-revolutionaries in Petrograd. He would be traveling there Thursday night and could introduce him to the most important figures next day. Berzin agreed to go—he had to review the Sixth Latvian Regiment in Petrograd anyway in his capacity as a military inspector.[32] He would leave tomorrow. Reilly gave him an address in Petrograd where they could meet safely between eleven o'clock and noon on Thursday. It was the Torgovaia Street apartment where he posed as the married businessman, Constantine Massino, with Elena Mikhailovna Boguzhevskaia, his mistress who was masquerading as his wife.

What happened next is unclear. Avotin, reporting what Sprogis/Shmidkhen told him, claimed that before catching the train for Petrograd, Berzin first consulted with Peters and Dzerzhinsky at the Lubianka. Perhaps one of Lockhart's men spotted him entering the building, or one of Reilly's men did. At any rate, Reilly found out. Thursday, before he left on the night train for Petrograd, he confronted Sprogis/Shmidkhen in a towering rage: "Your protégé is cavorting with the Cheka and deserves a bullet." The young Lett tried to pass it off: he said that commanders of the Latvian Riflemen were summoned to the Lubianka all the time for all sorts of reasons. In fact, he was deeply worried and, once his dangerous colleague had gone, quickly consulted with Peters too, no doubt taking proper precautions on his way to meet him. Peters sent off a telegram of warning, via the Petrograd Cheka, but it appears to have reached Berzin too late to affect subsequent events.

In his report a week later, Berzin made no mention of any of this, but then his carelessness did not cast him in a favorable light. In his coerced 1938 testimony, however, he said that he did indeed speak with Peters just before leaving for Petrograd—about how to better serve Lockhart and Reilly, which was what his Stalinist interlocutors wanted him to say. Still, conceivably, he and Peters did confer just before he made the journey, in which case, conceivably Reilly did come to know what he had done, as Avotin believed.

On Friday, August 30, Berzin (now in Petrograd) went to Reilly's Torgovaia Street address at 11 a.m., as directed. The concierge had instructions to admit "Mr. Massino's" "brother," but the apartment was empty because "Massino's" "wife" had gone to work and "Massino" had not yet arrived. Berzin took this opportunity to search it. In a drawer in a desk in the bedroom he found an envelope addressed to Elena. Inside he found the business card of Sidney George Reilly, and an address: Sheremetyevo Alley 3, Apt. 85 and some scribbled numbers. The address turned out to be a Moscow safe house used by the American agent Xenophon Kalamatiano. So far as the Cheka was concerned it was another link in the chain connecting the Allied Secret Services to Lockhart's plot.[33] Indeed when Berzin gave the card to Dzerzhinsky, it made possible the Cheka's first step in winding up Kalamatiano's network of agents and sub-agents, and his eventual arrest.

Also in the envelope was a second card on which Reilly had written to Elena: "Accept my tender gratitude for having filled 'that chalice that sparkles' today." Berzin then found a piece of paper on which was written: "Central Foodstuffs Directorate, Iosif Iosifovich Khrizhanovski." This had meaning to a man who knew the Allies and their counter-revolutionary friends intended first to starve and then to feed his countrymen.

Perhaps luckily for Berzin, Reilly did not appear. At noon the Latvian left the apartment and then, by chance, spotted the "Ace of Spies" riding in a horse-drawn cab, headed for Torgovaia Street. When he saw Berzin, Reilly stopped the vehicle and jumped out. He explained that his train had arrived extremely late. Berzin asked when he could meet the White leaders. Reilly told him to come back to the apartment at six o'clock that evening; a White Guard officer would be there then. What he was to do during the interval was not specified, but the typescript of Berzin's 1918 report in the Lockhart Collection at Stanford ends: "Further Berzin went on to describe...his meeting with the conspirators as well as with their British leader Cromy [sic]..."[34] If such a meeting did take place, the most likely time for it would have been that afternoon, August 30. What transpired at the meeting must remain a matter of speculation.

Anyway, Berzin reappeared at the Torgovaia Street flat at 6 p.m., punctual as ever, but no White Guard officer was present. Reilly made excuses; it does seem as if he no longer trusted the Latvian. Avotin wrote that Berzin "received a rejection, but thankfully no bullet." Reilly and Berzin then agreed to meet again in Moscow on the following Monday. By now, or anyway soon, Berzin would have received Peters' warning. He would not see Reilly in Moscow, or ever again. He had played his part, an important one, in the Lockhart Plot, but he would have no future role; and events were just about to reach their climax.

* * *

Marchand had told Dzerzhinsky about the meeting at the American consulate a day or two after the August 25 meeting there. Dzerzhinsky, who had just resumed command of the

Cheka, conferred with Lenin, and they hatched the plan about the letter to President Poincaré. Dzerzhinsky sent an emergency telegram to the heads of all Cheka branches throughout the country. He wanted to concentrate under his command "the necessary number of [Cheka] corps soldiers for the struggle against the counterrevolution that is rearing its head, and for the defense of revolutionary order in Moscow."[35] Now he wrote to his wife: "We are soldiers on active service...Here we have a dance of life and death—a moment of truly sanguinary struggle, a titanic effort..."[36]

From the other side, American Consul-General Poole sent a cyphered telegram (the Bolsheviks had not broken American codes) to Washington, DC. He anticipated acts of sabotage carried out by the conspirators, then Allied intervention, clashes between Whites and Reds and between General Poole's advancing army and the Reds. The telegram said in part: "every effort must be made to remove allied functionaries and nationals from that part of Russia controlled by the Bolsheviks...this territory must be regarded as hostile." He added: "Mr. Lockhart [who, of course, was not sending cables home because the Bolsheviks could read them] concurs in the foregoing and requests that it be communicated to the British Foreign Office."[37]

On Wednesday August 28, Berzin took the train to Petrograd, as we have seen. Reilly followed the next night. On Friday, the 30th, Reilly had the meetings (in the street and in his flat) with Berzin, whom perhaps he no longer trusted. According to his best biographer, he met sometime that day with Captain Cromie as well.[38] So may have Berzin, separately, as noted above. Cromie, with Petrograd's White Guards, had been plotting the destruction of Russia's Baltic fleet, the overthrow of the Archangel Soviet, linking up with White Guards in Nizhnii Novgorod to the east of

Moscow (this recalls Garstin's earlier connection with Whites in that city) and Tambov to the south,[39] and finally an insurrection in Petrograd, as a counterpart to the one scheduled for Moscow. Presumably, the "Ace of Spies" and the naval attaché brought each other up to date on their respective plans; possibly Cromie likewise explained matters to Berzin. What happened next in Petrograd is difficult to piece together.

Recall that Cromie had triggered the Lockhart Plot about three weeks earlier when he sent Engel'gardt/Shtegel'man and Sprogis/Shmidkhen with a note for the British agent in Moscow. Dzerzhinsky and Peters, however, needed Engel'gardt/Shtegel'man in the former capital, where he could take advantage of his connection with Cromie to further penetrate the counter-revolutionary movement there. They sent him back and chose Berzin to take his place in Moscow. The Latvian captain went with Sprogis/Shmidkhen for the initial, portentous meeting with Lockhart on August 15.

Before Engel'gardt/Shtegel'man returned to Petrograd, however, another Bolshevik agent had knocked on Cromie's door. He claimed to be Lieutenant Sabir of the Russian Baltic fleet. He said he had worked under Admiral Shchastny, whom the Bolsheviks had executed for treason two months earlier. "No notice was taken of [Sabir]," wrote Harold Trevenen Hall, later identified as a civilian, but in fact a British agent working with Cromie.[40] Then, Hall remembered, Engel'gardt/Shtegel'man reappeared with a letter from Lockhart asking Cromie "to assist bearer in all his military operations." No source mentions a meeting between Lockhart and Engel'gardt/Shtegel'man yet apparently one had occurred, further evidence of Lockhart's continuing role in the affair. Now back in Moscow, Engel'gardt/Shtegel'man vouched for Sabir. He "whitewashed" him in Hall's phrase.[41] As a result Cromie accepted them both as co-conspirators. Cromie had provided a letter of introduction for two false conspirators to Lockhart; the latter now had returned the favor, a curious example of reciprocal misplaced credulity. The results would be disastrous.

Sometime in mid-August, just as Lockhart was meeting with the Latvians in Moscow, Cromie met with Engel'gardt/Shtegel'man and the "whitewashed" Sabir in Petrograd. They claimed to be leaders among the Finnish White Guards. Cromie brought them both into his plot. They were the Petrograd counterparts of Berzin and Sprogis/Shmidkhen in Moscow, equally convincing, equally false.

A century later it is impossible to say what were the details of the Petrograd conspiracy whose principals meant to keep it secret, except that Cromie's "plans may have included the destruction of certain bridges,"[42] that he was "interested in several [Petrograd counter-revolutionary] organizations," "that considerable sums of money were being spent,"[43] and that some of the money probably supported counter-revolutionary agitation in the First Division of the Red Army stationed in the former capital.[44] Cromie, who had been funneling Whites to Archangel to assist General Poole's march south, also promised to supply him with armored craft for rivers and lakes.

Whatever the plan, Cromie's new acquaintances said they could assist. Sabir claimed to be commander of a Mining Division. He said he had a battalion of White Guards ready to help take over Petrograd by capturing all the Bolsheviks' armored cars. Cromie gave him an additional task: blow up the Okhta railway bridge, which linked two crucial Petrograd rail stations. That would impede a German invasion from Finland; equally it would impede the Reds when they tried to suppress his insurrection. Engel'gardt/

Shtegel'man said he controlled 60,000 Finnish White Guards including railway, telegraph, and telephone officials. He said he had in Russia 25,000 Latvians "who at a given moment would assemble at a settled point." They were just waiting for the signal to march on Petrograd, in concert with Allied soldiers descending from Murmansk and Archangel. Cromie thought he could work them into his plans too. He promised to introduce his new accomplices to the leading Petrograd Whites, including General Yudenich. "Stecklemann [sic] and Sabir were very keen on this."

*　*　*

The backdrop in Petrograd to Cromie's plotting was increasing tension and hardship in that city, not least for those connected to Britain and France. All were subject to arrest at any time. None were allowed to use the telegraph. None could leave. The chairman of the Petrograd Soviet, Grigory Zinoviev, threatened to intern all of them when (not if), Allied soldiers took Vologda.[45] Already he was rounding up former Tsarist officers and imprisoning them. Near famine conditions prevailed; the price of food on the black market continued to soar. This is when Cromie began to look thin and worn, and in order to avoid arrest took to spending nights in the secret attic room at the home of Reverend B. S. Lombard, the British chaplain in Petrograd. At about this time he wrote a letter to a friend: "I am sick of politics and lies and deceit. I want to get back to Arcadia...and so perhaps find peace..."[46] Lockhart thought he "had a presentiment of his death. He wrote to me in a letter...that 'he felt he was going out' one of these days."[47]

Reverend Lombard's diary vividly portrays the strains and anxieties of the period and place, and of the British community's shocked reaction. He wrote at 1:20 a.m. on August 6: "The bell has just rung violently. Went down in a dressing gown with a revolver, found Bobby…When he got home he found Red Guards watching for him, one at the back door and one at the front. They said they had come to arrest him…One had a rifle and the other a revolver. He turned on the one with the rifle, and floored him, and the other bolted, and he took to his heels and came straight here and is comfortably in bed next door."[48]

Eighteen hours later, Lombard turned to the diary again: "The news this evening is that three barge loads of prisoner officers whom they took to Kronstadt have been sunk. Three hundred in each!!!" He went to the British embassy the next afternoon: "everyone very jumpy, expecting to be sent away." He wrote on Thursday, August 8: "Friends on all hands are searched and robbed. The poor Hilton Browns are in trouble. He was arrested this morning. No one knows where he is. Jim Maxwell also, and Arthur Macpherson." In these conditions it is not surprising to find the chaplain finally writing: "For Poole to march down with 100,000 men and take Moscow and Petrograd would mean the settlement of the Russian problem and incidentally [?] crown ourselves with glory."[49] But Poole didn't have one hundred thousand men. He did not have ten thousand.

On about August 24, Cromie tried to arrange a meeting at the Hotel de France for his two new accomplices, Shtegel'man and Sabir, with the other chief Petrograd plotters. Only Lieutenant Sabir showed up. That was just before Felix Dzerzhinsky resumed leadership of the Cheka. A day or two later, the new recruits told Cromie they needed "to inspect their various posts." Harold Trevenen Hall reported: "they were away about three days."[50] That was just enough time to travel to Moscow for a meeting with their restored chief and to get back to Petrograd. Assume they met with

Dzerzhinsky, talked everything over, and returned on the 30th with his instructions. By now the Cheka leader had most of the threads of Lockhart's Moscow plot in his hands, but not yet the threads of Cromie's in Petrograd. The two Cheka agents, however, had directives. Then, the next day, two almost certainly unrelated events, unexpected as claps of thunder and bolts of lightning on a blue-sky day, altered everything.

CHAPTER 15

THE DEFEAT OF THE LOCKHART PLOT

In fact, the day dawned foggy and damp in Petrograd on August 30. At nine o'clock in the morning, a slight, good-looking young man wearing an officer's cap and leather jacket sat nervously in the crowded ground floor waiting room of the Cheka headquarters in Palace Square. Leonid Kannegisser had dark hair obscured by the cap, full lips and a long, sensitive, poet's face. He was 24 years old, the author of dreamy but credible verse. His bearing and dress revealed him to be a child of privilege and, in fact, he was the son of a millionaire. Previously he had been an ardent supporter of Kerensky; now he was an anti-Bolshevik socialist with links to White counter-revolutionary groups. Conceivably one of them put him up to the deed he was about to perform, but nobody has found evidence linking him directly with Cromie or Reilly, let alone with Lockhart. Probably, what the young poet intended to do was entirely separate from their conspiracy, and singularly ill-timed from their point of view.

It would have been sticky and warm at that time of year in that roomful of supplicants waiting for news of loved-ones under arrest, with armed guards, including one with a machine gun, watching over them.[1] The young poet may well have been sweating under his cap and leather jacket. But he did not take them off.

Figure 24. Leonid Kannegisser

In fact, he kept the jacket tightly closed. Beneath it he had hidden a Colt pistol. He was waiting for Moisei Uritsky, the head of the Petrograd Cheka. He intended to kill him.

Moisei Uritsky had played a prominent part in organizing the revolution; now, a member of the Central Committee of the Bolshevik Party, he oversaw the Petrograd secret police. By most accounts, the chief of the Petrograd Cheka did not thirst for blood; indeed, his reign had been comparatively mild, and if he had had his way it would have been milder still. Kannegisser, however, thought Uritsky did have blood on his hands, including the blood of one of his best friends.[2] The young romantic believed it was innocent blood. According to his father this, and not political conviction, was his motivation.[3]

At about eleven o'clock, very near the time that Captain Berzin was entering "Mr. Massino's" unoccupied flat on Torgovaia Street, Uritsky was arriving at his headquarters in a chauffeur-driven automobile. He entered the building, nodded at the crowd, and headed for a staircase at the other end of the room. Kannegisser let him pass. Perhaps he took a deep breath. Then he pulled out the gun and opened fire, hitting his man in the body and head. Onlookers screamed. Uritsky fell. Kannegisser fled. Cheka officers drew their weapons and ran after him. They too began shooting.

The young man had left his bicycle outside. The scene that followed evokes Keystone cops, but it was real, and real lives were at stake. The young poet sprang onto his bike and sped off, pedaling furiously. Shots rang out in historic Palace Square; bullets ricocheted. As he raced around the Winter Palace, then along the Neva Embankment into Millionnaya Street, his cap flew from his head and one of the pursuers stopped to pick it up. Did the assassin, for that is what he had just become, momentarily lose his pursuers? He did manage to get off the bike and, according to some accounts, dash into an "English Club"; or, according to others, gain entrance into the British embassy itself. According to Kannegisser's own testimony, he ran into the courtyard of Number 17, Millionnaya Street, and then through the first door that caught his eye. An early report said that was the house of "the Northern English Society," where the Petrograd English Association had its premises.[4] Ransome, interpreting events from Stockholm a few days later for the Daily News, corrected this account. Number 17 was not the address of the English Club but did contain a "flat belonging to some members of the British mission."[5] Major R. McAlpine, who had worked closely with Cromie arranging the coup in Archangel, also lived on Millionnaya Street, at Number 10. This is as close to an English connection as has ever been established for the poet assassin. Perhaps it means something, but equally, perhaps it does not.

Somehow, Kannegisser managed to acquire a coat, for purposes of disguise. It cannot have been much of a disguise, however. Within minutes Cheka agents tracked him down and arrested him. They identified him in part by the cap, which they now held and which they had seen him wearing only minutes earlier. Also, the young man did not deny the charge. He had achieved his purpose: Moisei Uritsky was dead.

* * *

That evening, August 30, Vladimir Lenin addressed a meeting of workers in the hand grenade shop of the Michelson Armaments factory in Moscow. If he did not have the Lockhart Plot specifically in mind when he spoke, certainly he had in it Leonid Kannegisser and the threat posed by counter-revolutionaries, although he made no mention of events in Petrograd that day. His subject: "liberty and equality"; his conclusion: "We have only one alternative: victory or death." At this grimly resolute declaration the crowd broke into "stormy applause passing into ovation."[6] Afterward, the Bolshevik leader made his way from the factory to his car. Part of the crowd followed. One woman was trying to tell him about her nephew whose allotment of flour had been confiscated. He stood with one foot on the running board of the automobile, surrounded by admirers, patiently listening to her. It was a little after 8 p.m.

(At that moment in Petrograd, despite earlier events, Reilly probably would have been dining with his "wife" at a restaurant or entertaining her on Torgovaia Street. Berzin would have been thinking of his return to Moscow by train the next morning. Cromie would have been headed for the safety of Reverend Lombard's secret attic room. And, in Moscow, Lockhart and Moura would have been dining together in the flat at 19 Khlebnyi pereulok for nearly the last time.)

Close to the factory exit just used by Lenin, across from the car, stood a booth. A small woman lingered unobtrusively behind it. Fanny Kaplan had not attended the speech but waited outside.

She might once have been pretty. Now she had black hair, great black circles under her eyes, large ears, a pointed chin and a face etched by years of hardship. She wore a wide-brimmed white hat, held a briefcase in one hand and a green umbrella in the other. Later it would be said that she had kept a gun in the briefcase, or in her pocket. A few people noticed her, but none paid her much attention.

Ten years earlier, Fanny Kaplan had been an anarchist. The Tsar's police had arrested her in 1906 for planning terrorist activities involving bombs. The Tsar's judge had sentenced her to "eternal" hard labor. According to possibly unreliable records gathered by the Bolsheviks in 1918, she had quit the anarchists during her imprisonment to join the Socialist Revolutionary Party.

Eleven years of harsh incarceration nearly broke Fanny Kaplan's body. She suffered from debilitating headaches; she grew deaf; she went temporarily blind and recovered her eyesight only imperfectly. But she remained a defiant if nervously distracted and balky individual. The first Russian revolution, the moderate one of February 1917, set her free. Eventually, she moved to Moscow, where she stayed with left SR friends she had made in prison. Then came the second Russian Revolution, the communist one of October 1917. She did not favor Bolshevism. Ten months later, August 1918, she and all the other left SRs believed the Bolsheviks already had sold out the peasantry, had knuckled under to German imperialism; in short, had betrayed socialism.

It is unlikely, but not impossible, that the conspirators whose plot we have been tracing had advance knowledge of what was about to take place. After all, both Reilly and Lockhart had maintained contact with the Socialist Revolutionaries, both left and right. It is inconceivable, however, that they would have approved it, a week before their own coup was scheduled; the timing was

Figure 25. Fanny Kaplan

wrong from their point of view. "The fools have struck too early," exclaimed one of Reilly's contacts when he learned what Kannegisser had done. He would have said the same when he learned about Fanny Kaplan.[7] As with the assassination of Uritsky, the attempted assassination of Lenin almost certainly was seren-dipitous as far as Bruce Lockhart was concerned, and singularly ill-timed.

Now, on a warm summer night outside a factory, the leader of the Bolsheviks stood amid a scrum of well-wishers, talking with a woman about flour shortages. Fanny Kaplan stood at the back of the crowd. Crack, crack, and crack: like a car backfiring: Lenin lay crumpled on the ground. One spent bullet rested beneath his collarbone having first passed through his neck and part of his lung; another lodged in his shoulder, less dangerously; the third had ripped through his overcoat and hit a woman standing next to him. The crowd panicked and scattered. What happened next is in dispute. One witness said that Kaplan ran with the rest; another said she remained standing motionless under a tree. Red Guards arrested several suspects, including the wounded woman, and someone, probably assistant military commissar, 5th Moscow Soviet Infantry Division, Batulin, grabbed Kaplan. She seemed odd to him. He searched her but found nothing suspicious. "Why do you want to know," she asked when he began to question her, which seemed odd yet again. He brought her to the local police station. Suddenly she stood up from the couch on which she had been sitting: "I shot Lenin. I did." She refused to say anything more.[8]

Meanwhile aides had lifted the grievously wounded Bolshevik leader into his car. It raced toward the Kremlin. No one knew whether the architect of the Russian Revolution would live or die.

* * *

News of the assassination of Mosei Uritsky by Leonid Kannegisser in Petrograd reached the Lubianka in Moscow by lunchtime, eight or so hours before Lenin would be speaking at the armament factory. Felix Dzerzhinsky conferred with the Bolshevik leader. It is inconceivable that they did not discuss what might be the connection between Kannegisser of Petrograd and the organization of Whites led by Captain Cromie also in Petrograd, and note that their agents, Engel'gardt/Shtegel'man and Sabir, had just returned to that city. They must have noted too that Kannegisser had fled along Millionaya Street, close to the British embassy, the "English Club," and the flats of numerous embassy personnel. Lenin instructed the head of the Cheka to "find the threads and links among the counterrevolutionaries."[9] Even before the assassination of Uritsky, "Comrade Dzerzhinsky [had] intended to travel to Petersburg [sic] to investigate," reported an official communication released a few days later.[10] After consulting with Lenin he pushed the plan forward, rushed to the railway station and onto the train. He had before him a journey of 450 miles, perhaps an eight-hour trip.

Agents of the Petrograd Cheka met him at the station and brought him to the prisoner. By now it would have been early evening, August 30, just before Lenin was to speak in Moscow. Dzerzhinsky conducted a brief interrogation. Did the young poet belong to a conspiratorial group? Did he belong to any particular political party? How had he obtained his revolver? There is no record that Dzerzhinsky asked about links with the foreign conspirators but he surely did. In any event, Kannegisser only shook his head. He admitted that he had shot Uritsky; other questions he would not answer.

Perhaps Dzerzhinsky broke off for a brief supper; then back to work, but a second session with Kannegisser proved no more illuminating than the first. Then the thunderbolt at the darkest hour: news from Moscow of the attempt on Lenin, and the Soviet leader's life hanging in the balance. Felix Dzerzhinsky rushed to take the next train home. As it rocketed through the countryside he would have been sitting wide awake (for he rarely slept) and ramrod straight (for he never bent). He would have stared out the window, his gray-blue eyes unseeing, his quick, cold brain analyzing pluses and minuses, context and history. Savinkov's risings at Yaroslavl, Murom and Ryabinsk; the left SR assassination of Mirbach; the developing civil war with the Whites to whom the fearsome Czech Legion was offering support; and all this funded, at least in part, by Allied diplomats whose masters now had established three strategic military outposts on Russian soil. How could he not have concluded that the two recent shootings fit within a wider pattern? How could he not believe that those same Allied diplomats must be at the root of the two most recent assaults? He had thought he had Lockhart and his accomplices under control. He had thought he would soon have Cromie's organization under control too. Events of the day forced him to rethink.

Dzerzhinsky on the train: he concluded it was time for decisive action. He would collect and print Marchand's letter about Allied agents sabotaging the revolution.[11] His agents would pick up Lockhart, and Captain Cromie. In fact, they would sweep up all British and French nationals in Moscow and Petrograd who might be involved with the conspirators, including consuls, vice consuls, and members of military missions. It was time to meet White terror with systematic all-encompassing Red Terror. When his train pulled into Moscow, Dzerzhinsky rushed to the Lubianka.

* * *

Earlier that night, Fanny Kaplan sat in a cellar room beneath the Cheka's dreaded headquarters. She was high-strung, distracted, but also in a state of nervy exaltation. Someone described her at about this time as "a holy idiot." Had she really been the one to pull the trigger? If so, had she acted alone? Could she have been a decoy, and the real assassin have escaped? Three hard men, high-ranking officers of the national Cheka, one of them Jacov Peters, confronted her, but they got as little from her as Dzerzhinsky had gotten from Kannegisser.

"To what party do you belong?"
"Don't belong to any party."
"Who sent you to commit the crime?"
"Committed the attempt on my own behalf."

"Why did you shoot at Comrade Lenin?"

"I regard him as a traitor. The longer he lives the further he will push back the idea of socialism....I made up my mind to shoot Lenin a long time ago. I was the one who shot him. I decided to take this step back in February."

She would not tell them how she obtained the gun. She never said how she shot it, while holding briefcase and umbrella. No one asked how, as dusk turned dark and she partially blind already, could see to shoot at all. A hundred years later no one knows whether the SR mounted a serious attempt to kill Lenin, and if so whether Kaplan was the shooter or accepted responsibility for an act she did not commit.

*   *   *

That same night, while Dzerzhinsky rode the train, Jacov Peters anticipated his thinking and ordered raids on the French consulate and on the residences of its staff and agents. One Cheka squad went for René Marchand's letter. Another squad went for Colonel Henri de Verthamon, French demolition expert. The Cheka had de Verthamon under close watch,[12] but nevertheless, he heard them coming up the stairs and escaped through an attic window over the rooftops. Then the squad took his flat apart, ripping up chairs, sofas, and clothing. They found a cipher key and ciphered letters; also 28,822 rubles; also "a ton of General Staff maps of Murmansk, Odessa, Kiev, and regions occupied by the Czechoslovaks." Then they found thirty-nine capsules for dynamite sticks hidden in four coffee-cans.[13]

In Petrograd the Cheka scooped up the British consul, Arthur Woodhouse, and the assistant naval attaché, George Le Page when they went for a late-night stroll, but they missed Cromie who likely had holed up again with the Reverend Lombard.

*   *   *

The next morning, Saturday, August 31, Cromie made his way to the embassy, a sanctuary he thought, protected by diplomatic immunity and therefore inviolable. Others of the embassy staff trickled in. No one knew where the consul was. Everyone, however, knew about the death of Moisei Uritsky.

Also that morning, the Petrograd Cheka communicated with Lieutenant Sabir and Engel'gardt/Shtegel'man, possibly after consultation with Felix Dzerzhinsky back in Moscow.[14] It may have had evidence linking Uritsky's murder with the Anglo-French.[15] At any rate, the shooting the previous day demanded a swift, pitiless, coordinated response. It was time to reel in all the counter-revolutionary conspirators. Undoubtedly acting on instructions, Engel'gardt/Shtegel'man telephoned the British embassy. He spoke with Harold Trevenen Hall. He had "very important news," he told him.[16]

Hall reported to Cromie. Cromie instructed him to find out what the news was. Hall "went to them about mid-day." Engel'gardt/Shtegel'man told him "it was very important to get in touch with the other organizations at once...the time for action was ripe and could not be delayed [for more than] two days at a maximum." Hall took the bait. He did not dispute. He promised to organize a meeting of principals. The two Bolsheviks (but of course Hall did not know that is what they were) suggested the conference take place at the Hotel de France. Hall preferred the embassy. Perhaps he thought they all would be safer there. The Russians should come at four o'clock that afternoon. Just as

Sidney Reilly had failed to hear warning bells when they chimed in Moscow, so now Harold Trevenen Hall failed to hear them chiming in Petrograd.

Nor did Captain Cromie hear them. Hall returned to the embassy, they conferred again, and the naval attaché agreed the meeting should go forward. According to Reilly's autobiography, Cromie failed to turn up for a noon meeting with him. Possibly the naval attaché was too busy. When the Reverend Lombard stopped by the embassy to see him, Cromie said with relish: "things have begun to move." He dispatched Hall to pick up one of the chief conspirators, presumably a Frenchman, identified only as "Monsieur Le General." He sent another of the embassy staff and a chauffeur to pick up General Yudenich. Other plotters would make their way to the embassy on their own. The Bolsheviks later claimed that these were meant to include Savinkov and one of his chief associates, M. M. Filenenko.[17]

The hands on the clock ticked forward inexorably. It was a little after four p.m. Hall returned to the embassy to report that "Monsieur le General" was not home. But at least a few of the counter-revolutionaries had arrived, including "a famous financier," Duke Shakhovski, whose presence at the embassy, Ransome would cable to the *Daily News* a few days later, was "quite enough to justify Soviet suspicions of some sort of dealings going on with anti-Soviet parties."[18] (Ransome called him Prince Shakhovskoi.) Another conspirator present may have been someone called "Mukhanov," as later the Cheka would question witnesses about him.[19] By now the building was crowded, which was odd because, since the departure of the ambassador and most of his staff, usually fewer than a dozen people worked there. Then Engel'gardt/Shtegel'man and Lieutenant Sabir walked in.

They made small talk with Trevenen Hall for a few minutes. Then Sabir excused himself: "Our organization has detectives posted outside and I am going to tell them to keep a sharp lookout." In retrospect, Hall thought this suspicious and probably he was right. Sabir reappeared. He and Engel'gardt/Shtegel'man and Cromie and Hall, found a room on the second floor of the building and "started talking" again. Seven or eight minutes passed. The two Britons did not know it, but already "Comrade [Semen Leonidovich] Geller," an officer of the Petrograd Cheka, and a detachment of secret policemen led by him, had arrived. Geller and a few others had entered the building, guns drawn, and occupied the ground floor. Quite possibly when Sabir had gone outside a little earlier, he had done so to tell them it was time to act.

The four men in the second-story room heard a car outside; simultaneously someone tried their door. Hall thought it would be General Yudenich. He went to open it. Cromie stood and walked over to look out the window. What he saw must have alarmed him. At the same time Hall opened the door, saw a stranger with a gun, and slammed the door shut again. Cromie pulled a revolver from his pocket. He told Hall: "Remain here and keep the door after me." He then pulled open the door: "Clear out you swine." These were the last words he ever uttered.

Precisely what happened next cannot be discovered, and anyway the details are unimportant. Cromie, gun in hand, drove before him the man who had tried to open the door. If there had been only one intruder perhaps all would have ended well for him. But there were many, and they had come upstairs, and someone began shooting. Who fired first cannot be ascertained. Most accounts say Cromie alone among the Britons fired a gun, but this is not certain either. In the end one or possibly two Bolsheviks died, and so did Captain Cromie in a hail of bullets. As Cromie lay dying, Reverend Lombard tried to help him; the Cheka pulled him away. Two women went to him; the Cheka would not let them give succor either.

The Bolsheviks had committed a breach of international law by entering an embassy whose occupants were supposed to be automatically protected. Cromie has gone down as a defender of international law. Of course, with his anti-Bolshevik plotting, he had been breaking international law for months. This the Chekists had finished. Now they confiscated "a mass of weapons," and "massive correspondence." They began herding everyone in the British embassy into various rooms to be interrogated. They would arrest between thirty and forty people including twenty-five "English agents" and five Russian "counterrevolutionaries."[20] For most of them a difficult period was about to commence. According to a British report, the Cheka, most oddly, soon released Prince Shakhovskoi.[21] However, the *Petrograd Pravda* reported on September 6 that he was being held as a hostage and, along with the other hostages, would be shot "if the Right SRs and White Guards kill but one more Soviet official."

*   *   *

Midnight in Moscow eight hours after Cromie's death: streets deserted and dimly lit; most people at home lying in bed, catching up on sleep in lieu of food; or lying awake, anxious and ruminating on events of the day. No one knew precisely what would happen next in the city, or the country, except that it would be bloody. "Let the iron hand of the rising proletariat fall on the vipers of expiring capitalism," Yakov Sverdlov, head of the Soviet Central Committee, had just demanded.[22] No one doubted the iron hand part.

Jacov Peters was not lying in bed. Despite the hour, he sat at his desk in his office at the Lubianka. Earlier he had taken part in the questioning of Fanny Kaplan. Now, he reached for the telephone and requested that the operator make a connection. At the other end, a phone began to ring. Pavel Malkov picked up. Although only 31 years old, a year younger than Peters, he too was a long-time Bolshevik, promoted to be commandant of the Kremlin, and despite the hour he too was still at his desk.

Peters spoke: "Drive over at once, I've urgent work for you." The younger man cradled the receiver, fixed "his invariable Colt" to his waist, summoned his chauffeur, and hurried to his automobile. The chauffeur spun the crank, the engine caught, the two men jumped into the rumbling car. Through darkened empty streets they sped. "I ran up to Peters' study," Malkov remembered. By now it was after one o'clock in the morning. The Cheka man rose from his desk and handed to Malkov "Search and Arrest Warrant 6370," dated September 1, "good for a day."[23] "'You will go and arrest Bruce Lockhart,'" Peters commanded.

Malkov left the Cheka headquarters and returned to the automobile. Across the dimly lit city he flew again, this time to Khlebnyi pereulok.[24] He and the driver exited the car, found the building superintendent who let them into the building, and accompanied them up the stairs, which they illumined with flashlights. Malkov knocked at door number 24. This woke Moura, but not her lover. She went to the door, opened it slightly, still on the chain, saw the men outside and would not let them in. Hicks now appeared, however, in his dressing gown and slipped the chain. They all went to wake the sleeping envoy. "Mr. Lockhart," Malkov announced, "by order of the Cheka you are under arrest."[25]

CHAPTER 16

DÉNOUEMENT

They searched the flat and confiscated "various correspondence," 369,500 rubles (equivalent to £4,666 then, which inflation renders at nearly £250,000 today), and three pistols. They arrested everyone present: two servants, Lockhart, Hicks, and Moura. Lockhart and Hicks, they bundled into a car, brought to Cheka headquarters, and made to sit in a poorly lighted, barely furnished, waiting room, guarded by stone-faced men with guns. It was not yet dawn. Lockhart did not know what had become of the servants. As for Moura, he knew only that she had been put into a separate automobile and taken elsewhere. At one point the guards brought into the waiting room a pale woman with dark circles under her eyes. It was Fanny Kaplan: the Cheka wanted to see if their prisoners recognized each other. She never spoke but only gazed out the window at the gray light of the dawning day, perhaps realizing that she would see morning only once or twice more. Eventually they took her away.[1]

After many hours, Peters summoned his main prisoner for interrogation. By now it was eight o'clock, cloudy and dreary. "The frightened face of Lockhart...I still recall as if it had been yesterday. He thought he was being charged with the assassination of Vladimir Ilyitch [Lenin]."[2] The Cheka deputy leader wrote this in 1924.[3] Lockhart, too, described the confrontation: in his memoir and in a report to the Foreign Office written just after returning to England.[4] Where the three versions overlap must be as close to where a true account of the meeting lies as we can get.

Thus, we know Peters told Lockhart something like: "There had been serious trouble in Petrograd. A band of British and Lettish conspirators had been arrested in our embassy." That is when the British agent learned that things had gone very wrong in the former capital, and it must have given him a bad moment. Peters then acknowledged that his prisoner had the right to remain silent but put four questions to him anyway. He showed him the pass Lockhart had made out to Krysz Krankl and asked if the handwriting on it was his. And he asked whether Lockhart knew Shmidkhen, or Berzin, or Konstantine—not whether he knew "the Kaplan woman," as Lockhart's memoir would have it.

Lockhart refused to answer any questions. Truthful replies would have been self-incriminating, as not only he, but Peters too, well knew. But then according to Peters, Lockhart made a significant admission. "When after the description of his conversation with comrade Berzin and the other acts of the Plot, and when he was offered his letter on behalf of Latvian rifles captain Krysz Krankl, then he admitted that this is all so, but that he acted not on his own initiative but on the suggestion of his government."

Of course, Peters wanted Lockhart to have made such an admission, but it was crucial and revelatory, if he really said it. The plot had blown up in his face. Was he now regretting it? Was he regretting his cynical decision to join the anti-Bolshevik plotters? Had he, deep in his heart, always believed that Anglo-Bolshevik rapprochement was the best way forward? Could he, even now, recoup not his position, but his conscience at least? There is evidence that he was asking himself such questions. Five weeks later, when he finally gained release from prison and from Russia and arrived safely in Stockholm, Arthur Ransome was waiting at the railway platform to greet him. "The first words I head from Lockhart," recalled the journalist, were "You know, in spite of everything I am still against Intervention."[5] But when, that day at the Lubianka, Peters asked him to admit what he had done in writing, Lockhart refused. Nor did he make the admission in his reports to Whitehall or in his memoir, for obvious reasons.

Peters sent his captive back to the waiting room. There, Lockhart and Hicks talked only of inconsequential matters; they both knew to say nothing important because they would be overheard. Eventually somebody told them they could go. The two men found themselves on the rainy Moscow streets at nine o'clock on a Sunday morning. But where was Moura?

She was at the Butyrka Prison, where the Tsar had held Dzerzhinsky only a year and a half earlier, and where Dzerzhinsky had kept Colonel Briedis. During her interrogation, the examiner accused her of holding a "pro-English orientation." He demanded that she disclose "secrets," and warned that she might be shot.[6] But he was young, polite, inexperienced, and she began to gain confidence. "They were still very untrained in strictness of interrogation…I felt that I could get the better of him at any moment."[7] Note that she did not say in this remembrance half a century later that she had known no secrets. But she implied that she divulged none.

Unlike Lockhart and Hicks, who soon would be on their way home, she could not claim diplomatic immunity. But if she had been working for the Cheka all along would it not now have released her? It did not, which suggests that she had not yet come into their employ. After her interrogation, she found herself with fifty-two other women in a barred and filthy room that could not fit half that number. "Prison...brings you down to realities. You see people naked, with all their fears, with all their real reactions and emotion." Apparently, she held hers inside, although she must have had real fears too. The prisoners received only potato soup for nourishment, and not enough of that. They slept on the floor. She could bear it. "Prison wasn't fun, but I must say that on the whole it is a remarkable school for life." After a few days, her jailers moved her into a cell by herself. A rat appeared every night. She claimed to enjoy the company. She claimed never to have despaired. "Everyone should go to prison for a short time."

Those were her memories fifty years later. That she had extraordinary self-possession, and that she bore physical hardship with fortitude, the rest of her life surely demonstrated. Nevertheless, there is evidence to suggest that the experience was much more traumatic for her than she ever admitted. She worried much about Lockhart, whom she had not seen since the Cheka had pulled her from the apartment. Given pencil and paper, she scrawled from her cell a line to a friend outside: "Do you think one could enquire at the Foreign Office if Lockhart was arrested or not?" And the next day, having heard nothing, and perhaps thinking she would soon be released: "Baby...I've got to enquire whether you are safe or not. Please wait in the flat or leave a message."[8] Do not forget that she was pregnant.

Lockhart indeed had returned to 19 Khlebnyi perolouk with Hicks. He consulted with the Dutch consul, William Jacob Oudendyk on the evening of his release, and learned the details of Cromie's death. On the next day, he met with DeWitt Clinton Poole. It must have been plain to them by now that their conspiracy had been entirely defeated. It had been betrayed, but by whom? They did not yet suspect the Latvians. Poole thought Reilly was the traitor. All serious scholars dismiss the charge, as did Lockhart himself. Increasingly, however, he worried about Moura. He knew now where she was, but not when she would get out.

On September 3, *Izvestia* printed a furious, bitter, perhaps fearful, but not essentially mistaken account of the entire conspiracy. That day Dzerzhinsky co-signed, with Zinoviev and two lesser lights, a statement of defiance in the *Petrograd Pravda*. It said in part: "The Anglo-French capitalists, through hired killers, have organized a range of terrorist attempts on representatives of the workers' government. Our native cities are crawling with Anglo-French spies. Sacks of Anglo-French gold are being used for bribing various scoundrels." Discount the hyperbole; the charges were close to the mark. Lockhart must have known the Cheka would soon come for him. Nevertheless, on September 4 he went back to Peters. "When he received me, I tackled him at once about Moura.... He looked me straight in the face. 'You have saved me some trouble. My men have been looking for you for the last hour. I have a warrant for your arrest.'"[9] Lockhart found himself back in the Lubianka, a prisoner once again. This time he had good reason to be frightened.

*   *   *

The Cheka was rolling up Allied agents. They detained six of de Verthamon's men although, as we have seen, they failed to capture de Verthamon himself. From Berzin they had Xenophon Kalamatiano's safe house address, and from that they began tracking down American agents too. At DeWitt Clinton Poole's urging, the Norwegians agreed to place the American consulate under their protection, and raised their country's flag above it. This made the place inviolate; the Bolsheviks still respected diplomatic niceties with the neutral powers; they did not enter the building although they laid siege to it. It became a sanctuary for Allied officials and agents—if they could get inside. Eight French officials including Grenard and Lavergne succeeded, among others. But then they could not get out. General Lavergne tried. Red Guards, led by a young woman with two revolvers stuck in her belt, confronted him. Lavergne "backstepped into garden, redguards followed him to vestibule of consulate one drew revolver threatened fire but another restrained."[10]

The unfortunate Kalamatiano could not get inside at all. He had been in Siberia on an evidence-gathering mission when the crackdown commenced. When he returned to Moscow and learned what had happened, he made a dash for the consulate's front door. The Cheka intercepted and arrested him. He carried a walking stick, which they confiscated. Then they inspected it closely, because he kept glancing at it. Eventually they discovered it was hollow, and held papers concerning Red Army movements curled within. Now they had still more evidence against the Allied conspirators, and more leads to follow. They would hold Kalamatiano for a long time.

As for tracking down British agents: the Cheka arrested one of Reilly's "girls," Yelizaveta Otten, at her flat—just before Maria Fride appeared carrying documents for her. So, the Cheka got them both, and the documents, and soon enough they had Fride's brother, Alexander, as well. A little later they swooped down upon another of Reilly's "girl" agents, Olga Starzhevskaia. But the Cheka did not find Sidney Reilly or George Hill.

On September 1, the "Ace of Spies" was still in Petrograd. Cromie's tragedy at the British embassy would have been fresh in his mind, but he knew nothing of events in Moscow. He did not realize the plot had been betrayed. He still thought it could go forward. He wrote out a full report for Lockhart on "what he considered had happened." That would be an illuminating document to read, but it is not to be found. If a copy ever reached the Foreign Office someone removed it or put it in a section not open to researchers.[11] Using one of his aliases, Reilly caught a sleeper train for the capital that evening, traveling in a first-class compartment. Only upon arrival in Moscow next morning did he grasp the enormity of the disaster confronting the plotters. He saw his name in the newspapers as Lockhart's chief deputy in a plot to overthrow the government, and the address of one of his safe houses. Immediately he went to ground in another bolt hole, "two rooms at the back end of town."

George Hill knew of Cromie's death because the newspapers carried stories about it starting on September 2. At first, he assumed the Cheka had arrested Reilly along with everyone else at the embassy in Petrograd. Nevertheless, at this stage he too still thought the plot could proceed. He himself was living underground, and the Cheka had no idea where. Moreover, they had not put his name on any published list. He sent a message to the recently freed Lockhart: "I had got all Lt. Reilly's affairs under my own control, and provided I could get money it would be possible to carry on...a lot might yet be done in destruction."[12] But Lockhart never received this message. The Cheka had just rearrested him. Somehow the Bolsheviks failed to pick up Hicks, who then made it into the protected American consulate building. By this time the Cheka was trying to arrest anyone who could possibly be connected to the plot, and many thousands besides, and shooting a lot of them. A Red Terror had begun.

*   *   *

Four months ago, a determined, ruthless, Felix Dzerzhinsky had said of the Cheka, his creation and instrument: "We represent in ourselves organized terror…We are terrorizing the enemies of Soviet power in order to strangle crimes in their germ."[13] Yet everywhere the White armies continued to recruit and to prepare for counter-revolution, and the Allied armies to loom menacingly alongside them, and their agents to organize and suborn and conspire. He had thought he had the most important foreign agents in his power—and now this: Uritsky dead, Lenin's life hanging by a thread. Iron Felix, cold-blooded and pitiless but shaken mightily, had sat ruminating as his train hurtled through the black night from Petrograd towards Moscow. He knew now: discriminate terror must be supplemented by terror that was indiscriminate; only that could save a Revolution menaced as Russia's was. The man who lived to serve others, who dreamt of making in Russia an earthly paradise—and who saw himself as a soldier engaged in a fight to the death to create it—would help to open the floodgates and let loose a sea of blood.

The Bolsheviks did open it. They saw themselves beset upon all sides. They *were* beset upon all sides. What transpired in Russia in the aftermath of August 30, 1918, was worse than anything previous—and a terrible portent, a decisive step in the development of what would become the Soviet police state. Red Guards and Chekists swept through cities and towns. In Moscow and

Petrograd, they tried to detain every 15- to 48-year-old British and French male national. They kept them in appalling conditions, hostages against Anglo-French intervention. But the Cheka arrested not only foreigners, and not only counter-revolutionary plotters and their sympathizers, but also entire categories of the population. "A considerable number of hostages should be taken from the bourgeoisie and [former army] officers," ordered Grigory Petrovsky, People's Commissar of Internal Affairs. "The least opposition, the least movement among the White Guards, should be met with wholesale executions."[14] Martin Latsis, a senior Chekist, instructed his agents not to "'look in the file of incriminating evidence to see whether or not the accused rose up against the Soviets with arms or words. Ask him instead to which class he belongs, what is his background, his education, his profession. These are the questions that will determine the fate of the accused."[15] This approach would culminate only weeks later in Grigory Zinoviev's chilling pronouncement: "We must carry along with us 90 million out of the 100 million of Soviet Russia's population. As for the rest...They must be annihilated."[16]

The newspapers began printing the names of hostages as well as the names of hostages dispatched; the British Consul General, miraculously still free on September 7, sent Whitehall a summary of the list: "late ministers Khvostov, Bieletsky, and Scheglovitov...five Grand Dukes...several important bankers, many generals and officers...512 shot up to date." That was in Moscow only, and only during the first few days of the officially sanctioned Terror, which began on September 5. Estimates of the number detained and killed during the remainder of 1918 vary wildly, from a few thousand to many thousands.

Whatever the precise number, the practice was shocking. DeWitt Clinton Poole, whom the Bolsheviks did not arrest because they still hoped against hope that America would treat them better than America's allies did, sent a scathing denunciation to Chicherin, who had replaced Trotsky as People's Commissar for Foreign Affairs (Trotsky had left the office in order to build the Red Army, which he succeeded in doing against all odds and expectations).[17] Neutral diplomats likewise protested strenuously. On one extraordinary occasion, German and Austrian representatives accompanied the neutrals to condemn "in the name of humanity" both the Terror and the wholesale arrest of British and French nationals, their enemies in the World War still ongoing.[18] But of course the Bolsheviks replied that it ill-became agents of nations that had sent many millions to their deaths in an imperialist conflict to discover they had humanitarian scruples after all. Governments did what they had to in order to survive. The Red Terror continued.

*　*　*

There were sporadic shootings day and night. People listened fearfully for the sound of automobiles stopping before their homes after midnight, and then a knock at the front door. Early on the morning of Wednesday, September 4, another of Reilly's "girls" brought George Hill by a circuitous route through terrorized Moscow to the "Ace of Spies." The two men discussed their next moves. The Lockhart Plot was finished, they both now recognized. Hill's name still had not been mentioned in the press. He must just stay quiet and not draw attention to himself. Once Russia agreed to repatriate British officials, he would come out of hiding, resume his identity as a British officer, and leave the country under his own name and with his real passport. Reilly, however, was implicated in the plot. He was one of the most wanted men in the country and would have to get out of it surreptitiously. The northern route appealed: Petrograd–Finland–Stockholm–Britain. Hill agreed to provide his friend with "passports, some new clothing and, as the place he was staying was entirely unsuitable, a fresh lodging."[19]

Everything that followed burnished the Reilly myth. He claimed in his "autobiography" to have taken refuge in a Moscow brothel for the next few days; Hill recorded that he found him quarters "at a Soviet office," which seems almost equally *de trop*. Either place would have been a characteristic hideaway for the "Ace of Spies." As for the passport: it bore the name George Bergmann, a Baltic German from Riga. Hill had intended to use it himself. It entitled the bearer to ride the train to Petrograd in a special compartment reserved for subjects of the Reich. As Reilly somehow obtained a railway ticket that originally had been intended for a member of the German embassy, he left Moscow with typical panache—at least that is how he wrote it in the memoir.[20]

What Reilly did next no one has been able to discover. His own accounts varied, even the official ones he gave to his superiors in London. Where he stayed in Petrograd is also uncertain; so is what he did there; so is the name under which he did it; so is how long he stayed; and finally, so is the means of his leaving the place. A Dutch captain may have taken him from Kronstadt to Tallin, from which it was easy enough to reach Stockholm, or it may have been a Finnish captain, or it might have been a Russian smuggler. He may have been disguised as a priest. The route may have been different. At any rate he surfaced in Sweden on about October 20, having written another disorienting chapter in a biography no one has quite been able to chart.

*   *   *

Neutral observers thought Lockhart would be shot. The Dutch consul, William Oudendyk, went to Lev Karakhan, Chicherin's Deputy Commissar for Foreign Affairs, on the evening of the day the British agent had been rearrested. He sat waiting for Karakhan for a long time. "You must do something, Mr. Karakhan, and do it now," he said when he finally saw him. "Please telephone [Cheka headquarters] at once." Karakhan made the call and began to speak. Then, according to Oudendyk he paled. "What?...Do nothing tonight. Wait until tomorrow morning." Oudendyk wrote: "I had arrived in the nick of time. Undoubtedly Lockhart would have been shot had I been made to wait much longer."[21] A week later the British minister at Christiana was still warning that Lockhart's life was "in imminent danger."[22]

According to the Danish consul, the Cheka were keeping their prize prisoner alive only long enough for him to incriminate himself. They had moved him from the Lubianka to the Kremlin where they held him "in solitary confinement...He is not permitted to read or write or occupy himself in any way. Bolsheviks are trying with every means in their power to break his spirit, and English here fear in [the] condition in which he is, he may disclose something damaging to England."[23] Then the Cheka weekly journal printed a letter written jointly by the chief, and deputy chief, of the Nolinsk branch, Viatka Province: "Why didn't you subject...Lockhart to the most refined tortures in order to extract evidence...to tortures the very description of which would have filled counterrevolutionaries with cold terror?...A dangerous scoundrel was caught. Get out of him what you can, and send him to the next world."[24]

"This is horrible," wrote the Whitehall mandarin George Clerk.[25] The British government was desperate to get Lockhart out—to save his life of course, but also to prevent him saying "something damaging to England." It did not know all that Lockhart had plotted but feared that Russia did. Ransome reported that Radek said he had enough evidence against Lockhart to shoot him. American officials warned that the Bolsheviks had Lockhart's and Cromie's documents;[26] according to another American those included "Cromie's lists of Russians to be recruited, etc."[27] It seemed to the Foreign Office just a matter of time before Lockhart, confronted by the Bolsheviks with proof of his activities, would crack, and tell all, perhaps in a show trial broadcast to the world.

How to save him—and the other British nationals, imprisoned and said to be suffering from ill health and slowly dying of starvation? Sir Ralph Paget, British ambassador in Copenhagen, thought he knew. "It would be advisable at once to arrest a certain number of notable Bolsheviks in [British] occupied [Russian] districts and publish their names....I would propose publication of a declaration stating that 5 principal Bolsheviks will be shot for every peaceful Allied citizen killed." He was recommending a British version of Terror.

* * *

Meanwhile Lockhart languished in prison, no longer at the Lubianka (that much the Danish informant had right), but in a suite of rooms at the Kremlin previously occupied by a former minister in the Kerensky government who had just been shot. Somehow Moura, who was still imprisoned at the Butyrka, learned of the transfer. Either she knew that no captive taken by the Bolsheviks to the Kremlin had emerged alive, or she was profoundly relieved to learn that at least her lover had not yet been executed. Either way, the reaction was profound. A few cynics have supposed Moura did not care deeply for Lockhart, but rather ensnared him on orders from the Cheka, and then spied on him. In fact, the revelatory news that he was still alive, although possibly still in terrible danger, proved so overwhelming for her that she miscarried her baby. That must have been a terrible business given the conditions in which she was kept. "It happened unforeseen in prison when I learned you were moved to the Kremlin."[28] But she had no opportunity as yet to tell him about it.

The move to the Kremlin seemed an ominous precedent, but actually it was a sign that the moment of his greatest peril had passed. The new accommodations were much better than the last. The rooms were small but clean; they had no windows but were decently furnished; he had a private bathroom, albeit with no bath; and a servant to tidy up after him and prepare his meals. Moreover, he could walk daily in the Kremlin grounds. It was a far cry from the Peter and Paul fortress in Petrograd, where so many of the British embassy staff continued to suffer real torment; or the Butyrka in Moscow, where Moura and several dozen British nationals endured their incarceration. It bore no relation at all to how the British government thought he was being treated.

Upon arrival, he was disconcerted to discover that he would be sharing the suite with none other than Jan Sprogis/Shmidkhen, whom he still thought of as a fellow conspirator. Of this he made no mention in the report he prepared for the Foreign Office, but he wrote in his memoir that "We spent thirty-six hours together during which we were afraid to exchange a word. Then he was taken away."[29] In fact, almost certainly Sprogis/Shmidkhen did manage to get Lockhart talking, although probably not enough to incriminate himself. Jan Avotin recorded that he brought his "imprisoned" friend a head of Dutch cheese: "We met at the Borovitskaia Tower of the Kremlin, behind the gates of which Sprogis was taking a walk with Lockhart." It is doubtful that the companionable pair walked and ate in silence. And there is an interesting titbit about the end of their relationship. At the close of the month, when Lockhart gained his freedom, so did Sprogis/Shmidkhen. Returning to the quarters he shared with Avotin and Buikis, the Cheka agent exultantly showed them "a recommendation written out by Lockhart addressed to the Speaker of the English Parliament asking him to furnish in England every aid and assistance. The paper was adorned by the large round seal of the English consulate."[30]

It is a curious point that while Lockhart remained in prison Felix Dzerzhinsky left all dealings with him to Jacov Peters. But since Peters was the Chekist with whom Lockhart mainly dealt, it was to Peters that Lockhart appealed for news of his lover. It is another curious point that Peters responded sympathetically. Or perhaps it is not so curious: the leaders of the Cheka appear to have had yet another scheme in mind when it came to Moura and Lockhart, or perhaps two schemes. Peters told Lockhart that he could write a letter to his lover.

The Chekist brought it to her at the Butyrka. She opened the envelope and began to read. Peters gave her pen and paper and she dashed a quick reply: "My dear, dear, Baby, I have just received your letter through Mr. Peters. Please don't be anxious about me,

I am quite well and my only trouble is about you." In truth she was not "quite well" at all. She had just miscarried. She did not know tensions were relaxing, and feared her lover might be shot at any moment. She must have feared that she would be shot too. Her appearance betrayed her: she looked awful.[31] She stood before Jacov Peters after a week or more in a terrible prison, alone, miserable, and frightened—completely at his mercy. And then he offered to set her free, and to let her ease her lover's situation, and even to visit him.

Did Jacov Peters and Felix Dzerzhinsky demand a quid pro quo from their helpless detainee? If ever Moura would have agreed to an arrangement with the Cheka, this was the time. Decades later she explained her conduct during the revolutionary period to H. G. Wells, who repeated to his son, Anthony West, what she had said: "Not to do what has to be done at such times is to elect not to survive."[32] Moura was a survivor. And what was it the Cheka wanted from her in return for her life? With Lockhart's admission to Peters still fresh in their minds (if he really had made one), perhaps they thought he continued to suffer from a guilty conscience over his counter-revolutionary plotting and could be persuaded to testify in a public trial against the plotters. In that case, Moura could be the persuader. Or, perhaps they merely thought she could provide general information on her lover and his milieu before his imprisonment and during it—and maybe even after.

Moura wrote to Lockhart: "Mr. Peters has promised to release me today. I will be able to send you linen and things and perhaps he will arrange for me to see you."[33] A few hours later she found herself on the street, so bewildered by the unexpected turn in her situation that she headed off in the wrong direction at first and walked several blocks before realizing her mistake.

Immediately, Lockhart's situation improved. Moura went to the prison twice daily, although she did not see him each time. She brought him many books. She brought him all sorts of foods: fruits, vegetables, cheeses, condensed milk; and many other little luxuries, including "velvet tobacco," playing cards, pens and paper, scissors, razor, and shaving soap. Such items in revolutionary Moscow were rare and very expensive, and could be purchased only on the black market, which was illegal. Yet she wrote to him every day about these items, listing them fearlessly, in letters vetted by Peters. People were shot for frequenting the black market. This suggests again that Moura had reached some sort of understanding with the authorities.

Her letters to Lockhart disclosed little except her continuing fierce love for him. She mothered him; worried about his health; asked continually what she could send to ease his discomfort; and told him time and again that she loved him. Two examples will suffice:

> Friday [September 13], My Baby, My Beloved Baby, I have seen you at last and my heart is bleeding at the thought of you being there all alone, all the time. Baby, baby, did you think me a coward for crying? I couldn't help it…my heart was breaking.
>
> Wednesday night [September 18]…You are just all my life. You are all my happiness, all my joy of existence. So, I walk about and breathe and pretend to live, but all my soul, my heart, is with you all the time.

To their great frustration Peters would only let them be together when he was there to chaperon.

On September 22, Moura and Peters visited Lockhart, not for the first time. The Chekist and the British agent sat at a small table facing each other. Moura stood behind. Peters was in a reminiscent mood. It was his birthday. While he spoke of his youth and conversion to socialism, Moura caught Lockhart's eye, held up a note and slipped it into a book. Peters never saw, because she stood behind him.

This is a more important incident than it might first appear to be. Lockhart wrote in his memoir that the note contained only six words: "Say nothing—all will be well."[34] Possibly so, and interesting if true: Why was Moura cautioning him to remain silent? Did she fear that he would not? Had he confided to her that he was suffering pangs of conscience? Could he have been about to make a clean breast of things? Did she want to save him from that? Or, more simply, had she just learned that he would soon be released?

In the report he prepared for the Foreign Office once he returned to Britain, Lockhart did not mention Moura's note to him, but rather another. "I had received a secret message in a book brought in to me that Reilly was safe."[35] Who could have brought him such a message? Aside from Moura, and aside from the Red Guards who watched him, only four individuals appear to have been in a position to do so. The man who had arrested him, Pavel Malkov, as commandant of the Kremlin, checked him daily, but would never have brought his prisoner a book.[36] The Swedish Consul General visited him once, but would never have endangered his position by carrying to Lockhart a book with a secret message inside. Peters and Karakhan came to him on their own more than once, but it is inconceivable that they carried him messages in books; they could have conveyed them verbally, much less risky.

That leaves Moura again. She must be the one who brought the book with the message about Reilly to him. Conceivably, she carried the message unwittingly, but that would mean that someone had placed her in grave danger without warning her, which seems unlikely. If she had agreed to carry it, however, or if, which seems much more plausible, she wrote the note herself after consulting perhaps with George Hill, then that suggests that she was privy to more secret information than just the news about Reilly, including secret information about the entire Lockhart Plot. It suggests that Lockhart kept her informed not only of his activities before he launched the plot, but afterwards as well. Certainly, it suggests that she was more deeply involved in the plot than her biographers give her credit for being. Finally, it suggests that if she had come to an arrangement with Peters and the Cheka, her first loyalty remained as always to her lover.

So: two instances of information conveyed by Moura to Lockhart by means of a note in a book. There is a possible third instance of information conveyed, although in this instance it probably was conveyed verbally. On September 16, Lockhart wrote a string of Malay words in his diary. Translated, they mean roughly: "he [she?] told me once that all the letters were taken secretly to the big Dutch house in the city."[37] It is obscure even in English, but one may guess it is a reference to his own documents, and that somehow they had come under Dutch protection and now were lodged at the Dutch consulate or embassy. Who could have brought him such news except Moura, who we know from later letters had dealings with Oudendyk? This too suggests that she knew more than a little of her lover's business. For Lockhart, it would have been a relief to learn the documents were safe, and it may explain why the Foreign Office began receiving reassurances that in fact the Bolsheviks had obtained none of his papers after all, but only Cromie's. It may also explain in part why the Bolsheviks did not bring him to trial: he had successfully hidden the evidence of his participation in the plot; he had one less reason to ease his conscience by testifying.

But we are dealing with secrets of long ago. We can only guess that Moura, more formidable than some have thought, knew some of Lockhart's secrets; that Peters and Dzerzhinsky offered her a chance to free herself for a price; that she agreed to pay the price in order to save herself and her lover; that she remained true to him even while working for the Cheka; and that she brought him messages, some hidden in books. This is a plausible interpretation of events; it may have happened—and that is all. There is no proof.

On September 23, Lockhart recorded in his diary that he had received from Moura "very sad news." It can only have been the letter about her miscarriage, and he took it badly. "I am much upset," he wrote in his diary, "and wonder how everything will end." He wrote her a letter in return: "Our illusions were all in vain." He must have been referring to their plans for a life together with their baby. Moura had made progress settling her Russian affairs. She thought that when Lockhart was repatriated he would wait for her in Stockholm and she would quickly join him. Now he wrote that they must change this plan. She did not understand. "Why does this alter your plans as regards Sweden?" she asked. "I want you to understand that if you don't want me to go with you I do not insist, and am prepared to wait—but why have your plans changed after you knew this to have happened? I am so afraid that your love for me has diminished."[38]

"Don't be sad," she entreated him in a second letter; it would make it harder for her to bear the miscarriage if he was sad. "There is no need to grieve. I pray God that I will become pregnant again."

Moura remained a woman desperately in love—but he may already have begun envisioning a future in which she did not figure. Perhaps he felt fewer obligations to a woman who had miscarried his child than he would have to one expecting to give birth to an infant he had fathered. Perhaps he had begun to think that he should leave Moura behind when released from prison—just as he had left behind Amai and "Madame Vermelle."

* * *

During his imprisonment, Lockhart met fairly frequently with Peters or Karakhan alone. He sparred with the latter in surprisingly pleasant, even jocular, political discussions, and gained the impression that Chicherin's deputy was trying to discover how to induce Britain to end her intervention in his country. This Lockhart duly reported to Balfour when he got home. His interactions with Peters were more psychologically complex, and he wrote about them in his memoir only. Peters showed him what the Okhrana had done to his hands. Lockhart thought this helped explain his devotion to Bolshevism. "He told me that he suffered physical pain every time he signed a death sentence."[39] Lockhart believed him. He deemed Peters to be a Puritan idealist, enthralled by Marxism, struggling to build socialism in a hostile world. Although never a Bolshevik, Lockhart sympathized with the Bolshevik desire to renew and revamp Russia. And Peters, hearkening back to Lockhart's seeming ambivalence about the plot, and possibly encouraged by Moura who might have told him that Lockhart was thinking hard about his situation, appears to have believed the young Scot was redeemable. He tried to persuade Lockhart to make a new life with Moura in Moscow.

"You can be happy... We can give you work to do. Capitalism is doomed anyway."[40]

Lockhart wrote about this offer: "Tempted, but this time heard the referee's whistle."[41] Was he tempted because he was still experiencing pangs of conscience which he could have assuaged by staying and working in Russia, thus making up for the plot? Moura would cheerfully have gone with him to the ends of the earth. Here was his opportunity to do for her what he knew she would do for him. But the whistle: who was blowing it? Was it Arthur Balfour, representing the British way of life and what he supposed to be Lockhart's ineradicable commitment to it? Is that what finally persuaded Lockhart not merely to leave Russia behind, but Moura as well? Or was it the thought of his wife Jean, representing family and British convention? He wrote fifteen years later that had he not been arrested, "I think I would have stayed in Russia forever."[42] This may be doubted. Had Moura not miscarried, had she given birth to his child, had his conscience really been troubling him, then perhaps he would have stayed, although even this seems doubtful. We know that Lockhart ignored referees when it suited him; he bent the rules of the game when self-interest dictated that he should; but he never turned the entire game upside down. That is what staying in Russia with Moura would have amounted to.

When the Russian government finally agreed to let Lockhart go, Peters asked a favor of him. "When you reach London will you give this letter to my English wife?" He handed to Lockhart a sealed package, also a signed photograph of himself to keep as a souvenir. Lockhart, when he returned to London, did indeed deliver the package. His final verdict on his jailer: "There was nothing in his character to indicate the inhuman monster he is commonly supposed to be."[43]

Years later, Peters wrote less charitably about Lockhart during his stint at the Kremlin. "He resembled a donkey standing between two bundles of hay—on the one hand, British and world imperialism—on the other, the new world that was coming into being. And each time he was told about this new world...and about his, Lockhart's, abnormal position in the world he served, he would take up the pen to make a clean breast of it, but after a few minutes the poor donkey would reach out for the other bundle and drop the pen."[44] This grates in comparison with Lockhart's fond tone. But the Scot had disappointed his jailer who, like most men, may have had a soft spot for Moura and therefore may have been jealous of the man she favored. He may have disapproved of the way Lockhart finally treated her.

*   *   *

Worried that Lockhart would "say things damaging to Britain," but not knowing precisely what they might be since the details of his plot were unknown, and moreover afraid that he faced imminent execution, the Foreign Office worked overtime to secure his release. Its first impulse was for "strong action, which unfortunately has at present to be confined to threats."[45] Actually, there was one strong act the government could and did take: it arrested Maxim Litvinov, the very man who had written Lockhart an introduction to Trotsky at the Lyons Corner House, Trafalgar Square, nine months earlier, and it arrested his Russian assistants, and it refused to allow some twenty-five additional Russian nationals who had been on the verge of returning home to leave Great Britain. Then, hostages in hand, it opened negotiations with Georgy Chicherin.

This hostage-taking cut across the grain of hundreds of years of European diplomatic practice, for it contained an implicit threat:

that Britain would do to its innocent prisoners whatever the Bolsheviks did to theirs. Would they have really? One Foreign Office mandarin soon would be arguing that "Mr. Litvinov and his friends were not of great value as hostages, none of them having been directly responsible for the crimes committed in Russia."[46] Possibly cool heads, like this one, would have prevailed in London, even if worse came to worst. Whether they would have prevailed in Moscow must be an open question. The Bolsheviks would shoot many hostages in the future.

Possibly working against the clock, then, Balfour and Chicherin worked out the details of a formal exchange. Litvinov and his associates would be released from jail in London at precisely the same time as Lockhart and the imprisoned British officials in Russia. Then the Litvinov group, and the twenty-five Russian nationals, would sail in a British ship from Aberdeen to Bergin, Norway, just as the Britons got underway by train in Russia for the Finnish frontier. Litvinov and party would disembark in Bergen but remain in place until Lockhart and party crossed the border, at which point the Russians would continue their journey home. The question of additional imprisoned British nationals would be dealt with separately.

As the process unwound, the British government had to deal with a series of minor problems that could have ruined everything: for example, a railway strike, and a vessel that proved to be unseaworthy.[47] They coped, however, and in the process managed to satisfy their exceedingly suspicious hostages. In the end, Litvinov agreed that "he had been comfortable and well treated and had nothing to complain of," except that some of his account books had gone missing. These do not appear to have been important.[48]

At the other end things went more smoothly. At six o'clock on Saturday evening, September 28, a smiling Jacov Peters entered the little suite of rooms at the Kremlin, again with Moura (also smiling perhaps, but probably a bittersweet smile), to announce that Lockhart would be freed three days hence, on Tuesday, October 1. He would have that day and the next to pack and would leave for Britain by train on Wednesday night. "The reaction," Lockhart wrote, "was wonderful."[49] And Moura? She had a fever higher than a hundred degrees to which she paid no attention.

On Tuesday, two Red Guards brought him from the Kremlin back to 19 Khlebnyi pereulok. Moura joined him. The flat was in chaos. Searching for compromising documents after his second arrest, the Cheka had slit chair and sofa linings, and pulled down wallpaper. Agents had stolen his pearl studs, silver cufflinks, and money. They had drunk all the wine. He wrote a letter of complaint to Peters who immediately offered compensation, which Lockhart refused. He could not leave the house, but he could receive visitors, among them the Swedish consul, and then Hicks' Russian fiancée who happened to be the niece of his old friend, Chelnokov. She asked him to ask Peters to let her that day marry Hicks, who was still holed up at the protected American consulate, so that she could accompany him to England as his wife. Lockhart did as she requested and Peters then did the kind thing, as six short months ago Betty Beatty might have predicted he would do. He expedited the marriage process, so that the couple could wed, and leave the country together.

Wednesday night at 9:30 a small detachment of guards, and Jakov Peters, brought Lockhart and Moura to Nicolaevski Station. That is where the couple said their goodbyes. His train, steaming in the dark, waited at a platform in the goods depot about half a mile beyond. It was just visible, the platform illuminated by oil lanterns, and a line of figures moving toward it from the station proper, some in uniform for there were Red Guards on sentry duty. It was chilly: the sleet of the day had turned to ice crystals. It was still possible for Moura to dream they would soon be reunited; perhaps Lockhart felt the same way. He took her in his arms and whispered: "Each day is one day nearer to the time when we shall meet again."[50] She would keep repeating these words to herself long after he had forgotten them.

Then he left her. Surrounded by his guards he headed for the steaming train. "Make way, make way," the guards shouted. On the platform by the train he passed George Hill, in uniform again, safe, and on his way out of Russia. Lockhart "winked and grinned. 'See you in a minute Hill.' The escort swept him past me into the carriage."[51]

Moura waited in the station for another hour, until whistles blew and steam clouded the air in great billows. Then, as she wrote to him the very next day, she watched sorrowfully as "the train faded out of sight into the darkness."[52] What to do next?

CHAPTER 17

EPILOGUE

With the defeat of the Lockhart Plot, the prospect of effective Allied counter-revolutionary intervention in Russia lapsed forever. Perhaps it had always been a pipedream. When the combatants in the West agreed to a ceasefire on November 11, the Allies no longer needed to revive the Eastern Front. Thus, the main original rationale for their intervention in Russia disappeared. So did the related rationale for keeping supplies in Vladivostok, Murmansk, and Archangel from German hands. What remained was anti-Bolshevism. That stayed strong as ever in the minds of most members of the Allied governing classes, but it was not so strong among their countrymen and women. Even those among the French, British, and American populations who shared it had little stomach for continued warfare.

The Allies did not withdraw their forces from Russia all at once, however. Sporadic clashes between Bolshevik and Allied forces continued for more than a year, all across the great Eurasian landmass. Nevertheless, by the end of 1919 most foreign troops had departed, although not all of the Czech Legion left until 1921, and some Japanese soldiers remained in the Russian Far East as late as 1925.

The Western Powers still did sympathize with the anti-Bolshevik Whites, and continued to fund their counter-revolutionary efforts, but the finance was insufficient to the purpose. Lockhart and Robins and Ransome had been right at the start; the White Russian forces arrayed against Bolshevism were weak, disorganized, and prone to splits, while the opposite could be said of the Bolsheviks. Once rule out massive aid for their opponents, and strong military intervention against them, as the Allies did in the aftermath of the Lockhart Plot, and then Lenin and Trotsky were likely to prevail.

Or rather, their government would prevail. Lenin would be dead within a few years and Trotsky on the run. As a very brief résumé: the undisputed Bolshevik leader recovered from the wounds for which Fanny Kaplan claimed responsibility, although one bullet, after ripping through his lung, remained lodged in his collarbone, and the other at the base of his neck. It is said that when he was able to speak and function again, two weeks after the attempt on his life, his first words were "Stop the Terror," and it did then come to a halt. Historians have pointed out, however, that Lenin had spoken previously in favor of systematic Terror, and that he would do so again.[1] Moreover, a regime that successfully employs such methods once often will find reason to re-employ them, as the Bolsheviks certainly did.

It is not clear what killed Vladimir Lenin. He seemed to recuperate fully during 1919, but then began increasingly to suffer ill health. He had high cholesterol; he had hardening of the arteries. He endured a number of strokes in 1922 and 1923, and then a seizure, and finally died of a massive stroke in January 1924, probably as a result of his diseases. Some believe that Stalin poisoned him, however, and it is a fact that someone issued an order that no toxicology be performed on his tissues, so that the matter must remain always in doubt.[2]

As for Lenin's second in command: Leon Trotsky performed prodigies of organization to build the Red Army, and then of generalship to help lead it to victory over the counter-revolutionaries, sometimes against great odds. His achievements are deservedly legendary, which is not to say that he opposed government-sponsored Red Terror either—in fact, he defended it unabashedly as part of the revolutionary process in a famous exchange with the left SRs early in 1918 when he predicted guillotines in the near future, and more completely in his *Terrorism and Communism* (1920). How Stalin, who obviously likewise believed in Terror, outmaneuvered him during the years after Lenin's death, has been the subject of many books. Exiled from Russia, Trotsky lived for a time in Turkey, then in France, then in Norway, until landing in Mexico in 1937. There one of Stalin's assassins finally killed him in 1940.

Lenin and Trotsky's chief British opponents during the Revolutionary era, Lockhart's masters, Lloyd George, Lord Milner, Arthur Balfour, and Robert Cecil, lived and died in much easier circumstances. All continued as leading political figures except for Milner, who stepped down from the cabinet shortly after the conclusion of the Paris Peace Conference. In 1925, he died at home after a visit to South Africa where he had contracted sleeping sickness. He was 71 years old. Balfour continued to serve his party and government more or less actively until 1929, collecting many honors, degrees, and chairmanships. He died at age 82 in 1930. His cousin Robert Cecil lived twenty-eight years past that, becoming, after World War I, Britain's leading advocate for the League of Nations. And Lloyd George, re-elected prime minister in a landslide in 1918, lost power in 1922, never to hold office again. He remained a powerful force from the backbenches for the rest of his life, "a giant without a job," always fertile with ideas and plans. Seduced for a time by the charisma and energy of Adolf Hitler, he came to realize that an Anglo-Soviet alliance might deter the German Fuhrer from war and would help Britain win should one nevertheless break out. Lenin would have smiled, probably Trotsky did. Lloyd George died shortly before the end of World War II; the Anglo-American–Soviet alliance he favored had saved his country.

* * *

The trial of arrested men and women accused of having played a role in Lockhart's plot began on November 29, 1918. Twenty defendants appeared, the most important of whom were Xenophon Kalamatiano and Colonel Alexander Fride. Several of Reilly's "girls" appeared too: Maria Fride, Yelizaveta Otten, and Olga Starzhevskaia. At least eight of Kalamatiano's agents sat in the dock. So did Colonel de Verthemon's landlady, a French teacher in whose rooms explosives had been found; so did a man who had supplied Reilly with automobiles; and so did Mr. Higgs of the firm Camber-Higgs. He was the British businessman who had exchanged Lockhart's checks in pounds sterling for rubles in cash and had performed like services for Reilly and for Kalamatiano.

Four crucial figures did not appear at the trial: Lockhart, Reilly, de Verthemon, and Grenard, all now safe in their home countries. They would be tried in absentia, their guilty verdicts and death sentences a foregone conclusion.

Moura, who still believed that she and Lockhart would soon be reunited, clipped newspaper accounts of the trial and sent them to her lover in London. She thought: "P[eter]'s report is, after all, rather mild concerning you, and rather vague."[3] That is further indication that Lockhart had covered his tracks well. He had destroyed his cyphers in early August, when the Bolsheviks first began seriously cracking down on Allied officials in Russia; he had sent no telegrams during the crucial period before the coup would have taken place; and if he had not done so before, probably he still had time the day after the attempt on Lenin's life to burn whatever incriminating documents remained or perhaps to give them to the Dutch for safekeeping. As a result, Peters had little evidence against him, not that this affected his demand for the death penalty in absentia. "You are either a fool or very clever," he told Lockhart, shortly before letting him go.[4] Lockhart was no fool. In the end, Dzerzhinsky and Peters could defeat his plan, but not the man himself.

Xenophon Kalamatiano had not been as clever as Lockhart. The Cheka had the papers from his walking stick, and as a result they had many of his agents too. The tribunal sentenced Kalamatiano to death. But he was a national of a country with which Russia still hoped to do business. His captors did their best to make his life a misery, notifying him more than once that his day had come, and taking him out of his cell for mock execution. But they released him in 1921. Returned to the United States, he suffered severe frostbite on a hunting and fishing expedition in Minnesota. This led to an infection that brought about his premature death in 1923.

Colonel Alexander Fride confessed to having worked for Kalamatiano and for Reilly, and received a bullet in the back of his head. The other seven of Kalamatiano's agents received sentences of five years at forced labor. Fride's sister, Maria, and Yelizaveta Otten were freed. Olga Starzhevskaia, who like the other two claimed she had no knowledge of Reilly's activities, only of his charm, received a three-month sentence and was prohibited for life from working for the government. The Russian purveyor of automobiles, and the British businessman Mr. Higgs, and de Verthemon's French landlady, all were acquitted.

Kalamatiano's lawyer put up a good defense for his American client. He wanted to depose René Marchand, whose testimony was so damning, but Marchand too had left the country. Where was "one Shmidkhen," the lawyer also wanted to know? It was a good question, which the prosecution did not even attempt to address. The Cheka was determined to protect the identity of its agent. Peters did not let him testify. He never told Berzin that Sprogis/Shmidkhen had been working with him, not against him.

Ian Sprogis' eventual fate is obscure. He brought to Felix Dzerzhinsky the letter to the Speaker of the House of Commons that Lockhart had given him. Dzerzhinsky advised him to take advantage of it. The Cheka would provide funds "for the purchase of a house and an automobile for a worry-free life in England, in the role of our undercover agent." Sprogis consulted the two Ians: "What do you think?" They declined to give advice and never saw him again. He may have been shot in 1921 as a smuggler and spy for Poland. Or that may have been disinformation intended to erase his former identity completely, and to smooth his way in Britain, in which case who knows what he got up to in that country?[5]

*   *   *

At first, Jacov Peters disapproved of what he termed "the Hysterical Terror," of November 1918, although he signed many orders condemning prisoners to death.[6] Even several years later, when he once again saw the American journalist Louise Bryant, he told her that he wished to God he had never seen or used a gun.[7] By then he had divorced his British wife and remarried, telling May Freeman what he had done only after she and her daughter appeared in Russia expecting a reunion. He spent the rest of his life working hard for the Cheka. His trajectory and Dzerzhinsky's were similar. But his cold-blooded assiduity would not save him from Joseph Stalin, who in 1937 accused him of being a Latvian nationalist, not a true Bolshevik internationalist. By now Stalin had read in translation *British Agent*, Lockhart's 1932 memoir of his stint in Russia. He had underlined passages that particularly interested him, including Peters' 1918 admission that signing death warrants caused him physical pain.[8] Perhaps this sign of scruples was a sign of weakness or even guilt to the dictator. At any rate, after interrogation, the tenor of which has never been described but which may be imagined, Peters confessed to all charges. He had been an English agent all along. He had helped Sidney Reilly in 1918, because the British promised to free Latvia. The People's Commissariat for Internal Affairs (NKVD) may have shot him then; otherwise the Germans did in 1942, when they overran his prison camp. Rumors that he survived the war do not appear to be credible. Eventually he was rehabilitated as a "Hero of October."[9]

In 1919, Captain Edouard Berzin left the Latvian Rifle Brigade to join the Cheka too. A few years later, he was chosen to oversee construction of, and then management of, a gulag called the Vishlag, where paper and cellulose were produced. Apparently, he made a success of this job without employing the dreadful methods usually associated with the gulag system. In 1932, Stalin sent him to develop the Kolyma region in the far eastern and northern part of the Soviet Union. Again, Berzin proved successful, again apparently shunning the most awful means. He has been described as a loving husband and doting father during these years. Yet like Peters, he too fell afoul of the Stalinists, and at the same time and for the same reason. Tried in December 1937, he too confessed to being a Latvian nationalist, and to having tried to help the plotters of 1918. It is said that he endured torture before his confession; perhaps he first resisted confessing to something so obviously untrue. They shot him in the Lubianka prison in August 1938.

Of the Russian protagonists involved in combatting the Lockhart Plot, loyal Bolsheviks all, Dzerzhinsky did not live long enough to run afoul of Stalin, but of those who did, Peters received a bullet (probably Russian but maybe German) in the back of the head, as did Berzin, and as, possibly, did Sprogis. Of the Russian Bolsheviks we have met in previous pages but who did not take an active part in foiling the plot: Chicherin died in 1930 before the purges began, Trotsky was murdered, Karl Radek was shot after the 1938 purge, so was Karakhan, and so for that matter was the left SR leader, Maria Spiridonova. Here in a nutshell was Stalin's plan for "old Bolsheviks," and for their allies during the October Revolution.

Whether Boris Savinkov was murdered or committed suicide remains an open question, but one way or another they got him too. The great conspirator fled Russia in 1919, first for France, later for Poland, but always he remained determined to return to the country of his birth, and to overthrow the Bolsheviks. He courted world leaders and particularly impressed Winston Churchill who wanted to help him "strangle Bolshevism in the cradle." For a time Savinkov and his movement prospered. He remained, therefore, a significant threat to the Soviets. But to his great cost, Felix Dzerzhinsky was even more wily, dogged and resourceful than he.

One great conspirator confronted another, and as might have been predicted, the Bolshevik won. He developed an entire false anti-Bolshevik organization known as "The Trust," with a false subsidiary body called the "Liberal Democrats (LDs)." Representatives of the LDs established contact with Savinkov and carefully, over time, convinced him of their counter-revolutionary bona fides. Then they offered him leadership of the bogus group, and lured him home, where immediately the secret police scooped him up. His two-day public trial in Moscow in August 1924 was a sensation. At it, he appeared to acknowledge not merely that the Bolsheviks had bested him, but that he had been wrong from the start to oppose them. He received the death sentence, which then was commuted to ten years behind bars. Shortly thereafter, he either jumped from a window to his death, or someone pushed him.

* * *

Having escaped Russia by an undetermined route, Sidney Reilly reappeared in England in November 1918, and almost immediately wrote to Lockhart: "I consider that there is a very earnest obligation upon me to continue to serve...in the question of Russia or Bolshevism....I should like nothing better than to serve under you."[10] Lockhart was no longer interested, but the British SIS was. It sent him, and George Hill, right back into the lion's mouth (or rather the bear's), to the Black Sea area this time, looking for information that would be useful at the Paris Peace Conference. Reilly advocated British military assistance to the Whites of the region.

When he again returned to England, he joined several above-ground anti-Soviet bodies, but also, he developed close ties with Boris Savinkov. He sold off his unrivalled collection of Napoleonic memorabilia to help finance Savinkov's efforts. He maintained contact with Lockhart, and more closely with the SIS men he had known in Russia, George Hill especially. Increasingly, however, he focused upon the murky and ever more desperate White under-ground. As always, he lived high; as always, he kept a string of women. He bigamously married his fourth wife, Nelly Louise "Pepita" Burton, an actress, in 1923.

In 1925 he traveled in secret to Russia, to meet with the leaders of the anti-Bolshevik resistance. Only his travel was not so secret, because the men with whom he met belonged to the same Potemkin organization that had tricked Boris Savinkov the previous year. Reilly's arrest followed swiftly, but there would be no trial; he had been tried in absentia seven years before and the sentence had been delivered. It remained only to carry it out.

They held him at the Lubianka, grilled him day and night, threatened him with immediate death, indeed went so far as to call in the executioner and have him load his pistol. For some obscure purpose Reilly kept a brief prison diary, written with pencil in tiny handwriting on cigarette papers. He knew it would be found. He wrote: "I am glad I can show them how an English Christian understands his duty."[11] He was not English and he was not Christian, and he did not do his duty, which was to keep silent. Rather, he wrote a letter to Felix Dzerzhinsky, offering to tell all he knew about the British SIS, and even to work for the Joint State Political Directorate (OGPU), in exchange for his life. Dzerzhinsky did not answer. Perhaps he realized Reilly kept to a bargain only so long as it suited him. They shot the "Ace of Spies" on November 5, 1925.

George Hill lived long enough to write his friend's biography, but could never sell it.[12] While holding a string of unfulfilling jobs during the interwar period, he did manage to publish two memoirs, enlarging upon—which is to say, embellishing—his exploits in wartime Russia. The SIS brought him back into service when World War II began, and returned him to Moscow to coordinate espionage efforts in occupied Europe with the NKVD. Historians judge this mission to have been a failure. After the war he became a director of a British-owned German mineral water company: "a strange finale for a man who was never known to have refused a drink."[13] He died in 1968.

*　　*　　*

Of Lockhart's closest friends and associates in Russia, two merit a few more words. The first of them, Raymond Robins, had failed to change American Soviet policy when he returned home in June 1918, and although forceful, energetic and well connected as ever, never played a major political role again. He did have some influence in Chicago during the 1920s as an advocate of clean government. He also became an apostle of prohibition and world disarmament during this period. In 1932, while traveling to meet President Hoover, whom he knew from the Red Cross campaign to feed starving Russia, he disappeared without a trace, only to turn up three months later living in a boarding house in Whittier, North Carolina, the victim of total amnesia.

From this odd experience he made a full recovery, but the rest of his life was a sad comedown for the confidant of Lenin and Trotsky, the intimate friend of Teddy Roosevelt, the former progressive candidate for the US Senate in Illinois. Yet Robins did have one last moment in the sun. He helped to persuade Franklin Roosevelt to recognize the Soviet Union formally, and to exchange ambassadors. At a victory dinner at the Waldorf Astoria in New York City, he delivered what Lockhart termed "the speech of the year." But Lockhart had not been present. Robins refused to invite the man he claimed "had ratted over intervention after he left Moscow." When Lockhart went to the USA on a book tour after publication of his *British Agent*, the two men lunched together. It was an uncomfortable occasion.[14]

Bad luck dogged Robins. While pruning a tree on his Florida estate, he fell to the ground and injured his spine. He never recovered, and remained an invalid, dying in 1954.

Arthur Ransome's story, post-1918, was much more eventful, and, after he divorced his first wife and married "the big girl," Evgenia Shelepina in 1924, much happier. When the Cheka broke up Lockhart's plot, Ransome was in Stockholm, directing the Bolshevik news service referred to in Chapter 14, cabling dispatches to the *Daily News* in London about Russian events, and sending reports on Russia to the Foreign Office. In his newspaper dispatches he doubted that those accused of the plot could have been so stupid as even to plan it. He wrote that the appointment of Dzerzhinsky and Peters to investigate the affair practically guaranteed fair treatment for the accused. He did write privately to Radek, urging him not to harm the plotters and to free them all; any other course would result in terrible publicity for the revolutionaries. British officials in Sweden bombarded the Foreign Office with telegrams asking what to do with, or about, this near Bolshevik British journalist.

The Foreign Office, and indeed the Secret Intelligence Service itself, did not know what to do with Arthur Ransome, because they remained always in two minds about him. The files of S.76, as he was known to SIS, bulge with contradictory assessments of his character and loyalty. The following is perhaps the most accurate, but not the most typical: "He has, I think, no special political views. But through his association with the Bolsheviks in Moscow, he became intensely interested in their idealism, and in certain aspects of their work, and also in certain personalities.... S.76 may be regarded as absolutely honest.... He will report what he sees, but he does not see quite straight."[15]

Ransome remained on good terms with Bruce Lockhart for the rest of his life although they did not often see each other. In the spring of 1919, he applied to him again for help getting his lover into Britain, and for the second time, Lockhart did right by her, and by his friend.[16] To no avail: the authorities would not permit the couple to live in England for five more years. In the meantime, Ransome traveled to and from Russia several times with Evgenia or to meet her, often courting great danger, often escaping dire consequences by great good luck. He left the *Daily News* for the *Manchester Guardian*, for which he became until 1930 a roving foreign correspondent, although always with a primary interest in Russia. He reviewed Lockhart's *British Agent* for that newspaper in November 1932, and Lockhart immediately wrote to him: "You heap coals of fire upon my head and I thank you from the bottom of my heart. No one is more fitted to write the review than you. No one, I am sure, will be half so kind as you have been."[17]

Even before returning to Britain with his bride in 1925, Ransome spent every spare moment fishing or sailing or bird watching, or writing about those pursuits, until finally he began the *Swallows and Amazons* series of children's books that made him even more famous than he was already. By then he had left politically engaged journalism and political pamphleteering far behind. He grew stout, then fat, but remained cheery. He owned a cottage in the Lake District, where he lived out his life unostentatiously and happily with his Russian sweetheart now his wife. She cared for him in his final illness, which took him in 1967. She lived on until 1975.

* * *

Felix Dzerzhinsky was exhausted and ill in the fall of 1918. At the beginning of October, just as Lockhart was boarding the train for the Finnish frontier, he was setting out for Switzerland to try to recuperate, and to see his wife and son. There is a story, probably apocryphal, that he and Lockhart actually came face to face on

Figure 26. Felix Dzerzhinsky, wife and son

Lake Lugano: it is said that the erstwhile British agent stood on the deck of a steamer approaching the jetty, Dzerzhinsky, with his family, was just about to board a different craft. "The eyes of the two men met. Fortunately, Lockhart did not recognize Dzerzhinsky."[18] It is a piquant but unlikely tale, as Lockhart almost certainly was in London at that time.

The trip to Switzerland may have been restorative for Dzerzhinsky, but he never regained his health. Nor did he ever change his modus operandi or his fundamental outlook. He wrote to his brother-in-law in 1919: "I am always in motion, in the thick of the changes and the creation of a new life…I want and must take part in its creation…until I reach the end—eternal rest."[19] Long before he reached the end, in fact only months after returning from wife and son to Russia, he sent instructions to his subordinates in the Cheka throughout the country. They said in part: "1. Make out a list of the entire population from which hostages can be taken, namely former landowners, merchants, factory owners, industrialists, bankers, large real-estate owners, officers of the old army, important officials of the tsarist and Kerensky regimes, and relatives of persons who are fighting against us…2. Send in these lists…"[20] He reserved to himself and other top Cheka officials the right to choose who would live and who would die. Perhaps this was his attempt to control unbridled Terror. If so, it cannot have reassured many.

A little later, he oversaw the translation of the Cheka first into the State Political Directorate (GPU) and then, when the Soviet Union came into being in 1923, into the OGPU. Ostensibly subordinate to the Council of People's Commissars, really the OGPU was a further enlarged secret police, with power to oversee and coordinate intelligence and counter-intelligence activities throughout the entire Soviet Union. But here is the other side to the extraordinary man who led this terrifying body until his death: at the same time as he was directing it in a ruthless war against the Whites and other enemies of the state, he was creating a national program to care for all the orphans of the civil war.

He died in 1926, two years after the death of Lenin, immediately after having delivered an important speech defending the economic policies of the Stalinist majority on the Politburo, and harshly attacking its critics who were led by Kamenev and Trotsky. It was a raucous occasion, and as Dzerzhinsky answered hecklers his face beaded with sweat and turned pale. "I never spare myself…never," he answered them defiantly. "If I see something is going wrong I come down on it with all my strength." But he had no strength left. He had to be helped from the hall when he had finished, and then back to his apartment at the Kremlin, where he collapsed. The doctors could not resuscitate him.

The Bolsheviks tried to build a cult around their dead hero. The Futurist poet, Mayakovsky, wrote: "To a young lad plunged into meditation after whom to model his life just commencing, I would say without hesitation—model it on Comrade Dzerzhinsky." The OGPU placed an effigy of his body, dressed in uniform, with death masks of his face and hands, in a glass coffin at its officers' club, a kind of shrine. Lubianka Square in Moscow became Dzerzhinsky Square. Forty years after "Iron Felix" had defeated the Lockhart Plot, Khrushchev's regime erected a towering statue of him there. But thirty years after that, the citizens of Moscow tore it down. Still Russia is not yet done with Felix Dzerzhinsky: in 2015 the Moscow Soviet agreed to hold a referendum on whether the statue should be restored.

*   *   *

And finally, Moura Benckendorff and Bruce Lockhart: she had watched sorrowfully as his train disappeared from the Nikolaevski Station and then returned to an empty apartment. He maintained a poker face among the newly liberated, jubilant, British and French officials boarding the train with him. Indeed, he flashed an insouciant smile, according to George Hill. But Lockhart wrote that when the steaming locomotive pulled slowly away from the station, he felt "a leaden feeling in my heart," just as Moura did.[21]

Yet there was this great difference between his situation and hers: she would continue to live in a country wracked by civil war, terrorized by rampant secret police, plagued by shortages of everything essential for decent living; he was returning to a country about to reap the fruits of victory in a great war, and in which the established norms of civil society prevailed. Of course, he faced challenges: his career and marriage were in jeopardy, or maybe even ruins, but she faced tests far more daunting than his.

There was another great difference. She had given him her heart, forever. He thought he had given his to her, and had told her so, and she believed him. In fact, he was incapable of such devotion, as both his previous history and the rest of his life would demonstrate. Moreover, he was returning to his wife, who would soon know about the affair, if rumors of it had not reached her already. She would undoubtedly do her best to help him put it behind him. Blinded by love, Moura had not yet fully assessed her lover's character, had not realized his inability to resist the temptations and distractions soon to confront him, and did not foresee what was about to happen.

In the wake of her miscarriage, he had told her she should not accompany him on the voyage home. Upon arrival in England, with memories of her still fresh in his mind, with his wife perhaps pale in comparison, he appears to have reconsidered and to have suggested that Moura immediately come to him after all. Too late: now she could not do so. Her mother was gravely ill. Moura planned a rendezvous with him in Stockholm instead. Her plan fell through, for complicated reasons.

She wrote to him nearly every day for several years; he replied regularly at first, although the post in Russia was unreliable and the letters arrived in batches and sporadically. Sometimes friends carried the letters for them, to avoid the censors. But his letters began to tail off; after two years they ceased to arrive at all.

He saved the ones she wrote him; at some point she destroyed his. Three of hers during the 1918–21 period stand out as signposts in the alteration of their relationship. She wrote the first on May 9, 1919, when she still thought they would soon be reunited. It was shortly before her mother passed away. In this letter, she told him that something terrible had happened. "My husband has been killed…by some Estonians [sic]…In what a hopeless, endless muddle of conflicting emotions I am plunged."[22] When her mother died only a few weeks later, she really was alone. But if she thought that meant there would be fewer obstacles to their meeting she was mistaken. His letters were petering out.

She wrote the second notable letter to him on June 24, 1921, two years after having heard from him last. During the interval she had begun to make a life for herself without him, but she continued to dream that someday they would be together again. When he finally broke silence, however, it was to convey devastating news. She wrote back to him: "There is no use asking you why and how and when, is [there]? As a matter of fact…this letter is of no use at all, only that there is something in me that aches so intensely that I must shout it out to you. Your son? A fine boy?…I thought I'd forgotten how to cry." She knew now that he had left her forever. Still she could not stop loving him.

The third letter dates from early August 1924, and it marks the moment when he finally summoned the courage to say they were done for good in so many words and to her face. She had managed a meeting after all (in Vienna as it happened), but she might almost have wished it had never occurred. Precisely what he said to her cannot be recovered, although he wrote about it in one of his memoirs (but of course that was a sanitized version). Afterward he wrote to her, not for publication, "the thrill is gone, never to be revived," and told her he was living "another life than that of six years ago." She replied: "I will not speak of the triumphant feeling of knowing love that was stronger than death. All this is something which from now on belongs to me alone."

She was right. He only thought he had experienced that feeling at the height of their romance. Eventually, in 1933, she would move to London. They began to meet regularly again. They would lunch, dine, drink, gossip, and reminisce. She would never cease to love him. She would call him "Baby" when she wrote to him, and he would sign his letters to her with that same endearment. But he had ended the affair, and, once she understood that it could never be resurrected because he no longer loved her as she did him, she resolutely closed the book and went on with her life.

* * *

Lockhart never again experienced the giddy drama of Russia in 1918. He had fallen from a great height. Soon he realized that the Foreign Office would not let him climb the ladder again, and after a few years as a commercial secretary in Prague, he switched to international banking. It bored him. But his charm, quick brain, and uncanny knack for befriending important people remained. While in Prague he got to know well both Thomas Masaryk, Czechoslovakia's first president, and his son, Jan, who became the country's ambassador to Britain; also, he befriended Eduard Benes who would serve as Czechoslovakia's president and prime minister.

On the other side of the ledger, he began, in Prague, to gain a reputation for lavish spending, heavy drinking and, if he did not already have it, womanizing. He would hire a gypsy band for an evening, not once but several times in a week. He would spend a night visiting not one nightclub or cabaret, but several. He drank too much, would vow to quit, and then immediately break the vow. He went into debt, first a little, then a lot, and could not think how to get out of it. He suffered bouts of depression. He often felt ill or "seedy," as he put it in his diary. He did not get on well with his wife, even after she had borne him a son, but then again, he did not often see her.

Robert Bruce Lockhart had extraordinary talent. Everything came easily to him. He could measure his natural abilities against those of the great men he knew, and not feel small. Probably he thought he could have been great himself, and perhaps he could have been. He had nearly achieved world-shaking results in 1918. Yet his career was stalled, and he saw no way to restart it. The bad behavior betrayed his frustration and unhappiness. In his memoirs he would reveal himself to be his own harshest critic. But self-knowledge was not enough. He could not change his mode of operation, and he knew that too. The self-knowledge prompted something that sometimes approached self-loathing.

To supplement his income he began to write, which returned him to the attention of Max Aitken, Lord Beaverbrook, owner of a chain of newspapers. Beaverbrook, whom he had first met shortly after his return from Russia in 1918, was a fabled character, a political fixer, disreputable, ruthless, ambitious, and sly. He played his hunches, usually successfully. Now, on a hunch, he hired Lockhart to write the "Londoner's Diary" column in his London newspaper, the *Evening Standard*. As was often the case with Beaverbrook, the hunch proved to be an inspired one, at least from his own standpoint. Lockhart could write, he could beguile, he moved easily in almost any circle. His column became essential reading for those interested in the intersection between high society and high politics in late 1920s and early 1930s Britain.

Lockhart also conducted more serious journalism. For example, he became the first English journalist to interview the former German Kaiser. He interviewed the German Foreign Minister, Gustav Stresemann. He wrote many of the *Standard*'s leaders, and the leaders for Beaverbrook's other newspapers. But he never enjoyed journalism and, after the success of his *British Agent* (1932) which mainly recounted his adventures in Russia, he quit it except on a freelance basis. Instead he wrote books: about his life and further adventures, about fishing, which (like Arthur Ransome) he loved, about Central European politics and affairs. He did continue to consult occasionally with the Foreign Office, although he no longer had a formal connection with it. A few people in Whitehall still knew enough, however, to take advantage of his deep knowledge—not only of Russia, but now of Central, Eastern, and Southern Europe too. The Foreign Office would continue to consult him as the international situation worsened over the decade.

His marriage had gone sour. His wife, as extravagant as he, suffered from what were then termed "nerves." He began spending a lot of time with Vera Mary (Tommy) Rosslyn, the beautiful third wife of the dissolute Harry, fifth Earl of Rosslyn. Twenty years earlier, he had contemplated converting to Islam to make life easier with Amai in Malaya. Now, influenced by Tommy, he did convert to Catholicism. Thus, he joined the church that Felix Dzerzhinsky had abandoned as a youth.

Tommy had entrée to reaches of British society even higher than the ones he inhabited. Through her, he came to know the Prince of Wales, soon to become Edward VIII. They golfed together and socialized. In London in the 1930s, it was for him as it had been in Moscow during the golden years before the war: financial, industrial, scholarly, artistic, literary, political, and aristocratic lions and lionesses all enjoyed his company. He enjoyed theirs too, and if he did not match Sidney Reilly's long string of adulterous affairs, nevertheless he conducted many.

But he was wasting his talents and he knew it. In Moscow before the war his contacts made it possible for him to help shape British policy towards Russia. In London they made it possible for him to write what was, in the last analysis, merely a gossip column. By this stage the drinking had become a serious problem; so had the extravagance. He condemned himself in his diary time after time; resolved to improve; broke his resolutions. Moura, too, knew that he was wasting himself. She sent him a letter in reply to one of his: "I have just shown the envelope of your letter to a man here who is a wonderful graphologist." The expert had discerned "callousness" in Lockhart's handwriting. He told Moura: "This man has developed such an indifference to his moral self that this callousness is like a beard that no razor can remove anymore."[23]

After a long separation, Lockhart and Jean divorced early in 1937. He moved in with Tommy, whose husband finally had passed away, but they argued about money and soon separated, never having married. In 1942 he married his secretary, Francis Mary (Mollie) Beck. It appears to have been a marriage of convenience. He told his son the marriage would not interfere with his continuing to see Moura. Probably he was seeing other women too.

World War II brought him back into government service and right into the center of things again. It was, briefly, a resurrection. Because he knew Benes and Jan Masaryk, he served for a time as Britain's representative to the Czech government in exile in London. More significantly, he became director general of the Political Warfare Executive, in charge of coordinating propaganda in enemy countries. Here was a job to tax even his abilities: in the end, he oversaw a department of 8,000 people. He was performing important, interesting work and it consumed him; but it lacked the immediate edge, danger, and romance of his assignment in Russia a quarter century before. After the war, he immediately made clear that he wanted no more government work.[24]

Then came the sad coda. He retired with his second wife to Edinburgh, but the climate did not agree with him. They moved to Falmouth in Cornwall. There he felt isolated, grew sentimental and depressed, found it difficult even to write. He went on seeing Moura whenever he traveled up to London. She always tried to brace him. In the 1960s he began to suffer increasing dementia. He died in 1970.

* * *

Moura proved tougher. She endured not merely the privations of revolutionary Russia but overcame and transcended them. Sometime in 1919, she managed to obtain an introduction to Russia's greatest living writer, Maxim Gorky, friend of Lenin, critic of Bolshevik excesses. He lived in a vast flat in Petrograd. People came and stayed, or passed through it, as they pleased; it was a hippie commune before the term "hippie" had been invented. Moura, the daughter of a great Ukrainian landowner and widow of a Russian diplomat and aristocrat moved in. She became Gorky's muse and lover, and because while still a child she had learned English and French and German, she soon became Gorky's translator and business agent for foreign rights as well. She was no longer wealthy; the Bolsheviks had dispossessed her, as they had stripped her entire social class of its wealth and belongings, but she earned sufficient income as a translator.

Probably she had made an arrangement with Jacov Peters and the Cheka in September 1918 in order to get out of Butyrka Prison and to save her lover. The Cheka seems to have given Moura an assignment once she came to know Gorky. The literary lion did not belong to the Bolshevik Party yet. He was a genuine maverick, principled and uncontrollable, but also untouchable because of his longstanding friendship with Lenin. The Cheka instructed Moura not to harm Gorky, but to spy on him and his friends, and to report back. Only once she got to know the great man, she could not do it. He fascinated and attracted her. "He was an entire world," she said. She confessed to him what the Cheka wanted her to do. Gorky went to Lenin and persuaded him to tell the Cheka to leave Moura alone.

Also, during this period, Moura married a young Estonian nobleman, the Baron Budberg. Love had nothing to do with it. Marriage to him procured her an Estonian passport, which in turn made possible foreign travel, which made possible her work and income. As for the Baron: he moved to South America and spent the rest of his life playing cards. She rarely, if ever, saw him again.

When Gorky left Russia, first for Central Europe and then for Sorrento, Italy, where he lived for many years, Moura joined him, traveling on the Estonian passport. By now she was acquiring manuscripts for a firm that published foreign works in Russian. Sorrento was her base, but she criss-crossed the continent meeting Europe's leading authors—and not only them. As much as Bruce Lockhart, she had a talent for attracting men with power, or men close to power. She slept with many of them.

Also, she traveled in and out of Russia. Why? How? Rumors flew about her: that she worked for Russian intelligence, for British intelligence, for German intelligence. Perhaps she still had a connection with the Russian NKVD, as it now was, but there is no hard evidence. Once, she met Mussolini and complained about Italian surveillance of Gorky. "We are not watching him," the Italian dictator replied. "We are watching you." When Gorky died in 1936, she returned to Russia for his funeral. There is a film showing her standing next to Stalin, near Gorky's coffin. Thus, rumor compounded. The rumors never ceased. When, in 2010, Nick Clegg, leader of the Liberal Democrat Party, became deputy prime minister in David Cameron's coalition government, newspapers soon discovered that his grandmother had been Moura's half-sister. He was, the *Daily Mail* blared, the grandnephew of Russia's Mata Hari.[25]

In 1920, the great English novelist, H. G. Wells, had visited Russia and stayed with Gorky at the vast flat in Petrograd. There he met Moura. (Possibly, he had met her once before, in 1914.) She entranced him; he interested her. One night she came to his room and they made love. He returned to England and to his own notoriously amorous existence there, but he did not forget the beautiful and intriguing Russian woman. "She had magnificence," he was to say. In 1931, she traveled to Britain on business, and the two resumed relations. In 1933, Gorky returned to Russia, hoping to protect authors from increasingly brutal repression. Moura did not go with him. Gorky told her not to because he was not sure he could shield her from the Stalinists. (In fact, she may still have had some connection to the Stalinists.) But at Wells' urging, she moved to Britain and soon to London.

She no longer had any illusions about Bruce Lockhart, although she could see him often now, and did so. She made her peace with their changed relationship. Finally, she could understand him for what he really was: "a creature of childish and wise complexities."[26] She knew that he admired and felt shamed by her, and found their meetings crucial. It was Wells, however, with whom she now engaged in her primary romantic relationship. "H.G." left all his other women for her. He proposed to marry her more than once. She cared for him in every sense of the word, as she did for Lockhart, right up until Wells' death in 1945, but she would not consent to become his wife. Usually with women, Wells dominated. With Moura it went the other way.

Her circle in prewar Britain came to include most of the artistic, theatrical, and literary elite; also, important politicians. After the war, she continued to preside over an exceptionally wide circle: writers, poets, musicians, actors, directors, composers, journalists, important politicians, spies: she fascinated them all, and took many of them to bed. Aside from Lockhart, Gorky, and Wells, however, no one—except for family—could really touch her now.

She was always busy, always traveling, or writing, editing, translating, consulting, or entertaining and being entertained. She could drink any amount of gin and never show the effects. Lockhart had broken her heart, but not her appetite for life. In the end no one lived life more fully than she, especially not Lockhart, for whom excess had become a byword.

* * *

In May 1918, she told Lockhart that she would love him forever, unconditionally. In February 1970, Lockhart died. His family arranged the funeral. Two days later, more than half a century after that declaration of love, Moura, old and heavy and wrinkled, scheduled a memorial service for him at the imposing Russian Orthodox Church in Kensington, Ennismore Gardens. Under golden chandeliers hung high above the nave, a choir chanted unearthly music; a priest lit a golden censer; fragrant smoke drifted through the vast space. Moura was the only mourner under that great domed roof, alone except for her grief and memories. What combination of thoughts and remembrances rushed then through her mind?

When the service finished, she would have gotten up and walked out onto the Brompton Road. There were people to meet, parties to go to, theater and movies and concerts to attend, travel plans to perfect, books still to read, the whole fascinating business of life. She would carry on for four more years. When she died, the funeral took place at the same church. This time, the building was packed.

CHAPTER 18

CONCLUSION

It is a story of love and romance and idealism—and of their curdling. In 1918, Lockhart had known that Anglo-Bolshevik cooperation would be good for both parties. A friendly Russia would be good for Britain, not only in the war against Germany but after it, for economic reasons. A friendly Britain would be good for Russia, not only at present when Russia lacked for everything, but in the future, when she might temper the Bolshevik sense of beleaguerment and help to moderate Bolshevik polices. Lockhart also understood that the Russian counter-revolutionary movement was disunited, reactionary, ineffectual, even unworthy. He ignored what he knew.

After Raymond Robins returned to America, Lockhart could not resist the chance to advance his career by joining the interventionist camp. Neither could Cromie, Reilly, or any of the others among Lockhart's circle, except for Arthur Ransome—and Ransome worked for a newspaper, not a government. Bolshevik excesses made opposition to the regime easier, but it was the possibility of self-advancement that moved Lockhart and his colleagues most. The chance to wield power, and having wielded it successfully to be in a position to wield it again, was a great aphrodisiac. For Lockhart in the end it was a more potent aphrodisiac than even Moura von Benckendorff. But the cost of it! As Reilly said, the plotters would win only if they employed methods "as subterranean, as secret, as mysterious, as ferocious and inhuman"' as those employed by their opponents. That is what they planned to do.[1]

On the other side, Felix Dzerzhinsky and Jacov Peters personified the degeneration of Bolshevism. Dzerzhinsky personified it most starkly. Perhaps of all the former idealists in this book, he had farthest to fall. He saw the movement to which he had devoted his life, and its greatest achievement, the Soviet State, beset on all sides, completely isolated, likely to go under. There was nothing he would not do to save it. He would launch systematic terror. He would defend heaven, as he conceived it, with hell. Peters too: the man whose eyes once had brimmed with human tenderness became, according to a Dutch journalist, "the most awful figure of the Russian Red Terror, the man with the most murder on his soul."[2]

The story of the Lockhart Plot is a story of debasement on all sides then, and of fear, cynicism, opportunism—and futility. Even the great romance proved futile. Men and women make their own history, but not in conditions of their own choosing, and therefore rarely as they would wish it. Lockhart and his colleagues hoped their plot would represent a turning point in Russian, and even world history, but it was a turning point that failed to turn. Dzerzhinsky and his colleagues thought they were building paradise, but that is not what they built. History is not unknowable, except while it is being made.

Of course, the story of the Lockhart Plot is more than an authentic historical thriller. It transcends all the elements of the genre: suspense, treachery, violence, love and desire, larger-than-life personalities, to make a larger point. At a historical moment when literally everything in Russia was in the melting pot, all the protagonists, on both sides, understood what was at stake, but not one understood his own inconsequence. Perhaps Lenin had an inkling when he said of the plot, "It is like something in a novel," that is to say, fantastic, unrealistic. Perhaps he realized that the forces at work in Russia in 1918 were too vast for anyone to harness or channel, let alone divert into another channel altogether as Lockhart wished to do. With Lenin's guidance, the Bolsheviks managed to ride the raging torrent, but that was not preordained, as they themselves well knew.

And yet, the Lockhart Plot *might* have succeeded, in which case everything would be different, although we can only guess at the ways. But Dzerzhinsky and Peters prevailed, with consequences we can know: most obviously long-lasting Soviet distrust of the Western powers and a siege mentality that helped to justify creation of the Soviet police state. It is hard to imagine that is what they were aiming at—and of course it was not only the Lockhart Plot that led them there. But, when the Chekists slammed shut the door that the plotters were pushing to open, meaning to preserve Lenin's life, and Russia's right to self-determination, they also made more likely those disastrous consequences, all unforeseen and none inevitable. A century on, in the age of Putin and Trump, we may still hear ringing, however faintly, the echoes of the Lockhart Plot.

ACKNOWLEDGEMENTS

The path that brought me to an interest in the Lockhart Plot was long and indirect. In April 1981, I met John Grigg in New Haven, Connecticut. I was then an assistant professor of modern British history at Yale University. He was a prize-winning historian, a former lord who had given up his title to uphold democratic principles, a well-known columnist for important British newspapers, a Tory Radical who once had raised a storm by criticizing in print the young Queen Elizabeth for being out of touch with her subjects. He had receding white hair when I met him, a cherubic pink face, an invariable smile, and he seemed always to be inviting me to laugh with him. But he took me seriously when we discussed history or politics, which we did even on that initial occasion. He had first-hand knowledge of the British political world and he seemed to know everyone important. I was dazzled. For whatever reason, he took a kindly interest in me. Although he was twenty-five years my senior we became friends.

Usually when I went to London I would stay at the temporarily unoccupied home of one or another fellow academic who likewise had gone traveling. But in the summer of 1986, none of my friends left London, nor could they suggest accommodation with anyone else. In desperation, I wrote to John. By then I lived in Atlanta, Georgia. It was June, unbearably hot and humid, and when the kitchen telephone rang one steamy, sweltering afternoon, I was perspiring by the stove, unwisely boiling spaghetti for my two young sons who were dueling vigorously with plastic baseball bats in the living room. It was John. "I have a place for you to stay in central London," he announced cheerily. "But before you contact your new landlady, read her book." Next day I went to the library and found it: *A Little of All These: An Estonian Childhood*, by Tania Alexander. As I read, I realized my friend had done me a favor far greater than the one for which I had asked.

Although it was meant to be a memoir, the real subject of Tania's book was not her own life, remarkable though that had been and (as I would come to realize) continued to be, but rather the life of her mother, which was more remarkable still. Of course, her mother was Moura.

Beginning that summer, and for nearly twenty-five years after, whenever I went to London I would stay at Tania's little house in Knightsbridge. We too became friends. I had heard of the Lockhart Plot before I read her book, but after reading it I knew a good deal more. Talking with Tania over the years, I learned more still, more than any published work had ever disclosed. It was not until 2015, however, some years after Tania had passed away, while reading the first volume of Stephen Kotkin's projected multi-volume biography of Joseph Stalin, that it occurred to me I might write a book about it. The Lockhart Plot seemed to me to be an important subject; also, dramatic, romantic, intrinsically gripping; what was more, through Tania I had a tangential connection to it.

I knew that Russian sources would be difficult to access. I knew from Tania that Moura had left no papers. I knew from the myriad of published works mentioning the plot, that British government sources are silent on certain of its embarrassing aspects and that probably someone has weeded them. I decided to plow forward anyway. Today I have many people to thank for helping me pull the plow.

To begin with, I could not have pulled it at all without financial support from my home institution, the Georgia Institute of Technology, and here special thanks must go to Jackie Royster, Dean of the Ivan Allen College of Liberal Arts, who steered an exceptional research grant my way. Also, to Steve Usselman, chairman of the School of History and Sociology, who likewise found ways and means to support my work. They deserve special thanks, not only for helping me personally, but also for having done their best to create a supportive and humane atmosphere at Georgia Tech.

Other individuals also deserve mention. The first would be Andrey Shlyakhter, a Russian history graduate student who, by the time of publication of this book, will have obtained his doctorate from the University of Chicago. Andrey did not merely translate many hundreds of pages from Russian into English for me, although he would deserve many thanks just for that. But also, he helped me find Russian sources I would not have known even to look for. And then, when I was trying to figure out if Moura had worked for the Cheka, he put me in touch with senior members of the history faculty of the FSB Academy in Moscow; when I was trying to discover if Moura had a connection with Ukrainian Intelligence, he put me in touch with leading Ukrainian scholars of the subject in Kiev. He is a creative, resourceful, assiduous scholar himself, and I was extremely lucky to have his help.

I was lucky, too, to meet and to get to know Jamie Bruce Lockhart, great nephew of "wicked uncle Bertie" as he recalled him. Jamie was the literary executor of his uncle, Robin Bruce Lockhart, son of my protagonist. Robin, who inherited his father's papers, was the biographer of Sidney Reilly. He became an expert on the Lockhart Plot, but never wrote a book about it. The same may be said of Jamie.

Jamie was generous, sharing what he knew about the plot and about his great uncle with me, over meals and via an extended correspondence. He read and commented on my draft manuscript. I was shocked to read that he died in October 2018, never having had a chance to read this tribute to him.

Then, I was lucky, yet again, to make the epistolary acquaintance of Richard Spence, the author of important works on Sidney Reilly and Boris Savinkov. Although himself hard at work on a book of his own, Richard found time to answer my questions and, most generously, to find documents he had collected in Russia many years before, and to photocopy and send them to me. I thanked him at the time, and I take this opportunity to thank him again, in print.

Two friends, Peter Dimock and Marc Jaffe, both independent editors, helped me think about how to present this book. Its final shape owes much to their expert advice. And three more individuals also deserve special recognition. Another Russian history graduate student, Isaac Scarborough, carried out research for me at both the RGASPI and GARF archives in Moscow; Grace Segran, at a moment's notice, translated Lockhart's prison musings in Malay into English; and Murray Frame, a bare acquaintance, generously photographed and mailed to me Lockhart's application to join the British Consular Service from the National Archives.

While researching and writing the book I corresponded with various experts in the field. Every one of them responded to my questions with grace, patience, and good advice. I will thank them by name: the Russian scholars Vladimir Khaustov and A. A. Zdanovich, both connected to the FSB Academy; the Ukrainians, Tamara Vron'ska and Vladimir Sidak; the British-based Canadian, James Harris; and the Americans, David Shearer, Alexander Rabinowich, Arch Getty, and Hioraki Kuromiya.

I want to thank too the many archivists in the UK and USA with whom I had dealings. All of them did their best to help me. Special thanks must go to the staff at the National Archives in Kew, where I conducted much of the research for this book. I must have wearied them as day after day I requested they bring me volumes (no doubt hundreds in the end) from wherever they are stored in that enormous building. Sometimes I recalled volumes I had sent back only the day before. Still they brought them.

Friends and colleagues discussed the project with me over the years, and read portions of, or in a few cases even entire versions of, what eventually became this book. I thank in alphabetical order by last name: Daniel Amsterdam, Chris Clark, John Drucker, Murray Frame, Rob Harding, Ken Knoespel, John Krige, David Large, Terry MacFadyen, Lynn Olsen, Rose Rosiello, Paul Rowe, Seth Schneer, and Peter Shizgal. They helped me to think and rethink and saved me from numerous mistakes and infelicities of style. If they missed any, then I own them.

Three anonymous readers for Oxford University Press read what I thought would be the final draft of my manuscript and made many excellent suggestions for improving it. I have done my best to follow their advice and I take this opportunity to thank them for it. I am grateful, too, for the efficient and sympathetic approach of my OUP editor, Matthew Cotton.

My agents, Peter Robinson in London and George Lucas in New York City, provided advice, encouragement, even sustenance. Thank you both.

And finally, I want to thank my wife, Margaret Hayman. Once I get involved with researching and writing a book I develop tunnel vision. This cannot be pleasant to live with, but she never complains because she knows I like being in the tunnel, and better still, coming out of it and back to her.

JONATHAN SCHNEER
Atlanta, GA
February 5, 2019

LIST OF ABBREVIATIONS

CUL	Cambridge University Library
HLRO	House of Lords Record Office
KCLHC	King's College, Liddle Hart Centre
LUBL	Leeds University, Brotherton Library
OUNBL	Oxford University, New Bodleian Library
SUHI	Stanford University, Hoover Institute
TNA	The National Archives, London
UILL	University of Indiana, Lily Library
WSHS	Wisconsin State Historical Society

END NOTES

Chapter 1

1. SUHI, Lockhart Collection, Box 1.
2. *New York Times*, February 28, 1970.
3. LUBL, Russian Archive Shorter Collection, Lockhart to Shorter, January 16, 1914.
4. TNA, CSC 11/161, William Sime, his first employer in Malaya.
5. Bruce Lockhart, *Return to Malaya*, London, 1936, *passim*.
6. TNA, CSC 11/161. The referee was A. MacGregor.
7. SUHI, Lockhart Collection, Box 10, "Testimonial," March 31, 1911.
8. Pavel Malkov, *Reminiscences of a Kremlin Commandant*, Moscow, 1959: Malkov wrote of Lockhart that "he spoke fluent Russian with no trace of an accent," p. 269. Ian Buikis agreed in his "Proschet Lokkarta," in I. E. Polikarenkov (ed.), *Osoboe zadanie. Vospominaniia veteranov-chekistov*, Moscow, 1988, p. 81, trans. Andrey Shlyakhter.
9. Kenneth Bourne and D. Cameron Watt (eds.), *British Documents on Foreign Affairs: Reports and Papers from the Foreign Office Confidential Print*, Part II, Series H., 2 volumes, University Publications of America, 1989, Lockhart to Buchanan, June 11, 1917, Doc. 55, p. 111.
10. Ibid., Lockhart to Buchanan, n.d. (but sometime in August or September 1915 from internal evidence), Doc. 125, p. 92.
11. Ibid., Lockhart to Buchanan, September 27, 1915, Doc. 204, p. 184.
12. Ibid., Lockhart to Buchanan, January 22, 1916, Doc. 263, p. 282.
13. Ibid., Lockhart to Buchanan, January 22, 1916, Doc. 263, p. 281.
14. Ibid., Lockhart to Buchanan, July 23, 1917, Doc. 92, p. 166.
15. Ibid., Lockhart to Buchanan, January 22, 1916, Doc. 263, p. 283.
16. Ibid., Lockhart to Buchanan, May 1, 1917, Doc. 13, p. 63.
17. Ibid., Lockhart to Buchanan, May 8, 1917, Doc. 22, p. 74.
18. TNA, FO 371/2454/136408, Minute by G. Clerk, September 23, 1915.
19. TNA, FO 371/2455/149/853, Minute by G. Clerk, October 16, 1915.
20. But for a contrary view, see Sean McMeekin, *The Russian Revolution*, New York, 2017, pp. 93–4, who argues that neither conditions at the front nor at home were so dire as previous historians have argued.

21. UILL, Lockhart Collection, "Enclosure No. 1 in Acting Consul-General Lockhart's dispatch No 36 of the 23rd March, 1917."

22. HLRO, Lockhart Diaries, Volume 1, Wednesday, March 22 [1917].

23. Deborah McDonald and Jeremy Dronfield, *A Very Dangerous Woman*, London, 2015, p. 39.

24. I am grateful to Murray Frame for ferreting out this information.

25. I am grateful to Richard Spence for making this suggestion to me. He heard it from Lev Bezymensky, a Russian journalist occasionally employed during the 1980s and 1990s by the KGB to write about itself. He had access to their files and often copied them. But he only told the rumor to Professor Spence. He did not offer evidence.

26. Bruce Lockhart, *British Agent*, London, 1974, p. 188.

27. UILL, Lockhart Collection, X/33, Georgina Buchanan to Jean Lockhart, February 18, 1918.

28. See Catherine Merridale, *Lenin on the Train*, New York, 2016, for the most complete account of this episode.

29. McMeekin, *The Russian Revolution*, pp. 132–6.

30. Lockhart, *British Agent*, p. 197.

31. Ibid., p. 199.

32. TNA, FO 395/184, Memorandum on the Status of Mr Lockhart's Mission to Russia.

33. Lockhart, *British Agent*, p. 197.

34. Michael Occleshaw, *Dances in Deep Shadows*, New York, 2006, p. 184.

35. See, for example, TNA, WO 106/1150, Poole to McAlpine, April 25, 1918. Lockhart had directed McAlpine, the latter protested to Poole, who tried in this telegram to reassert his authority.

36. OUNBL, Selborne Papers, 80/285.

37. HLRO, Lockhart Diaries, Volume 3, Friday, January 4, 1918.

38. The team consisted of: Captain W. L. Hicks, an expert on poison gas who had recently returned from Russia, knew the country well and was anxious to get back; Edward Birse, a British-born Moscow businessman; and Edward Phelan, from the Ministry of Labour.

39. Lockhart, *British Agent*, p. 207.

Chapter 2

1. SUHI, Edgar Browne Collection, Russian Revolutionary Pamphlets.

2. SUHI, Gessin Collection, "Reminiscences," Volume 2, p. 32.

3. Ibid., p. 31.

4. TNA, FO 369/1017, Woodhouse to London, January 29, 1918.
5. TNA, KV 2/566, extract of letter from Morgan Phillips Price to ?, n.d., but January 1918 from internal evidence. The British intelligence service intercepted this letter.
6. Hugh Walpole, "Denis Garstin and the Russian Revolution: A Brief Word in Memory," *The Slavonic and East European Review*, Vol. 17, No. 51 (April 1939), p. 598.
7. Ibid., p. 600.
8. Ibid., p. 600.
9. SUHI, Edgar Browne Collection, "Special Correspondence of the *Chicago Daily News*," January 13, 1918.
10. Lockhart, *British Agent*, p. 217.
11. HLRO, Lockhart Diary, January 30, 1918.
12. UILL, Lockhart Collection, Box 1, Lockhart to Jean, February 2, 1918.
13. HLRO, Lockhart Diary, February 3, 1918.
14. SUHI, Browne Collection, "Petrograd, December (?) 25, 1917 ..."
15. Edgar Sisson, *One Hundred Red Days*, New Haven, CT, 1931, p. 182.
16. Ibid.
17. Rupert Hart-Davies (ed.), *The Autobiography of Arthur Ransome*, London, 1976, p. 231.
18. *Friendly Russia* (1915), *The Shilling Soldiers* (1918), both accessible online, and *The Cavalryman's Tale*, Amazon Digital Editions, 2014.
19. See David Tovey, "Cornish Artists and Authors at War (1914–1919)," at https://www.stivesart.info/cornish-artists-and-authors-at-war-1914-9/.
20. Walpole, "Denis Garstin and the Russian Revolution: A Brief Word in Memory," pp. 587–605.
21. For Cromie, see, especially, Roy Bainton, *Honoured by Strangers*, Shrewsbury, 2002.
22. David R. Jones (comp. and ed.), "F. N. Cromie's Letters, March 27th to July 11th, 1917," and "January 19th to August 14th, 1918," *Canadian-American Slavic Studies*, Vol. 7, No. 3 (Fall 1973), pp. 350–75; and Vol. 8, No. 4 (Winter 1974), pp. 544–62: Cromie's letters, p. 561, Cromie to Admiral Hall, August 14, 1918.
23. Cromie to Rear Admiral Phillimore, November 29, 1917, quoted in Bainton, *Honoured by Strangers* (Kindle 54%).
24. TNA, ADM 196/42, "Francis Allen Newton Cromie."
25. LUBL, Ransome Collection, Box 14, telegrams, *Daily News*, London, 33.2.
26. TNA, ADM 137/1731, Cromie to Admiralty, May 8, 1918.
27. Mark Steinberg, *The Russian Revolution, 1905–1921*, Oxford, 2017, p. 95.

28. TNA, FO 371/3283, March 18, 1918.

29. A. J. Plotke argues in *Imperial Spies Invade Russia*, Westport, CT, 1993, pp. 58–65, that this was an excuse for intervening. There were no massive caches of stores in Archangel, and there was little danger of German agents purchasing them from the Bolsheviks, let alone of German troops taking over the port.

30. TNA, WO 106/1560, Russia Committee Meeting, February 9, 1918.

31. Ibid., February 22, 1918.

32. See, for example, TNA, FO 800/205, Cecil to Balfour, May 13, 1918: after discounting the possibility of an Allied breakthrough on the Western Front, he wrote: "I see no answer except in the resuscitation of Russia."

33. TNA, WO 106/1560, Russia Committee, 33rd Meeting, February 22, 1918.

34. It is interesting to note that in fact the victorious Allies acted like "imperialist pirates" at Versailles after they had defeated Germany. Germany too bowed its head, and clenched its fist—and kept it behind its back for only a short time—to the world's great cost.

35. HLRO, Lockhart Diary, February 12, 1918.

36. TNA, FO 371/3284, Lockhart to Balfour, February 13, 1918.

37. Ibid., Balfour to Lockhart, February 15, 1918.

38. SUHI, Edgar Browne Collection, undated and untitled newspaper clipping, but internal evidence indicates that it was written in early January 1918.

39. HLRO, Lockhart Diary, February 15, 1918.

40. TNA, FO 371/3284, Lockhart to Balfour, February 16, 1918.

41. HLRO, Lockhart Diary, March 9, 1918.

42. Ibid., February 20, 1918.

43. Ibid., February 22, 1918.

44. OUNBL, Milner Collection, Dep. 109, Lockhart to Balfour, March 3, 1918.

45. TNA, FO 371/3283, March 30, 1918.

46. Ibid., April 6, 1918.

47. See Jennifer Siegel, "British Intelligence on the Russian Revolution and Civil War – A Breach at the Source," *Intelligence and National Security*, Vol. 10, No. 3, July 1995, pp. 468–85.

48. TNA, FO 371/3283, "The Delay in the East," by General Knox, March 18, 1918.

49. TNA, FO 371/3283, March 3, 1918.

50. Ibid.

51. OUNBL, Milner Collection, Dep. 109, Lockhart to Balfour, March 10, 1918.
52. TNA, FO 371/3283, March 18, 1918.
53. Ibid., March 21.
54. TNA, FO 371/3313, March 22, 1918.
55. TNA, FO 800/739/205, Cecil to Balfour, March 7, 1918.
56. Ibid., Lockhart to Balfour, March 21, 1918.
57. OUNBL, Milner Collection, Dep. 109, Lockhart to Balfour, March 31, 1918.
58. UILL, Lockhart Collection, Box 11, Leeper to Lockhart, February 12, 1918.
59. At just this time he was promising part of Palestine to his French allies in the war, and all of Palestine to Arab nationalists, and to Jewish nationalists, and to Turkish leaders if they offered favorable terms for a separate peace. All the while, he meant to keep Palestine for Britain. See Jonathan Schneer, *The Balfour Declaration*, New York, 2010, *passim*.
60. Quoted in Siegel, "British Intelligence on the Russian Revolution and Civil War – A Breach at the Source," p. 472.
61. Lockhart, *British Agent*, p. 289.

Chapter 3

1. SUHI, Lockhart Collection, Box 4, "My Europe," p. 7 of an unpublished outline for a book of that title.
2. Lockhart, *British Agent*, p. 241.
3. Paul Benckendorff and Steve Grieco, "The Memoirs of a Balt," p. 21. This is an unpublished manuscript held by the British Museum, call number Lf. 31.b.10168.
4. Quoted in Tania Alexander, *A Little of All These*, London, 1987, p. 31.
5. Benckendorff and Grieco, "The Memoirs of a Balt," p. 21.
6. Nina Berberova, *Moura*, New York, 2005, p. 9. But Helen Rappaport, *Caught in the Revolution*, New York, 2016, pp. 7–8, writes that Lady Georgina organized a "British Colony Hospital for Wounded Russian Soldiers" in the wing of Pokrovsky Hospital on Vasilievsky Island. Since Moura worked with MerielBuchanan perhaps this is the hospital with which she was affiliated.
7. McDonald and Dronfield, *A Very Dangerous Woman*, p. 29.
8. George Hill, *Go Spy the Land*, London, 1932, p. 87.
9. CUL, Boyle Collection.

10. Central Government (Special) Archive, a division of the Russian State Military Archive, or RGVA, USSR, fond 7, opis 2, delo 3529. This consists of the file on Moura kept by the French secret service. The Germans stole it from Paris in 1940; the Russians stole it from Berlin in 1945. I am grateful to Richard Spence for providing me with a copy.
11. Anthony West, *H. G. Wells*, London, 1984, pp. 75–7.
12. Hill, *Go Spy the Land*.
13. McDonald and Dronfield, *A Very Dangerous Woman*.
14. CUL, Boyle Collection, Alexis Sherbatov to Keyserlinge, 9/24/80.
15. McDonald and Dronfield, *A Very Dangerous Woman*, p. 35.
16. Alexander, *A Little of All These*, p. 37.
17. Hicks is an elusive figure whose role (if any) in the Lockhart Plot simply cannot be determined, at least by me. Lockhart chose him in London to be part of the small team accompanying him to Petrograd. They shared rooms in that city and then, later, in Moscow. On one occasion Hicks traveled to Siberia to report on conditions there, and to buttress Lockhart's opposition to Japanese intervention. I do not think Lockhart confided details of the plot to him. Hicks married a Russian woman literally on the date of his return home as part of Lockhart's entourage. He and his wife, and Lockhart, remained friends. They were present when Lockhart had his first reunion with Moura in 1923.
18. WSHS, Raymond Robins Papers, Box No. 42, Raymond Robins' Diary, March 6, 1918.
19. HLRO, Lockhart diary entries, February 17, 23, March 8, 12, 15.
20. Lockhart, *British Agent*, p. 242.
21. UILL, Lockhart Collection, Lockhart to Jean, January 22, 1918.
22. Ibid., Lockhart to Jean, February 28, 1918.
23. SUHI, Lockhart Collection, Box 1, Moura to Lockhart, n.d.
24. Lockhart, *British Agent*, p. 266.
25. UILL, Lockhart Collection, Lockhart to Jean, April 9, 1918.
26. Ibid., April 16, 1918.
27. WSHS, Robins diary entry, February 24, 1918.
28. Ibid., April 22, 1918.
29. TNA, WO 106/1186, "Russia" summary of Lockhart telegrams, p. 3.
30. TNA, FO 371, Lockhart to Balfour, April 25, 1918.
31. Ibid., Lockhart to Balfour, May 4.
32. TNA, FO 371/3286, Lockhart to Balfour, May 26, 1918.
33. Ibid., May 23, 1918.
34. Ibid., May 23, 1918.

35. Ibid., April 30, 1918.
36. Ibid., May 25, 1918.
37. Ibid., May 27, 1918.
38. Ibid., May 28, 1918.
39. WSHS, Robins' Diary, April 3, 1918.
40. Ibid., May 11, 1918.
41. Robert Bruce Lockhart, *Friends, Foes and Foreigners*, London, 1957, p. 148.
42. TNA, FO 371/3286, Lockhart to Balfour, June 11, 1918.
43. TNA, FO 175/3, Lockhart to Wardrop (?), July 10, 1918.
44. Sidney Reilly, *The Adventures of Sidney Reilly, Britain's Master Spy* (edited and completed by his wife), London, 1931, p. 20.

Chapter 4

1. Felix Dzerzhinsky, *Prison Diaries and Letters*, Moscow, 1959: Dzerzhinsky to Aldona, October 21, 1901.
2. Quoted in ibid, p. 46.
3. Ibid., Dzerzhinsky to Aldona, June 16, 1913.
4. Dzerzhinsky wrote an account of the escape. It appeared first in *Cerwony Sziandar*, No. 1, 1902. The account appears in Felix Dzerzhinsky, *Prison Diaries and Letters*, Moscow, 1959, pp. 163–74.
5. Dzerzhinsky, *Prison Diaries and Letters*, Dzerzhinsky to Zofia, August 14, 1912.
6. Ibid., Dzerzhinsky to Zofia, February 24, 1913.
7. Quoted in Donald Rayfield, *Stalin and his Hangmen*, New York, 2004, p. 66.
8. Quoted in Robert Blobaum, *Feliks Dzerzhinski and the SDKPiL*, New York, 1984, p. 215.

Chapter 5

1. Louise Bryant, *Mirrors of Moscow*, Westport, CT, 1973, p. 59; Bessie Beatty, *The Red Heart of Russia*, New York, 1918, p. 134.
2. Beatty, *The Red Heart of Russia*, p. 135.
3. Yakov Peters, Russian Wikipedia entry.
4. Beatty, *The Red Heart of Russia*, p. 136.
5. Clare Sheridan, *Clare Sheridan's Diary*, New York, 1921, p. 37.
6. International Institute voor Sociale Geschiedenis, Archief Sawinkow, Box 37, p. 12. See also Richard Spence, "The Tragic Fate of Kalamatiano:

America's Man in Moscow," *International Journal of Intelligence and CounterIntelligence*, Vol. 12, No. 3 (1999), 346–74, footnote 87.

7. *New York Times*, December 1, 1918.
8. Elena Syanova, "Under the Grounds of Charity," *Izvestia* (Moscow), October 14, 2003 (Google Chrome translation).
9. TNA, KV2/1025, *Daily Express*, October 3, 1918.
10. Beatty, *The Red Heart of Russia*, p. 137.
11. TNA, KV2/1025, file on Jacov Peters.
12. Ibid.
13. David Rumbelow, *The Houndsditch Murders and the Siege of Sidney Street*, London, 1988.
14. Private correspondence with Richard Spence, May 17, 2017.
15. TNA, file on Jacov Peters.
16. *Daily Express*, September 24, 1918.
17. Beatty, *The Red Heart of Russia*, p. 224.

Chapter 6

1. Quoted in Rayfield, *Stalin and his Hangmen*, p. 69. See also Arseny Tishkov, *Felix Dzerzhinsky*, Moscow, 1977, pp. 32–3.
2. Quoted in Tishkov, Felix Dzerzhinsky, p. 32.
3. Al'fred Avotin, *Shmidkhen: zatianuvshiisia maskarad*, 2010, p. 8, trans. Andrey Shlyakhter.
4. Jacov Peters, quoted in David Satter, *It Was a Long Time Ago and it Never Happened Anyway*, New Haven, CT, 2012, p. 15.
5. Avotin, *Shmidkhen: zatianuvshiisia maskarad*, p. 12.
6. Rayfield, *Stalin and his Hangmen*, p. 57.
7. Maria Spirodinova, quoted in I. N. Steinberg, *In the Workshop of the Revolution*, New York, 1953, p. 222.
8. Ibid., p. 223.
9. Dzerzhinsky to Zofia Dzerzhinsky, May 21, 1918, in Felix Dzerzhinsky, *Communist Morality*, New York, 2011, p. 19.
10. Beatty, *The Red Heart of Russia*, p. 302.
11. Bryant, *Mirrors of Moscow*, p. 51.
12. *Daily Express*, September 24, 1918.
13. Malkov, *Reminiscences of a Kremlin Commandant*, Moscow, p. 148.
14. See Lennard Gerson, *The Secret Police in Lenin's Russia*, Philadelphia, PA, 1976, pp. 30–1.
15. Lennard Gerson, "The Shield and Sword: Felix Dzerzhinsky and the Establishment of the Soviet Secret Police," PhD dissertation, George Washington University, 1973, p. 118.

16. Natalia Belskaya (trans.) et al., *Felix Dzerzhinsky, a Biography*, Moscow, 1988, p. 93.
17. Tishkov, *Felix Dzerzhinsky*, p. 37.
18. Gerson, "The Shield and Sword," p. 32.
19. Quoted in Gerson, "The Shield and the Sword," p. 95.
20. Nikolai Berdyaev, quoted in Satter, *It Was a Long Time Ago*.
21. G. P. Maximoff, "The True Reasons for the Anarchist Raids (Moscow 1918) (Analysis and Conclusions)," http://www.katesharpleylibrary.net/brv25k.
22. WSHS, Raymond Robins' Diary, April 9, 1918; William Hard, *Raymond Robins' Own Story*, New York, 1920, pp. 76–7.
23. See, especially, Paul Avrich, *The Russian Anarchists*, Chapter 7, "The Anarchists and the Bolshevik Regime," http://www.ditext.com/avrich/russian/7.html, 1967.
24. OUNBL, Milner Papers, Dep. 109, Lockhart to Balfour, April 12, 1918.
25. Malkov, *Reminiscences of a Kremlin Commandant*, p. 228.
26. Lockhart, *British Agent*, p. 239.
27. Quoted in William Henry Chamberlin, *The Russian Revolution, Volume 1: 1917–1918: From the Overthrow of the Tsar to the Assumption of Power by the Bolsheviks*, Princeton, NJ, 1987, p. 423.
28. Victor Serge, *Year One of the Russian Revolution*, ed. and trans. Peter Sedgewick, London, 1992, p. 216.
29. Lockhart, *British Agent*, p. 312.
30. Malkov, *Reminiscences of a Kremlin Commandant*, p. 230.
31. WSHS, Raymond Robins' Diary, April 12, 1918.
32. Quoted in Neil V. Salzman, *Reform and Revolution: The Life and Times of Raymond Robins*, Kent, OH, 1991, p. 260.
33. Lockhart, *British Agent*, p. 254.

Chapter 7

1. Lockhart, *British Agent*, p. vi.
2. Richard Spence, "Reilly, Sidney George [*formerly* Shlomo ben Hersh Rozenbluim]," *Oxford Dictionary of National Biography*, https://www.oxforddnb.com/view/10.1093/ref:odnb/9780198614128.001.0001/odnb-9780198614128-e-40834.
3. Spence, "The Tragic Fate of Kalamatiano."
4. SUHI, Lockhart Collection, Box 11, undated note from Hill to Robin Lockhart.
5. Norman Thwaites, assistant to Sir William Wiseman, quoted in Christopher Andrew, *Her Majesty's Secret Service*, London, 1987, p. 214.

6. SUHI, George Hill Collection, "Go Spy the Land," a radio production based on Hill's book, Part 6.
7. For most of the details of Reilly's April–October 1918 stint in Russia, I rely on Richard Spence's *Trust No One: The Secret World of Sidney Reilly*, Los Angeles, CA, 2002. Robin Lockhart's *Reilly, Ace of Spies*, London, 1992 and Andrew Cook's, *Ace of Spies*, Gloucestershire, 2002, are also useful.
8. Reilly, *The Adventures of Sidney Reilly*, p. 12.
9. TNA, WO 62/5669, April 4, 1918.
10. TNA, WO, 62/5669, "Situation in Russia," October 1, 1918.
11. TNA, FO 175/6, Report by ST1, June 14, 1918.
12. TNA, FO 370.3300, Lockhart to Foreign Office, June 26, 1918.
13. Lambeth Palace Library, Davidson Papers, Box 476. I am grateful to Adrian Gregory, a bare acquaintance, who generously sent me this helpful citation.
14. SUHI, Lockhart Collection, Box 10, Robin Lockhart, "Notes on Sidney Reilly." Robert Service, *Spies and Commissars*, New York, 2012, p. 122, writes only that Reilly and George Hill delivered over £200,000 worth of Russian rubles to the Patriarch. It seems fair to write they delivered them in a suitcase.

Chapter 8

1. S. A. Smith, *Russia in Revolution*, Oxford, 2017, especially pp. 161–96. For more on the Russian Civil War one might also consult, among many, Ronald Sinclair, *The Spy who Disappeared*, London, 1990, I. C. Dunsterville, *The Adventures of Dunsterforce*, London, 1932, N. Baron, *The King of Karelia*, London, 2007.
2. Geoffrey Swain, *The Origins of the Russian Civil War*, London, 1996, pp. 127–86, is very good on the plan and its context.
3. Walpole, "Denis Garstin and the Russian Revolution," p. 598: Garstin to ?, January 18, 1918.
4. Arthur Ransome, *On Behalf of Russia: An Open Letter to America*, New York, 1918, p. 27.
5. WSHS, Robins' Diary Entry, May 14, 1918.
6. William Hard, *Raymond Robins' Own Story*, New York, 1920, online version, Chapter V, "The Bolshevik 'Bomb,'" http://net.lib.byu.edu/estu/wwi/memoir/Robins/Robins5.htm
7. OUNBL, Milner Collection, Dep. 109, Box B, Lockhart to Foreign Office, May 10, 1918.

8. Walpole, quoting letters dated May 15, 1917, February 14, 1918, and July 17, 1918.

9. David S. Foglesong, "Xenophon Kalamatiano: An American Spy in Revolutionary Russia?" *Intelligence and National Security*, Vol. 6, No. 1 (January 1991), p. 162.

10. DeWitt Clinton Poole, *An American Diplomat in Bolshevik Russia*, ed. Lorraine M. Lees and William Rodner, Madison, WI, 2014, p. 142.

11. Michael Jabara Carley, "The Origins of the French Intervention in the Russian Civil War," *The Journal of Modern History*, Vol. 48, No. 3 (September 1976), pp. 413–39.

12. Serge, *Year One of the Russian Revolution*, p. 231.

13. UILL, Lockhart Collection, Bruce Lockhart, "The Counter-Revolutionary Forces," p. 3.

14. Winston Churchill, *Great Contemporaries*, London, 1937, p. 103.

15. Lockhart, *British Agent*, p. 288.

16. Churchill, Great Contemporaries.

17. TNA, WO 106/1186, Summary of telegrams on Russia; for Savinkov more generally, see, especially, Richard Spence, *Boris Savinkov*, Boulder, CO, 1991. For the promise to Savinkov made by Noulens, see UILL, Lockhart Collection, Bruce Lockhart, "The Counter-Revolutionary Forces," p. 4. For just how complicated this counter-revolutionary world really was, see Jonathan Smele, *The 'Russian' Civil Wars, 1916–26*, London, 2015.

18. TNA, FO 371/3332, Lockhart to Foreign Office, and notes on file, May 17, 1918.

19. TNA, FO 371/3313, Lockhart to Foreign Office, May 23, 1918.

20. TNA, FO 371/3348, Bruce Lockhart, "Secret and Confidential Memorandum on the alleged 'Allied Conspiracy' in Russia," November 5, 1918, p. 1.

21. They alleged it at the 1922 trial of right SRs. See N. V. Krylenko, *Sudebnye rechi. Izbrannoe*, Moscow, Iuridicheskaia literatura, 1964, pp. 157–8, trans. Andrey Shlyakhter.

22. G. E. Chaplin, "Dva perevorota na Severe (1918)," *Beloe delo: letoopis' Beloi bor'by*, vol. 4 (Berlin: Mednyi vsadnik, 1928), p. 14. This is an extract of the autobiography in Russian of G. E. Chaplin, who took part in the events discussed above (translation provided by Andrey Shylakhter). See also Benjamin Wells, "The Union of Regeneration: The Anti-Bolshevik Underground in Revolutionary Russia, 1917–19," DPhil thesis, Queen Mary College, University of London, 2004, p. 62.

23. TNA, ADM 137/1731, Cromie to Admiralty, June 14, 1918.
24. LUBL, Douglas Young Papers, Ms 1275/1, memorandum by Douglas Young, *passim*.
25. Ibid.
26. TNA, FO 371/3286, Lockhart to Foreign Office, May 25, 1918.
27. During the revolutionary period rampant inflation meant that the ruble lost value every day. It is difficult, therefore, to accurately convert rubles of 1918 to pounds sterling of 1918. After much digging I found a currency converter for 1918 which pegged £1 at 45 rubles during the first quarter of 1918; at 60 rubles for the second quarter; at 80 rubles for the third quarter and at 150 rubles for the fourth quarter of the year. Another currency converter pegs the value of £1 in 1918 at approximately £55 in 2019. I use these conversion rates throughout the text.
28. TNA, FO 371/3327, Military Intelligence office of the War Office to Wardrop, n.d.
29. TNA, FO 371/3323, Lockhart to Foreign Office, June 1, 1918.
30. Ibid.
31. Ibid., May 26, 1918.
32. TNA, FO 371/3286, Lockhart to Foreign Office, June 1, 1918.
33. Ibid.
34. SUHI, Lockhart Collection, Box 10, Robin Lockhart note to George Hill, n.d.: "In 1918, my father was…financing Savinkov…"
35. TNA, FO 371/3286, Lockhart to Foreign Office, May 26, 1918.
36. Ibid.
37. See, e.g., Richard Ullman, *Intervention and the War: Anglo-Soviet Relations, 1917–1921*, Princeton, NJ, 1961, p. 51.
38. Lockhart, *British Agent*, p. 179.

Chapter 9

1. Lockhart, *British Agent*, p. 288.
2. SUHI, Lockhart Collection, Moura to Lockhart, n.d.
3. HLRO, Lockhart diary entry, May 12, 1918.
4. SUHI, Lockhart Collection, Moura to Lockhart, Easter Day, 1919.
5. HLRO, Lockhart diary entry, May 19, 1918.
6. UILL, Lockhart Collection, Leeper to Lockhart, May 13, 1918.
7. Ibid., Clerk to Jean Lockhart, May 17, 1918.
8. Lockhart, *British Agent*, p. 277.

9. SUHI, Lockhart Collection, Moura to Lockhart, n.d., but from Lockhart's diary we know she returned to Petrograd on May 20, so this letter was probably May 21, 1918.
10. SUHI, Lockhart Collection, Moura to Lockhart, May 29, 1918.
11. SUHI, Lockhart Collection, Box 1, Moura to Lockart, n.d., but McDonald and Dronfield, *A Very Dangerous Woman*, claim "probably 31 May 1918," fn. 36, p. 353, and internal evidence suggests they are correct.
12. HLRO, Lockhart diary entry, June 4, 1918.
13. CUL, Andrew Boyle Collection, Add 9429/2B/125. Andrew Boyle interviewed Zinoviev on September 5, 1980.
14. Central Government (Special) Archive, USSR, Department 3, fond 7, Opis 2, Delo 3529. I am grateful to Richard Spence for making this source available to me. He reports that it was among files stolen by the Germans when they conquered France in 1940, and then stolen by the Russians when they conquered Germany in 1945.
15. TNA, KV2/979/1.
16. Ibid.

Chapter 10

1. For more on the left Socialist Revolutionaries, see Ettore Connella, "The Tragedy of the Russian Revolution: Promise and Default of the Left Socialist Revolutionaries," *Cahiers du Monde Russe*, 1997, pp. 45–82.
2. HLRO, Lockhart diary entry, July 5, 1918.
3. Walpole, "Denis Garstin and the Russian Revolution," p. 603.
4. Lockhart, *British Agent*, p. 297.
5. HLRO, Lockhart diary entry, July 4, 1918.
6. Quoted in James Bunyan (ed.), *Intervention, Civil War and Communism in Russia, April–December 1918*, Baltimore, MD, 1936, p. 203.
7. Morgan Philips Price, *My Reminiscences of the Russian Revolution*, London, 1921, p. 319.
8. Konrad H. Jarausch, "Cooperation or Intervention? Kurt Riezler and the Failure of German *Ostpolitik*, 1918, *Slavic Review*, Vol. 31, No. 2 (June 1972), p. 387.
9. This is now the interpretation accepted by most historians. See, e.g., ibid., and also Alexander Rabinowitch and Maria Spiridonova, "Maria Spiridonova's 'Last Testament,'" *The Russian Review*, Vol. 54, No. 3 (July 1995), p. 426.
10. TNA, FO 371/3287, Lockhart to Foreign Office, July 7, 1918.

11. Lockhart, *British Agent*, p. 297.

12. Ibid., p. 298.

13. A French agent had provided the grenade to the assassins. Serge, *Year One of the Russian Revolution*, p. 270: "I have been assured from several quarters that the latter [French military mission] supplied the grenades that were used in the murder at the German Legation." Savinkov made the same charge, *The Trial of Boris Savinkov*, Berlin, 1924, p. 19.

14. TNA, FO 371/3287, Lockhart to Foreign Office, July 7, 1918.

15. UILL, Lockhart Collection, Bruce Lockhart, "The Counter-Revolutionary Forces," p. 4.

16. *Trial of Savinkov*, p. 20.

17. Swain, *The Origins of the Russian Civil War*, pp. 171–2.

18. Quoted in Bunyan, *Intervention, Civil War and Communism in Russia, 1918*, p. 193.

19. TNA, FO 371/3287, Lockhart to Foreign Office, July 13, 1918.

20. Ibid., July 16, 1918.

21. SUHI, Lockhart Collection, Box 10, 'Questionnaire.'

22. TNA, FO 371/3324, Lockhart to Foreign Office, June 14, 1918.

23. Geoffrey Swain, "'An Interesting and Plausible Proposal': Bruce Lockhart, Sidney Reilly and the Latvian Riflemen, Russia 1918," *Intelligence and National Security*, Vol. 14, No. 3 (1999), p. 86.

24. Ibid., pp. 81–102. See also Geoffrey Swain, "The Disillusioning of the Revolution's Praetorian Guard: The Latvian Riflemen, Summer–Autumn, 1918," *Europe-Asia Studies*, Vol. 51, No. 4 (June 1999), pp. 667–86.

25. *Historia.lv atbalstitaji*, http://www.historia.lv/raksts/v-october-1917-october-1918, p. 12.

26. TNA, FO 371/3333, Lockhart to Foreign Office June 6, 1918.

27. See, e.g., TNA, FO 175/1, Lindley to Foreign Office, August 13, 1918, but referring to earlier organizing efforts.

28. Reilly, *The Adventures of Sidney Reilly*, p. 21.

29. "Report by…Peterson to VTsIK," quoted in V. A. Goncharov and A. I Kokurin (eds.), *Gvardeitsy Oktiabria. Rol' korennykh narodov stran Baltii v ustanovlenii I ukreplenii bol' shevistskogo stroia*, Moscow, 2009, p. 147, trans. Andrey Shlyakhter.

Chapter 11

1. Most think so, but not Yuri Felshtinsky, *Lenin and his Comrades*, New York, 2010, p. 115.

2. V. K. Vinogradov et al. (eds.), *Arkhiv VChK: sbornik dokumentov*, Moscow, 2007, trans. Andrey Shlyakhter, "The Lockhart Case: The Report of

Com. Peters about the History of the Genesis of the Lockhart Case," p. 490.

3. Avotin, *Shmidkhen: zatianuvshiisia maskarad*, trans. Andrey Shlyakhter, p. 14.

4. Buikis, "Proschet Lokkarta," pp. 77–8.

5. An extraordinary figure, apparently this individual would continue working for the Cheka until 1941, when he joined the Germans—and then after World War II somehow manage a transition to the United States, where he died in 1960. See http://swolkov.org/2_baza_beloe_ dvizhenie/pdf/Uchastniki_Belogo_dvizhenia_v_Rossii_26-EE.pdf.

6. See Roy Bainton, *Honored by Strangers*, London, 2002, p. 228.

7. Buikis, "Proschet Lokkarta," p. 78.

8. Ibid.

9. Avotin, *Shmidkhen: zatianuvshiisia maskarad*, p. 16.

10. A. A. Zdanovich, "Latyshskoe delo: niuansy raskrytiia 'zagovora poslov,'" *Voennoistoricheskii zhurnal*, Vol. 3, No. 57 (March 2004), pp. 25–32, trans. Andrey Shlyakhter.

11. Statement by Captain Berzin, 1918, Bezymensky Document (FSB Archive), file 302330. Berzin says Colonel Briedis introduced him to Sprogis/Shmidkhen in "May/June" 1918, trans. Andrey Shlyakhter. I am grateful to Richard Spence for directing me to this document. He obtained it from Lev Bezymensky, a Russian journalist and historian who wrote about the KGB and had access to Cheka files.

12. Zdanovich, "Latyshskoe delo," p. 27.

13. Tema Zdanovich, "'Zagovor Lokkarta' v istoricheskoi literature: nereshennye voprosy i vosproizvedenie mifov," *Klio*, no. 8 (2017), pp. 73–91.

14. Zdanovich, "Latyshskoe delo," p. 28.

15. Avotin, *Shmidkhen: zatianuvshiisia maskarad*, p. 17.

16. SUHI, Lockhart Collection, Box 11, Robin Lockhart to P. R. H. Wright, February 9, 1967.

17. Buikis, "Proschet Lokkarta," p. 79.

18. Lockhart, *British Agent*, p. 312.

19. Richard Pipes, *The Russian Revolution*, New York, 1990, pp. 654–5.

20. Statement by Captain Berzin, 1918, Bezymensky Document (FSB Archive), file 302330.

Chapter 12

1. LUBL, Douglas Young Papers, MS 1275/1, Young to Undersecretary of State, n.d.

2. KCLHC, General Poole Collection, Captain Hill's report showing work done from September 1917 to October 1918, p. 30.
3. LUBL, MS 1099, Lombard Papers, Lombard diary entries for much of early August 1918.
4. UILL, Lockhart Collection, Moura to Meriel Buchanan, October 13, 1918.
5. TNA, FO 371/3287, Lockhart to Foreign Office (via Paris), August 3, 1918.
6. TNA, WO 106/1155, "Details of Allied Forces on Russian Territory on 19.8.18."
7. TNA, ADM 137/1731, "A History of the White Sea Station, 1914–19," p. 31.
8. SUHI, Lockhart Collection, Box 1, Moura to Lockhart, "Easter Day, 1919."
9. UILL, Lockhart Collection, Moura to Lockhart, November 29, 1918.
10. SUHI, Lockhart Collection, Box 1, Moura to Lockhart, n.d.
11. Today this "architectural masterpiece in a high-profile Moscow neighborhood [has been] redesigned into deluxe housing."' See the Russian language website https://hleb-dom.ru/.
12. UILL, Lockhart Collection, Moura to Lockhart, December 16, 1918.
13. Ibid., October 24, 1918.
14. SUHI, Lockhart Collection, Box 1, Moura to Lockhart, March 10, 1919.
15. Poole, *An American Diplomat in Bolshevik Russia*, p. 169.
16. R. H. Bruce Lockhart, *Retreat from Glory*, London, 1934, pp. 5–6.
17. SUHI, Lockhart Collection, Box 1, Moura to Lockhart, May 28, 1918.
18. Ibid., Moura to Lockhart, n.d.
19. Ibid., Moura to Lockhart, January 25, 1919.
20. Ibid., Moura to Lockhart, n.d.
21. TNA, KV 2/979/1, "Baroness Budberg…"
22. SUHI, Lockhart Collection, Box 1, Moura to Lockhart, n.d.
23. Ibid., Moura to Lockhart, n.d.
24. Benckendorff and Grieco, "The Memoirs of a Balt," p. 8.
25. All these notes from Yendel may be found in Box 1 of the Lockhart Collection at SUHI.
26. SUHI, Lockhart Collection, Box 1, Moura to Lockhart, July 3, 1918. It is unclear if she knew this through Petrograd newspapers or through talking to Swedes in Petrograd.
27. Ibid., May 28, 1918.
28. Ibid., Moura to Lockhart, n.d.
29. Ibid., Moura to Lockhart, n.d.

30. Ibid., Moura to Lockhart, July 3, 1918.
31. Ibid., Moura to Lockhart, May 28, 1918.
32. Lockhart, *Retreat from Glory*, p. 5.
33. Ibid.

Chapter 13

1. TNA, WO 106/1184, Summary of Intelligence No. 18, for the period ending September 2, p. 3.
2. TNA FO 371/3310, "Situation at Moscow," July 9, 1918.
3. The best summary of historians' attitudes toward the Lockhart Plot is John W. Long's "Plot and Counter-Plot in Revolutionary Russia: Chronicling the Bruce Lockhart Conspiracy, 1918," *Intelligence and National Security*, Vol. 10, No. 1 (January 1995), pp. 122–43.
4. Lockhart, *British Agent*, p. 319.
5. Lockhart kept three diaries simultaneously all his life, but the two private ones are unavailable. Perhaps they contain revelatory information. TNA, FCO 12/121, Denning to Child, 2/23/71. However, Richard Spence acquired a copy of Lockhart's "private" prison diary for September 1918, and shared it with me. It is almost, but not quite, identical with the diary at the HLRO.
6. Jan Buikis "Proschet Lokkarta," p. 81, trans. Andrey Shlyakhter. In: I. E. Prolikarenkov (ed.), *Osoboe sadanie. Vospominaniia veteranov-chekistov*, Moscow, 1988, In fact, Buikis was not present at this first meeting although he claimed to have been, but he would have dealings with Lockhart later, and so his description is apt.
7. Perhaps Sprogis told this to Buikis, who wrote it in his "memoir" of the event.
8. Lockhart, *British Agent*, p. 312.
9. "Berzin's Statement" 1918, Bezymensky Doc, FSB Archive File 302330.
10. Peterson's report in V. A. Goncharov and A. I. Kokurin (eds.), *Gvardeitsy Oktiabria. Rol' korennykh narodov stran Baltii v ustanovlenii I ukreplenii bol'shevistkogo stroia*, Moscow, 2009, p. 148, trans. Andrey Shlyakhter.
11. The only identification I have for Peters' statement is its date, December 27, 1937.
12. The three historians are Arch Getty (University of California, Los Angeles), Hiroaki Kuromiya (Indiana University Bloomington), and James Harris (University of Leeds).
13. Private correspondence with the author, trans. Andrey Shlyakhter.

14. By the time he returned to London at the end of the year, the British government wanted nothing more than to forget about the Lockhart Plot. It was an embarrassment. To all intents and purposes, they denied it had ever happened. Lockhart tailored his report to suit Whitehall's mood. But many years later he admitted to his son that, "At the time *British Agent* was published, it was not politic for me to tell the whole truth": SUHI, Lockhart Collection, Box 11, Robin Lockhart, quoting his father's notes in a letter to F. R. H. Wright, December 30, 1966. Thirty years after that, in a diary entry, "he stressed yet again that the full story [of the Plot] had not been told": SUHI, Lockhart Collection, Box 10, Robin Lockhart to the Editor, *Sunday Times*, September 9, 1983. And at the end of the 1960s, he reiterated that the Russian version of events was more truthful than his own: SUHI, Lockhart Collection, Box 11, Robin Lockhart to F. R. H. Wright, February 9, 1967. None of this refers specifically to his description of that first freighted encounter, but we should read it with these caveats in mind.

15. TNA, WO 106/1165, Poole to War Office, August 13, 1918.

16. Lockhart *British Agent*, p. 313.

17. Ibid.

18. *Petrogradskaia Pravda*, September 3, 1918, trans. Andrey Shlyakhter.

19. Avotin, *Shmidkhen: zatianuvshiisia maskarad*, p. 21.

20. KCLHC, Poole Collection, Captain Hill's Report, p. 36.

21. Ibid., p. 25.

22. Ibid., p. 37.

Chapter 14

1. Avotin, *Shmidkhen: zatianuvshiisia maskarad*, p. 22.

2. Spence, "The Tragic Fate of Kalamatiano," p. 354.

3. Bezymensky Doc, FSB Archive File 302330, Berzin Statement of 1918.

4. Occleshaw, *Dances in Deep Shadows*, p. 204.

5. Sidney Reilly, *The Adventures of Sidney Reilly*, London, 1931, p. 30.

6. Ibid., p. 21.

7. Lockhart, *British Agent*, p. 313.

8. TNA, FO 371/3336, Clive to Foreign Office, September 7, 1918.

9. On a silver box he presented to Lockhart commemorating "events in Moscow in August and September 1918," SUHI, Lockhart Collection, Box 9.

10. TNA, FO 371/3319, French to Campbell, October 10, 1918.

11. SUHI, Lockhart Collection, Box 11.
12. Peterson's report in Goncharov and Kokurin, *Gvardeitsy Oktiabria*, p. 148.
13. Jacov Peters' report on the Lockhart Case, in Vinogradov et al., *Arkhiv VChK: sbornik dokumentov*, p. 513.
14. Buikis, "Proschet Lokkarta," p. 82.
15. Ibid.
16. See both the Berzin statement and Peters' in Vinogradov et al., *Arkhiv VChK: sbornik dokumentov*.
17. Buikis writes that Lockhart stressed the need to kill Lenin: "With Lenin alive, our undertaking will be a failure": "Proschet Lokkarta," p. 81.
18. KCLHC, Poole Collection, Report by George Hill, p. 46.
19. His real name was Martial-Marie-Henri de Verthamon, according to Gordon Brooke-Sheperd, *Iron Maze*, London, 1998, p. 41. Almost every other secondary source calls him Vertemont.
20. Service, *Spies and Commissars*, p. 155.
21. Harry Thayer Mahoney, "The Saga of Xenophon Dmitrivich Kalamatiano," *International Journal of Intelligence and CounterIntelligence*, Vol. 8, No. 2 (1995), p. 184.
22. Pamphlet, René Marchand, *Why I Support Bolshevism*, London, 1919, p. 46.
23. René Marchand, *Allied Agents in Soviet Russia*, Moscow, 1918, p. 4.
24. *Izvestia*, September 5, 1918, "A Conversation with Comrade Peters," trans. Andrey Shlyakhter.
25. Hugh Walpole, "Denis Garstin and the Russian Revolution: A Brief Word in Memory," *The Slavonic and East European Review*, Vol. 17, No. 51 (April 1939), p. 587.
26. OUNBL, Milner Collection, Dep 143, Foreign Office telegrams, February–October 1918, Thornhill to Poole, July 30, 1918.
27. Denis Garstin, *The Shilling Soldiers*, London, 1919, preface by Hugh Walpole, p. vi.
28. TNA, WO 339/13569.
29. Hugh Brogan (ed.), *Signalling from Mars: The Letters of Arthur Ransome*, London, 1997, p. 76: Ransome to A. G. Gardiner, August 11, 1918.
30. TNA, KV2/1903, Lockhart to Foreign Office, June 21, 1918.
31. TNA, KV2/1903, W. J. Oudendyk on Ransome, October 15, 1918.
32. This comes from Berzin's coerced confession in 1938, but seems unimportant enough to have been true.
33. Spence, "The Tragic Fate of Kalamatiano," p. 354.
34. SUHI, Lockhart Collection, Box 11.

35. A. V. Tishkov, *Pervyi chekist*, Moscow: Voennoe izdatel'stvo Ministerstva Oborony SSSR, 1968, p. 29, trans. Andrey Shlyakhter.
36. Dzerzhinsky, *Communist Morality*, p. 19.
37. TNA, FO 371/3336, Poole to Washington, August 26, 1918.
38. Spence, *Trust No One*, p. 227.
39. *Petrogradskaia Pravda*, September 5, 1918, trans. Andrey Shlyakhter.
40. TNA, FO 371/3336, Findlay to Foreign Office, September 17, 1918, mistakenly identifies Hall as a "civilian."
41. TNA, ADM 223/637. This is a report by H. T. Hall sent to London from Stockholm on November 19, 1918.
42. TNA, FO 371/3326, Lindley to Foreign Office, September 6, 1918.
43. TNA, FO 371/3348, Bruce Lockhart, "Secret and Confidential Memorandum on the Alleged 'Allied Conspiracy' in Russia," November 5, 1918.
44. TNA, ADM 137/1731, Cromie to Admiralty, August 5, 1918.
45. TNA, ADM 223/637, Cromie and Woodhouse (British Consul in Petrograd) to General Poole to Admiralty, August 9, 1918.
46. Quoted in Meriel Buchanan, *Ambassador's Daughter*, London, 1958, p. 195.
47. TNA, FO 371/3348, "Secret and Confidential Memorandum," Lockhart report, November 6, 1918.
48. LUBL, Lombard Additional, MS1099, diary entry for August 6, 1918.
49. Ibid., diary entry for July 13, 1918.
50. TNA, ADM 223/637, Cromie and Woodhouse (British Consul in Petrograd) to General Poole to Admiralty, August 9, 1918.

Chapter 15

1. A description of the waiting room may be found in William J. Oudendyk, *Ways and By-Ways in Diplomacy*, London, 1939, p. 278.
2. For Uritsky, see especially Alexander Rabinowitch, *The Bolsheviks in Power*, Bloomington, IN, 2007, *passim*.
3. Information on Kannegisser's assassination of Uritsky is taken mainly from Vasily Mitrokhin, *Chekisms: A KGB Anthology*, translated by Harry Spinnaker, Yurasov Press, 2008, pp. 43–64.
4. TNA, FO 371/3336, Wardrop to Foreign Office, August 30.
5. LUBL, Ransome Collection, Ransome cable to *Daily News*, n.d.
6. *Izvestia*, No. 188, September 1, 1918; published according to the *Izvestia* text; source: *Lenin's Collected Works*, volume 28, Progress Publishers, Moscow, 1965, pp. 51–2; trans. and ed. Jim Riordan.
7. Reilly, *The Adventures of Sidney Reilly*, p. 32.

8. According to the text reprinted by Mitrokhin, *Chekisms: A KGB Anthology*, p. 66, two different individuals claimed to have arrested Kaplan. But Semion Lyandres, "The 1918 Attempt on the Life of Lenin: A New Look at the Evidence," *Slavic Review*, Vol. 48, No. 3 (Autumn 1918), p. 439, has evidence showing that yet a third individual claimed the responsibility.

9. Quoted in Rabinowitch, *The Bolsheviks in Power*, p. 329.

10. *Izvestia*, "Official Communication," September 3, 1918, trans. Andrey Shlyakhter.

11. Marchand wrote the letter of September 6 according to George Hill: King's College, Poole Collection, Hill Report, p. 50.

12. Yulia M. Galkina, "K voprosu o frantsuzkom slede v 'dele Lokkarta': kto takoi Henri Verthamon?" *Klio*, Vol. 3, No. 135 (2018), p. 181.

13. State Archive of the Russian Federation (GARF), 1467/1/806; 6.

14. *Izvestia*, "Official Communication," September 3, 1918, trans. Andrey Shlyakhter.

15. That is what the "commandant of Petrograd," Shatov, told Dutch officials: TNA, FO 371/3336, Findlay to Foreign Office, September 17, 1918.

16. TNA, ADM 223/637.

17. *Izvestia*, "Official Communication," September 3, 1918.

18. LUBL, Ransome Collection, Ransome cable to *Daily News*, September 6, 1918.

19. TNA, FO 371/3336, Statement of Nathalie Bucknall, September 1, 1918.

20. *Petrogradskaia Pravda*, September 3, 1918, trans. Andrey Shlyakhter.

21. TNA, FO 371/3336, Findlay to Foreign Office, September 17, 1918, list of those arrested and held, including names of those released.

22. TNA, FO 371/3336, Wardrop to Foreign Office, August 30. The leading Bolshevik was Yacov Sverdlov.

23. "Search and arrest warrant No. 6370, 1 September 1918, Jacob Peters": Ia. F. Pogonii et al., *Lubianka 2. Iz istorii otechestvennoi kontrrazvedki* [*Lubianka 2: from the History of Domestic Counterintelligence*], Moscow: Mosgorarkhiv, 2001, p. 172, trans. Andrey Shlyakhter.

24. Malkov, *Reminiscences of a Kremlin Commandant*, pp. 264–72.

25. Ibid., pp. 264–7.

Chapter 16

1. Lockhart, *British Agent*, pp. 314–18.

2. UILL, Lockhart Collection, "Translation of 'Reminiscences of the Cheka in the First Year of the Revolution,' by Peters, Part 4: The Lockhart

Case." The sentences I have quoted do not appear in my translated paragraphs of the relevant portions of Vinogradov cited in the following footnote, but I think they must come from that same work.

3. Vinogradov et al., Arkhiv VChK: sbornik dokumentov, p. 513.
4. TNA, FO 371/3348, Bruce Lockhart "Secret and Confidential Memorandum...," p. 8.
5. Hart-Davis, The Autobiography of Arthur Ransome, p. 262.
6. UILL, Lockhart Collection, Moura to Meriel Buchanan, October 13, 1918.
7. British Library Recording, C1398/05404, James Mossman interviewer, February 4, 1970.
8. UILL, Lockhart Collection, Moura to Lockhart, two notes both undated.
9. Lockhart, British Agent, p. 322.
10. TNA, KV2/566, Beringer, Reuters dispatch, October 8, 1918.
11. KCLHC, Poole Collection, Hill Report, p. 44.
12. Ibid., p. 41.
13. Quoted in John J. Dziak, Chekisty: A History of the KGB, Lexington, MA, 1988, p. 28.
14. Quoted in Bunyan, Intervention, Civil War and Communism in Russia, 1918, p. 240.
15. Quoted in Dariusz Tolczyk, See No Evil: Literary Cover-Ups and Discoveries of the Soviet Camp Experience, New Haven, CT, 1999, p. 19.
16. Quoted in George Legget, The Cheka, Oxford, 1981, p. 114.
17. Poole, An American Diplomat in Bolshevik Russia, p. 165.
18. TNA, FO 371/3336, Oudendyk to Findlay, September 6, 1918.
19. KCLHC, Poole Collection, Hill Report, pp. 44–5.
20. Reilly, The Adventures of Sidney Reilly, p. 66.
21. Oudendyk, Ways and By-Ways in Diplomacy.
22. TNA, FO 371/3336, Sir M. Findlay to Foreign Office, September 11, 1918.
23. Ibid., Paget to Foreign Office, September 20, 1918.
24. Quoted in Gerson, The Secret Police in Lenin's Russia, p. 132.
25. TNA, FO 371/3333, 151517.
26. TNA, FO 371/3339, Clive to Foreign Office, September 19, 1918.
27. TNA, FO 371/3336, Clive to Foreign Office, September 7, 1918.
28. UILL, Lockhart Collection, Moura to Lockhart, n.d.
29. Bruce Lockhart, British Agent, p. 327.
30. Avotin, Shmidkhen: zatianuvshiisia maskarad, p. 26.
31. UILL, Lockhart Collection, Moura to Lockhart, n.d.. She refers to "my awful looks," in this letter and ascribes them to worry for Lockhart.

32. Anthony West, *H. G. Wells*, London, 1984, p. 141.
33. UILL, Moura to Lockhart, n.d., possibly September 6, 1918.
34. Lockhart, *British Agent*, p. 334.
35. TNA, FO 371/3348, Bruce Lockhart, "Secret and Confidential Memorandum."
36. Malkov, *Reminiscences of a Kremlin Commandant*, p. 287.
37. For this translation I am grateful to Jamie Lockhart, who got it from a Malayan High Commission press officer. Grace Segran translated the passage as follows: "Letters taken from beneath [or possibly to the cellar of] the important Dutch house in the city."
38. UILL, Moura to Lockhart, n.d., trans. Andrey Shlyakhter.
39. Lockhart, *British Agent*, p. 325.
40. Ibid., p. 337.
41. SUHI, Lockhart Collection, Box 4.
42. Lockhart, *Retreat from Glory*, p. 5.
43. Lockhart, *British Agent*, p. 325.
44. SUHI, Lockhart Collection, Box 11.
45. TNA, FO 371/3333/151517, Lord Hardinge memo, September 4, 1918.
46. TNA, FO 371/3336, War Cabinet 472, September 13, 1918. The speaker was Rex Leeper, who had arranged Lockhart and Litvinov's first interview, and who knew Litvinov well.
47. Since the National Union of Railwaymen had declared a strike, they could not bring the Russians to Aberdeen by train and then sail directly for Bergen, as originally they had told Litvinov and the others they would do. Instead the group should pick up a boat at Tilbury, twenty-six miles down the Thames from London. They arranged transportation to Tilbury by motorbus (and a separate limousine for Litvinov). The Russians objected, and had to be persuaded that this was not some nefarious ruse. Then, when the party reached Tilbury, it discovered that the waiting boat could not sail to Norway, but only to Aberdeen, from which a second vessel would carry them the rest of the way. Again, the Russians sensed a trap. They refused to board. They insisted on the original plan—but of course there was no train to take them to Aberdeen, because of the strike.

It took all day, but the authorities finally managed a train after all, to depart from King's Cross at 7 p.m. that evening. The train had no sleeping compartments. The Russians objected yet again, and somehow one was procured for Litvinov; the rest had to sit up all night. Fortunately, the passage from Aberdeen to Bergen aboard the *Jupiter* compensated for these hardships: all the Russians enjoyed first-class accommodations and excellent food.

48. TNA, FO 371/3337, N. Aall, "Report on my journey to Aberdeen 25–28 September 1918 and M. Litvinoff's departure," September 30, 1918.
49. Lockhart, *British Agent*, p. 337.
50. UILL, Lockhart Collection, Moura to Lockhart, October 3, 1918.
51. George Hill, *Dreaded Hour*, London, 1936, p. 24.
52. UILL, Lockhart Collection, Moura to Lockhart, October 3, 1918.

Chapter 17

1. See, e.g., Gerson, *The Secret Police in Lenin's Russia*, p. 135.
2. *New York Times*, May 27, 2012.
3. UILL, Lockhart Collection, Moura to Lockhart, November 30, 1918.
4. Lockhart, *British Agent*, p. 338.
5. Avotin, *Shmidkhen: zatianuvshiisia maskarad*, pp. 27–8.
6. See Ransome's dispatch to *Daily News*, October 9, 1918: LUBL, Ransome Collection, Box 1.
7. Bryant, *Mirrors of Moscow*, p. 260.
8. I am grateful to Andrey Shlyakhter for this tidbit, which he found on the Stalin Digital Archive: https://www.stalindigitalarchive.com/frontend/sda_viewer?n=111409
9. Rumbelow, *The Houndsditch Murders and the Siege of Sydney Street*, p. 191.
10. SUHI, Lockhart Collection, Box 11, Reilly to Lockhart, November 25, 1918.
11. "Sidney Reilly's Lubianka Diary," ed. Richard Spence, *Revolutionary Russia*, Vol. 8, No. 2 (December 1995), p. 182.
12. I am grateful to Richard Spence for telling me this.
13. Martin Kitchen, "Hill, George Alexander," *Oxford Dictionary of National Biography*, https://www.oxforddnb.com/view/10.1093/ref:odnb/9780198614128.001.0001/odnb-9780198614128-e-67487
14. Lockhart, *Friends, Foes and Foreigners*, p. 148.
15. TNA, KV 2/981, "Memorandum from S.8 re Arthur Ransome (S. 76)," March 17, 1919.
16. Ibid., Lockhart to Gregory, May 2, 1919.
17. LUBL, Ransome Collection, Lockhart to Ransome, November 2, 1932.
18. Tishkov, *Felix Dzerzhinsky*, p. 43.
19. Dzerzhinsky, *Communist Morality*, pp. 19–20.
20. Bunyan, *Intervention, Civil War and Communism in Russia, 1918*, pp. 264–5.
21. Lockhart, *Retreat from Glory*, p. 6.
22. SUHI, Lockhart Collection, Box 1, Moura to Lockhart, May 9, 1919.

23. Ibid., n.d.
24. Lockhart's published diaries and the introductions to them provide the details of his later life. See Kenneth Young (ed.), *The Diaries of Sir Robert Bruce Lockhart*, volumes 1–2, London, 1973 and 1980.
25. *Daily Mail*, March 26, 2011.
26. SUHI, Lockhart Collection, Box 1, Moura to Lockhart, "Thursday, 1933."

Chapter 18

1. Reilly, *The Adventures of Sidney Reilly*, p. 11.
2. *Daily Chronicle*, October 1, 1918.

BIBLIOGRAPHY

I. Primary Sources

Great Britain

British Library
Paul Benckendorff (unpublished ms)
Moura Budberg Interview (British Library Recording C1398/05404)
Cecil of Chelwood Papers
Harold Williams Papers

Cambridge University
CU Library: Hardinge Papers, Andrew Boyle Papers
Churchill College: Alexander Leeper Papers

House of Lords Record Office
Lockhart Diaries

Imperial War Museum
C. Budden Papers

Kings College, London, Liddell Hart Centre,
Spiers Papers, General Poole Papers

Leeds University (Brotherton Library)
Francis Lindley (unpublished autobiography)
R. H. Bruce Lockhardt [sic] Papers
Reverend Lombard Papers
Arthur Ransome Papers
Douglas Young Papers

The National Archive at Kew
Admiralty: ADM 12, 137, 196, 223
Civil Service: CSC 11

Foreign and Commonwealth Office: FCO 12
Foreign Office: FO 175, 369, 370, 371, 395, 566, 800
MI5: KV 2
War Cabinet: CAB 24
War Office: WO 32, 62, 106, 339

Oxford University
New Bodleian Library, Milner Papers

United States

Stanford University, Hoover Institute
Edgar Browne Papers
Georgy Chicherin Papers
I. V. Gessin Papers
George Hill Papers
R. H. B. Lockhart Papers
Marvin Lyons Papers
Eugene Prince Papers
Isaac Nachman Steinburg Papers

University of Indiana
Lockhart Papers

Wisconsin State Historical Society
Raymond Robins Papers

Russia

Russian State Archive of Social and Political History (RGASPI)
Dzerzhinsky Papers

State Archive of the Russian Federation (GARF)
Cheka Papers

Private Collection amassed by Professor Richard Spence
French Intelligence File on Moura Budberg

Berzin 1918 Statement on the Lockhart Plot
Berzin 1938 confession
Peters 1937 confession
"Search and arrest warrant No. 6370, 1 September 1918, Jacob Peters": Ia.
F. Pogonii et al., *Lubianka 2. Iz istorii otechestvennoi kontrrazvedki* [*Lubianka 2: from the History of Domestic Counterintelligence*], Moscow: Mosgorarkhiv, 2001, p. 172, trans. Andrey Shlyakhter.

Newspapers and Periodicals (1917–18)

Daily Express (UK)
Daily News (UK)
Izvestia (Russia)
Manchester Guardian (UK)
New York Times (USA)
Petrovskaia Pravda (Russia)
The Times (UK)

Pamphlets

Marchand, René, *Allied Agents in Soviet Russia*, London, 1918.
Philips Price, M., *The Old Order in Europe and the New Order in Russia*, New York, 1918.
Philips Price, M., *The Soviet, the Terror and Intervention*, New York, 1918.
Ransome, Arthur, *The Truth about Russia*, New York, 1918.
Ransome, Arthur, *On Behalf of Russia: An Open Letter to America*, New York, 1918.

II. Secondary Sources

PhD Dissertations
Gerson, Lennard, "The Shield and the Sword: Felix Dzerzhinsky and the Establishment of the Soviet Secret Police," George Washington University, 1973.
Wells, Benjamin, "The Union of Regeneration: The Anti-Bolshevik Underground in Revolutionary Russia, 1917–19," DPhil thesis, University of London, 2004.

Journal Articles

Avrich, Paul, "The Anarchists in the Russian Revolution," *The Russian Review*, 26, 4 (October 1967), pp. 341–50.

Avrich, Paul, "Russian Anarchists and the Civil War," *Russian Review*, 27, 3 (July 1968), pp. 296–306.

Avrich, Paul, "Sidney Reilly: materialy k biografi," *Iz glubinyb vremin*, No. 11 (St. Petersburg, 1999), pp. 282–91.

Carley, Michael Jabara, "The Origins of the French Intervention in the Russian Civil War," *The Journal of Modern History*, 48, 3 (September 1976), pp. 413–39.

Chamberlin, William Henry, "The Evolution of Soviet Terrorism," *Foreign Affairs*, 13, 1 (October 1934), pp. 113–21.

Connella, Ettore, "The Tragedy of the Russian Revolution: Promise and Default of the Left Socialist Revolutionaries", *Cahiers du Monde Russe*, 1997, pp. 45–82.

Debo, Richard, K., "Lockhart Plot or Dzerzhinskii Plot?" *The Journal of Modern History*, 43, 3 (September 1971), pp. 413–39.

Foglesong, David, S., "Xenophon Kalamatiano: An American Spy in Revolutionary Russia," *Intelligence and National Security*, 6, 1 (January 1991), pp. 154–95.

Galkina, Yulia M., "K voprosu o frantsuzkom slede v 'dele Lokkarta': kto takoi Henri Verthamon?" *Klio*, 3, 135 (2018), pp. 176–86.

Goldstein, Erik, "The Foreign Office and Political Intelligence," *Review of International Studies*, 14, 4 (October 1988), pp. 275–88.

Hafner, Lutz, "The Assassination of Count Mirbach and the 'July Uprising' of the Left Socialist Revolutionaries in Moscow, 1918," *The Russian Review*, 50, 3 (July 1991), pp. 324–44.

Jarausch, Konrad H., "Cooperation or Intervention? Kurt Riezler and the Failure of German *Ostpolitik* 1918," *Slavic Review*, 31, 2 (June 1972), pp. 381–98.

Jones, David R. (comp. and ed.), "F. N. Cromie's Letters, March 27th to July 11th, 1917," and "January 19th to August 14th 1918," *Canadian-American Slavic Studies*, 7, 3 (Fall 1973), pp. 350–75; and 8, 4 (Winter 1974), pp. 544–62.

Long, John W., "*Plot and Counter-Plot in Revolutionary Russia: Chronicling the Bruce Lockhart Conspiracy, 1918,*" *Intelligence and National Security*, 10, 1 (January 1995), pp. 122–43.

Long, John W., "Searching for Sidney Reilly: The Lockhart Plot in Revolutionary Russia, 1918," *Europe-Asia Studies*, 47, 7 (November 1995), pp. 1225–41.

Lyandres, Semion, "The 1918 Attempt on the Life of Lenin: A New Look at the Evidence," *Slavic Review*, 48, 3 (Autumn 1918), pp. 432–48.

Mahoney, Harry Thayer, "The Saga of Xenophon Dmitrivich Kalamatiano," *International Journal of Intelligence and CounterIntelligence*, 8, 2 (1995), pp. 179–201.

Pares, Bernard, "Review of Delo Borisa Savinkova (*The Savinkov Case*)," *The Slavonic Review*, 14, 12 (March 1926), pp. 760–9.

Rabinowitch, Alexander and Spiridonova, Maria, "Maria Spiridonova's 'Last Testament,'" *The Russian Review*, 54, 3 (July 1995), pp. 424–46.

Siegel, Jennifer, "British Intelligence on the Russian Revolution and Civil War – a Breach at the Source," *Intelligence and National Security*, 10, 3 (July 1995), pp. 468–85.

Spence, Richard (ed. and annotator), "Sidney Reilly's Lubianka 'Diary,' 30 October–4 November 1925," *Revolutionary Russia*, 8, 2 (December 1995), pp. 179–94.

Spence, Richard, "The Tragic Fate of Kalamatiano, America's Man in Moscow," *International Journal of Intelligence and CounterIntelligence*, 12, 3 (1999), pp. 346–74.

Swain, Geoffrey, "The Disillusioning of the Revolution's Praetorian Guard: The Latvian Riflemen, Summer–Autumn 1918," *Europe-Asia Studies*, 51, 4 (June 1999), pp. 667–86.

Swain, Geoffrey, "'An Interesting and Plausible Proposal': Bruce Lockhart, Sidney Reilly and the Latvian Riflemen, Russia 1918," *Intelligence and National Security*, 14, 3 (Autumn 1999), pp. 81–102.

Tynan, Kathleen, "The Astonishing History of Moura Budberg, A Flame for Famous Men," *Vogue*, October 1, 1970, pp. 162, 208–11.

Walpole, Hugh, "Denis Garstin and the Russian Revolution: A Brief Word in Memory," *The Slavonic and East European Review*, 17, 51 (April 1939), pp. 587–609.

Zdanovich, A. A., "Latyshskoe delo: niuansy raskrytiia 'zagovora poslov,'" *Voennoistoricheskii zhurnal*, 3, 57 (March 2004), pp. 25–32.

Zdanovich, Tema, "Zagovor Lokkarta' v istoricheskoi literature: nereshennye voprosy i vosproizvedenie mifov," *Klio*, 8 (2017), pp. 73–91.

Websites

http:/www.historia.lv/raksts/v-october-1917-october-1918, on Latvian Riflemen.

Avrich, Paul, "The Anarchists and the Bolshevik Regime," Ch. 7 in *The Russian Anarchists*, (1967) at http://www.ditext.com/avrich/russian/7.html

Maximoff, G. P., "The True Reasons for the Anarchist Raids," (1918) at http://www.katesharpleylibrary.net/brv25k

Books

Abraham, Richard, *Alexander Kerensky: The First Love of the Revolution*, New York, 1990.

Abraham, Richard, *Lubianka 2. Iz istorii otechestvennoi kontrrazvedki*, Moscow, 2001.

Alexander, Tania, *A Little of All These*, London, 1987.

Andrew, Christopher, *Her Majesty's Secret Service*, London, 1987.

Andrew, Christopher and Mitrokin, Vasili, *The Sword and the Shield: The Mitrokhin Archive and the Secret History of the KGB*, London, 1999.

Avotin, Al'fred, *Shmidkhen: zatianuvshiisia maskarad*, self-published, 2010.

Bainton, Roy, *Honoured by Strangers*, London, 2002.

Baron, N., *The King of Karelia*, London, 2007.

Beatty, Bessie, *The Red Heart of Russia*, New York, 1918.

Belskaya, Natalia (trans.) et al., *Felix Dzerzhinsky, a Biography*, Moscow, 1988.

Berberova, Nina, *Moura*, New York, 2005.

Blobaum, Robert, *Feliks Dzerzhinski and the SDKPiL*, New York, 1984.

Bonch-Bruyevich, M., *From Tsarist General to Red Army Commander*, trans. Vladimir Vezey, Moscow, 1966.

Bourne, Kenneth and D. Cameron Watt (eds.), *British Documents on Foreign Affairs: Reports and Papers from the Foreign Office Confidential Print*, University Publications of America, 1989.

Brogan, Hugh, *The Life of Arthur Ransome*, London, 1984.

Brogan, Hugh (ed.), *Signalling from Mars: The Letters of Arthur Ransome*, London, 1997.

Bromage, Bernard, *Man of Terror*, London, 1956.

Brook-Shepherd, Gordon, *Iron Maze*, London, 1998.

Bryant, Louise, *Mirrors of Moscow*, Westport, CT, 1973.

Buchanan, Meriel, *Ambassador's Daughter*, London, 1958.

Buchanan, Meriel, *Recollections of Imperial Russia*, London, 2015.

Buikis, Ian, "Proschet Lokkarta," in I. E. Polikarenkov (ed.), *Osoboe zadanie. Vospominaniia veteranov-chekistov*, Moscow, 1988, pp. 75–84.

Bunyan, James (compiler), *Intervention, Civil War and Communism in Russia, April–December 1918*, Baltimore, MD, 1936.

Chambers, Roland, *The Last Englishman*, London, 2009.

Chamberlin, William Henry, *The Russian Revolution, Volume 1: 1917–1918: From the Overthrow of the Tsar to the Assumption of Power by the Bolsheviks*, Princeton, NJ, 1987.

Chaplin, G. E., *Beloe delo: letoopis' Beloi bor'by*, Berlin, 1928.

Churchill, Winston, *Great Contemporaries*, London, 1937.

Cook, Andrew, *Ace of Spies*, Gloucestershire, 2002.

Day, Peter, *The Bedbug*, London, 2015.

Deacon, Richard, *A History of the Russian Secret Service*, London, 1975.

Deutscher, Isaac, *The Prophet Armed: Trotsky 1879–1921*, New York, 1985.

Dukes, Sir Paul, *The Story of 'ST 25,'* London, 1938.

Dunsterville, I. C., *The Adventures of Dunsterforce*, London, 1932.

Dzerzhinsky, Felix, *Prison Diary and Letters*, Moscow, 1959.

Dzerzhinsky, Felix, *Communist Morality*, New York, 2011.

Dziak, John, J., *Chekisty: A History of the KGB*, Lexington, MA, 1988.

Engelstein, Laura *Russia in Flames*, New York, 2017.

Felshtinsky, Yuri, *Lenin and his Comrades*, New York, 2010.

Fitzpatrick, Sheila, *The Russian Revolution*, Oxford, 1994.

Francis, David, *Russia from the American Embassy*, New York, 1921.

Garstin, Denis, *The Shilling Soldiers*, Moscow, 1919.

Gerson, Lennard, *The Secret Police in Lenin's Russia*, Philadelphia, PA, 1976.

Goncharov V. A. and Kokurin A. I. (eds.), *Gvardeitsy Oktiabria. Rol' korennykh narodov stran Baltii v ustanovlenii I ukreplenii bol'shevistkogo stroia*, Moscow, 2009.

Hard, William, *Raymond Robins' Own Story*, New York, 1920.

Hardyment, Christina, *The World of Arthur Ransome*, London, 2012.

Hart-Davis, Rupert (ed.), *The Autobiography of Arthur Ransome*, London, 1976.

Hill, George Alexander, *Go Spy the Land*, London, 2014 [1932].

Hill, George Alexander, *Dreaded Hour*, London, 1936.

Hingley, Ronald, *The Russian Secret Police*, New York, 1970.

Hoare, Samuel, *The Fourth Seal*, London, 1930.

Hughes, Michael, *Inside the Enigma*, London, 2003.

Jaxa-Roniker, Bogdan, *The Red Executioner*, London, 1935.

Kangaspuro Markku and Oittenin, Vesa (eds.), *The Problems of Stalinism*, Helsinki, 2013.

Kennan, George, *Russia Leaves the War*, Princeton, NJ, 1956.

Kennan, George, *The Decision to Intervene*, Princeton, NJ, 1958.

Kerensky, Alexander, *The Kerensky Memoirs*, London, 1966.

Krylenko, N. V., *Sudebnye rechi. Izbrannoe*, Moscow, 1964.

Latsis, M., *Dva Goda Bor 'by na vnutrennem fronte*, Moscow, 1920.

Lauchlan, Iain, "Young Felix Dzerzhinsky and the Origins of Stalinism," in Markku Kangaspuro and Vesa Oittinen (eds.), *Essays on Stalinism*, Helsinki, 2013.

Legget, George, *The Cheka: Lenin's Political Police*, Oxford, 1981.

Lerner, Warren, *Karl Radek*, Palo Alto, CA, 1970.

Levytsky, Boris, *The Uses of Terror*, trans. H. A. Piehler, New York, 1972.

Libby, James K., *Alexander Gumberg and Soviet–American Relations, 1917–33*, Louisville, KY, 1977.

Liberman, Simon, *Building Lenin's Russia*, Chicago, IL, 1945.

Lockhart, Robert Hamilton Bruce, *Memoirs of a British Agent*, London, [1932] 1974.

Lockhart, Robert Hamilton Bruce, *My Scottish Youth*, London, 1937.

Lockhart, Robert Hamilton Bruce, *Retreat from Glory*, London, 1934.

Lockhart, Robert Hamilton Bruce, *Return to Malaya*, London, 1942.

Lockhart, Robert Hamilton Bruce, *Friends, Foes, and Foreigners*, London, 1957.

Lockhart, Robert Hamilton Bruce, *The Two Revolutions*, London, 1967.

Lockhart, Robin Bruce, *Reilly, Ace of Spies*, London, 1992.

Lynn, Andrea, *Shadow Lovers*, Boulder, CO, 2001.

McDonald, Deborah and Dronfield, Jeremy, *A Very Dangerous Woman*, London, 2015.

McFadden, David, *Alternative Paths*, New York, 1993.

McMeekin, Sean, *The Russian Revolution*, New York, 2017.

Malkov, Pavel, *Reminiscences of a Kremlin Commandant*, Moscow, 1959.

Marchand, René, *Why I Support Bolshevism*, London, 1919.

Merridale, Catherine, *Lenin on the Train*, New York, 2016.

Milton, Giles, *Russian Roulette*, London, 2013.

Mitrokhin, Vasily, *Chekisms: A KGB Anthology*, trans. Harry Spinnaker, Yurasov Press, 2008.

Neilson, Keith, *Strategy and Supply*, London, 1984.

Noulens, Josef, *Mon ambassade en Russie sovietique, 1917–1919*, Paris, 1933.

Occleshaw, Michael, *Dances in Deep Shadows*, New York, 2006.

Orlov, Alexander, *The March of Time*, London, 2004.

Oudendyk, William J., *Ways and By-Ways in Diplomacy*, London, 1939.

Philips Price, Morgan, *My Reminiscences of the Russian Revolution*, London, 1921.

Pipes, Richard, *The Russian Revolution*, New York, 1990.

Platt, D. C. M., *The Cinderella Service*, Lancaster, 1971.

Plotke, A. J., *Imperial Spires Invade Russia*, Westport, CT, 1993.

Poole, DeWitt Clinton, *An American Diplomat in Bolshevik Russia*, ed. Lorraine Lees and William Rodner, Madison, WI, 2014.

Rabinowitch, Alexander, *The Bolsheviks in Power*, Bloomington, IN, 2007.

Rappaport, Helen, *Caught in the Revolution*, New York, 2016.

Rayfield, Donald, *Stalin and his Hangmen*, New York, 2004.

Reilly, Sidney, *The Adventures of Sidney Reilly* (edited and completed by his wife), London, 1931.

Rosenstone, Robert, *Romantic Revolutionary*, New York, 1975.

Rothstein, Andrew, *When Britain Invaded Soviet Russia*, London, 1979.

Rumbelow, David, *The Houndsditch Murders, and the Siege of Sidney Street*, London, 1988.

Sadoul, Jacques, *Notes sur la Revolution Bolchevique*, Paris, 1971.

Salzman, Neil, *Reform and Revolution: The Life and Times of Raymond Robins*, Kent, OH, 1991.

Satter, David, *It Was a Long Time Ago, and it Never Happened Anyway*, New Haven, CT, 2012.

Savinkov, Boris, *Memoirs of a Terrorist*, New York, 1931.

Serge, Victor, *Year One of the Russian Revolution*, ed. and trans. Peter Sedgewick, London, 1992.

Service, Robert, *Spies and Commissars*, New York, 2012.

Sheridan, Clare, *Clare Sheridan's Diary*, New York, 1921.

Sinclair, Ronald, *The Spy Who Disappeared*, London, 1990.

Sisson, Edgar, *One Hundred Red Days*, New Haven, CT, 1931.

Smele, Jonathan, *The 'Russian' Civil Wars, 1916–26*, London, 2015.

Smith, S. A., *Russia in Revolution*, Oxford, 2017.

Spence, Richard, *Boris Savinkov*, Boulder, CO, 1991.

Spence, Richard, "Sidney Reilly, Master Spy: A Reappraisal of his Role in the Lockhart Plot," in Steven Weingartner (ed.), *A Weekend with the Great War*, Proceedings of the Fourth Annual Great War Inter-Conference Seminar, September 16–18, Wheaton, IL, 1994, pp. 126–43.

Spence, Richard, *Trust No One: The Secret World of Sidney Reilly*, Los Angeles, CA, 2002.

Steinberg, I. N., *In the Workshop of the Revolution*, New York, 1953.

Steinberg, Mark, *The Russian Revolution, 1905–1921*, Oxford, 2017.

Sunderland, Willard, *The Baron's Cloak*, Ithaca, NY, 2014.

Swain, Geoffrey, *The Origins of the Russian Civil War*, London, 1996.

Thwaites, Norman, *Velvet and Vinegar*, London, 1932.

Tishkov, A. V., *Pervyi chekist*, Moscow, 1968.

Tishkov, Arseny, *Felix Dzerzhinsky*, Moscow, 1977.

Tolczyk, Darius, *See No Evil: Literary Cover-ups and Discoveries of the Soviet Camp Experience*, New Haven, CT, 1999.

Ullman, Richard H., *Intervention and the War: Anglo-Soviet Relations, 1917–1921*, Princeton, NJ, 1961.

Van der Rhoer, Edward, *Master Spy*, New York, 1981.

Vinogradov, V. K. et al. (eds.), *Arkhiv VChK: sbornik dokumentov*, Moscow, 2007.

West, Anthony, *H. G. Wells*, London, 1984.

Wollin, Simon and Slusser, Robert (eds.), *The Soviet Secret Police*, New York, 1957.

Young, Kenneth (ed.), *The Diaries of Sir Robert Bruce Lockhart, 1915–1938*, London, 1973.

Young, Kenneth (ed.), *The Diaries of Sir Robert Bruce Lockhart, 1939–1965*, London, 1980.

INDEX

Note: Figures are indicated by an italic 'f', respectively, following the page number.

For the benefit of digital users, indexed terms that span two pages (e.g., 52–53) may, on occasion, appear on only one of those pages.

Kornilov, Lavr (General) 35, 88, 107, 109, 117–18
  death 109–10
Krankl, Krysz 183, 230
Kravchenko, V. F. xii
Kuromiya, Hiroaki 305n. 12

'Landowners Union' 88
Latsis, Martin 236–7
Latvian Club (Petrograd) 151–3, 158
Latvian nationalism 180, 182–3, 196, 260–2
Latvian Rifle Brigade 92–3, 145f, 146
  anarchist combat 93, 145–6
  anti-Bolshevism 161
  Bolshevism 92–3, 145–6, 175–6
  Dzerzhinsky and 147–9
  left SR 'uprising' 141, 145–6
  Lockhart and 144–7, 161, 175–6
  Lockhart Plot 178–83, 189–91, 193–4
  October Revolution 145–6
  Russian counter-revolution and 146–8
  subordination 161, 175–6
  see also Berzin, Eduard Petrovich
Lavergne (General) 181, 233–4
  Lockhart Plot 189–90, 193–4, 197–9
Lawrence, T. E. 10
Le Page, George 223–4
Leeper, Rex 311n. 46
left SRs (Socialist Revolutionaries)
  1922 trial 140–1
  Allies-Russia cooperation 61
  anti-Bolshevism 135–8
  Bolsheviks and 35, 44
  Cheka and 134
  Kaplan, Fanny 218
  left SR 'uprising' 141, 145–6
  Lenin's regime and 134
  Lockhart's funding of 140–1
  Mirbach's murder 138–40, 221–2
  Ukraine and 137–8
  see also Spiridonova, Maria
Lenin (Vladimir Ilyitch) xvi, 134, 283–4
  assassination plot against 118, 121, 194–5, 307n. 18
  Brest-Litovsk Peace Treaty 40–1
  British attempt to replace Lenin 44
  death 256
  Dzerzhinsky/Lenin relationship 72

Gorky/Lenin relationship 278
Kaplan's attempted assassination of 218–23, 256
left SRs and 134
Lockhart Plot 196–7, 200, 283–4, 307n. 18
October Revolution 16–17, 75
Peters and 82–3
poisoned by Stalin? 256
Red Terror 256
return to Russia with German help 16–17, 75, 200
Russo-American trade 112
Sovnarkom 75–6
war declaration to Allied powers 163
Leninism 26
Litvinov, Maxim xvi, 17–18
  arrest by British authorities 251
  Balfour/Chicherin exchange of prisoners 252
  reference letter for Lockhart's mission 3–4
Lloyd George, David xvi, 13, 17–19, 257–8
  foreign policies 47, 293n. 59
  Lockhart/Knox disagreement 47
  on Lockhart's assignment 36
Lockhart, Bruce (Robert Hamilton Bruce) xvi
  birth 4–5
  Consular Service exam 7–8
  diaries 177, 305n. 5
  education 4–6
  family 4–5
  malaria (probably) 6–7
  marriages 8, 275–9
  Ministry of Overseas Trade, London 16
  passport 4–5f
  physical appearance 4, 178
  trip to Orient 6
  see also entries below related to Lockhart, Bruce
Lockhart, Bruce: British Agent 260–1, 265–7, 275
Lockhart, Bruce: character traits 4, 6–9, 16
  callousness 276
  guile 60–2
  persuasiveness 17
  recklessness 6

333